# STARTING A BUSINESS IN IRELAND

*A Comprehensive Guide and Directory*

*6th edition*

**Brian O'Kane**

www.oaktreepress.com

Oak Tree Press
19 Rutland Street, Cork, Ireland
www.oaktreepress.com
www.startingabusinessinireland.com


© 2010 Brian O'Kane


A catalogue record of this book is
available from the British Library.


ISBN 978-1-904887-37-9


First edition published 1993; Second edition 1995;
Third edition 1998; Fourth edition 2001; Fifth edition 2004.

Printed in Ireland by Colour Books.

# CONTENTS

# PREFACE

Yet again, in this the sixth edition of *Starting a Business in Ireland*, I am writing the *Preface* in a period of change – albeit as yet largely unrealised – in the enterprise support scene in Ireland.

Previous editions of the book coincided with the introduction of the **County & City Enterprise Boards**[1] (first edition, 1993); the formation of Forbairt (second edition, 1995), later to become **Enterprise Ireland** (third edition, 1998); with the shift towards 'soft supports' in lieu of cash grants as the focus of State support for start-ups and small businesses (fourth edition, 2001); and an entire new support landscape – the centrepieces of which are **Invest Northern Ireland** and **Enterprise Northern Ireland** – north of the Border (fifth edition, 2004). This sixth edition, following from the global economic / local property crises of 2008 / 2009, is written at a time when decisions based on the McCarthy / An Bord Snip Nua report are still awaited.

Much has changed since the first editions of this book, most of all public attitude towards enterprise, small business and start-ups. Where previously the 'proper job', one with a pension after a lifetime of service, was the be-all-and-end-all, there's a genuine interest across Irish society in entrepreneurship.

With all due modesty, *Starting a Business in Ireland* can lay claim to credit for some of Ireland's entrepreneurial success and for the more positive view in Irish society towards enterprise. It struck a chord with the Irish public right from its launch in 1993. It sells consistently well, month in month out, mainly by word-of-mouth and recommendation – the most effective form of marketing! And its companion website, **www.startingabusinessinireland.com**, attracts significant traffic. Of

---

[1]  The bold text indicates that more information on the organisation and its activities in support of start-ups is available in the *Directory of Sources of Assistance* at the back of this book.

course, I cannot (and would not) claim all the credit – the many people whose job (in some cases, their mission) it is to assist start-ups and small businesses deserve recognition, too.

But the real heroes in Irish enterprise are Irish entrepreneurs – the men and women who have taken the plunge and built successful businesses where none existed before. As I speak on courses, at conferences, or at exhibitions, I am always dumbstruck by the sheer inventiveness, innovation and enthusiasm of people whom I meet at these events, who have shared their dreams and ambitions with me (good luck to you all), and who have done me the honour of asking for my advice and opinion. To them belongs the lion's share of the credit.

## OAK TREE PRESS

In recent years, Oak Tree Press, too, has changed – refocusing its activities on micro and small businesses, and moving gently to encompass a broader view of publishing than just books.

## THE BOOK

Starting a business in Ireland is frustrating, time-consuming and difficult – I know, because I have done it – but it can also be highly satisfying and enjoyable.

The first edition of this book was born out of the frustration of dealing with the bureaucracy and information dead-ends that surrounded starting a business at that time – and, sadly, still do to some extent today. This sixth edition of *Starting a Business in Ireland* continues the formula of earlier editions by:

- Taking you step-by-step through the stages in going into business for yourself.
- Helping you to identify, from the many organisations that provide assistance to entrepreneurs, those that are likely to be appropriate to your needs.

The chapters are arranged to take you through the stages:

- Deciding whether you have what it takes.
- Researching your idea.
- Writing a business plan.

- Raising money to set up your business.
- Getting help from State and other agencies.
- Getting your business up and running.

*Chapter 9, Implementation* outlines some of the steps you need to complete in order to get your new business up and running.

The *Directory of Sources of Assistance* provides information (including contact details) for many organisations that may be of use to you as you go through the stages of starting your own business. The full directory, and now with nearly 1,000 entries for organisations North and South, is available and kept up-to-date on **www.startingabusinessinireland.com**.

## THANK YOU

A book such as this can never be the work of one person alone.

My idea lay fallow for several years, until David Givens (Oak Tree Press' first general manager, now managing director of his own business, The Liffey Press) pushed me to complete what I had begun – and so the first edition of *Starting a Business in Ireland* was written. David's encouragement is appreciated more than he realises.

Ron Immink, who researched and co-wrote the *Starting Your Own Business* workbook with me in 1997 for the **Department of Enterprise, Trade & Employment** (updated in 2009), and also, *TENBizPlan*, the *Steps to Entrepreneurship* series and the *Growing Your Own Business* workbook, deserves special thanks for his constant encouragement and unstoppable flow of ideas.

Despite my reluctance to delegate, someone always gets stuck with the job of checking the many entries in the *Directory* to ensure that they are all correct. This time, Anne Kennedy rose to the challenge.

I am also grateful to the staff of the many organisations listed in this book for their helpfulness, patience and support in preparing and checking this and previous editions and in recommending the book to so many people. I'd also like to thank the organisations that have advertised in this edition – please support them.

I am pleased and somewhat surprised to find *Starting a Business in Ireland* now in its sixth edition and well into its second decade! The reaction to its publication has far exceeded all my expectations.

I have enjoyed writing and updating this book – in all its editions. I hope it is of help to you, the reader, as you take your first steps on your journey. May the road always rise to meet you!

**Brian O'Kane**
**Cork**
**January 2010**

# DEDICATION

This book is dedicated especially to my wife, Rita, without whose constant support and encouragement none of this would have been possible, and to my children, Niamh, Conall, Kevin and Deirdre.

# 1 : GETTING STARTED

For some people, starting their own business is as obvious as the nose on their face. For others, it is a risk not to be contemplated.

For you, it is an idea in the back of your mind, one you cannot get rid of. You may already know what kind of business you want to be in. What you want from this book are a few short cuts to help you get there faster and with fewer problems.

On the other hand, you may simply be toying with the idea of starting a business of some kind, unsure of which direction to take. You are hoping that this book will present you with a ready-formed solution. The truth is that you must provide your own solution but this book can help by providing a structure for your thinking.

## THE STAGES IN A START-UP

The stages involved in starting a business include:

- Deciding whether you have the right temperament to start (and persevere with) your own business – a critical first step, often overlooked in the rush to get started.

- Finding an idea – it's worth taking time on this stage to explore all the options; sometimes your first idea is not always the best.

- Doing the market research – this involves finding out about your customers, your competition, how you will make your product or deliver your service, what price to charge, where your business will be located, how to market your product or service, what staff you require and with what skills, and so on.

- Writing a business plan – this draws together all the work you have done in the research stage and presents it in a form that is readily understandable.

- Finding the necessary money – since it's likely you won't have enough of your own capital to start, you'll have to raise money elsewhere.
- Identifying and accessing sources of assistance – as the *Directory* shows, there are hundreds of organisations dedicated to helping small businesses get started.
- Implementing your plan – this is where you put your plan into action.

### STAGES IN STARTING A BUSINESS

| | |
|---|---|
| **Self-assessment** | Are you suited to be an entrepreneur? |
| **Idea assessment** | Will your idea for a product or service work in the market? |
| **Market research** | Who? What? When? Where? Why? How? The operational details of your business. |
| **Business Plan** | Document your research in a plan, with back-up evidence. |
| **Finance** | How much do you need? Where can you get it? |
| **Assistance: State/Private** | Where can you find help in starting your business? Who provides what assistance? |
| **Implementation** | Lights! Camera! Action! It's time for the show to begin! |

Sometimes, in practice, these stages will not follow in the order set out above; in other cases, you will have to double-back, perhaps even several times, to adjust the results of a stage because of new information you find out later.

For instance, your idea might be to sell to the local community a product that you make yourself. After doing your market research, you write your business plan and look for money on this basis but, as you proceed, you find that there is a national demand for the product. To supply it, you need to plan on a larger scale and need more money – so you revise your plans and finances accordingly.

Most of these stages in starting a business are covered in this book. Some are dealt with in greater detail in other books published by **Oak Tree Press** and available from our website at **www.oaktreepress.com**. Other stages, like finding an idea, lie with you alone.

## ARE YOU SUITED TO LIFE AS AN ENTREPRENEUR?

Sadly, there is no fail-safe method of becoming a successful entrepreneur. Research, quoted in *You Can Do It* by Joyce O'Connor and Helen Ruddle (Gill & Macmillan, 1989 – currently out of print), shows that successful entrepreneurs have:

- Strong needs for control and independence.
- Drive and energy.
- Self-confidence.
- A point of view of money as a measure of performance.
- A tolerance of ambiguity and uncertainty.
- A sense of social responsibility.

and that they are good at:

- Problem-solving.
- Setting (and achieving) goals and targets.
- Calculated risk-taking.
- Committing themselves for the long-term.
- Dealing with failure.
- Using feedback.
- Taking the initiative.
- Seeking personal responsibility.
- Tapping and using resources.
- Competing against self-imposed standards.

How do *you* measure on these criteria? Be honest with yourself.

Very few entrepreneurs can lay claim to all of these characteristics. Making the most of your best characteristics and using ingenuity (including the skills of others) to bridge the gaps is perhaps the most frequently encountered entrepreneurial characteristic of all!

## YOUR SUITABILITY AS AN ENTREPRENEUR

Where are you on each of the following, on a score from 1 (weak) to 10 (strong)?

| | 1 | 2 | 3 | 4 | 5 | 6 | 7 | 8 | 9 | 10 |
|---|---|---|---|---|---|---|---|---|---|---|
| Need for control / independence | | | | | | | | | | |
| Drive and energy | | | | | | | | | | |
| Self-confidence | | | | | | | | | | |
| Money to measure performance | | | | | | | | | | |
| Tolerate ambiguity / uncertainty | | | | | | | | | | |
| Sense of social responsibility | | | | | | | | | | |
| Problem-solving | | | | | | | | | | |
| Setting (and achieving) goals | | | | | | | | | | |
| Calculated risk-taking | | | | | | | | | | |
| Committing for the long term | | | | | | | | | | |
| Dealing with failure | | | | | | | | | | |
| Using feedback | | | | | | | | | | |
| Taking the initiative | | | | | | | | | | |
| Seeking personal responsibility | | | | | | | | | | |
| Tapping and using resources | | | | | | | | | | |
| Self-imposed standards | | | | | | | | | | |

There are no correct answers to the exercise above but, obviously, the higher your scores the more likely you are to be suited to being an entrepreneur.

However, despite the great variety of people who end up as business-owners, probably the most important personal characteristic for an entrepreneur is determination.

It's easy to start a business; it's more difficult to keep it going. When you are faced with long hours, with working through nights and weekends, with extended periods away from your family, and with the horrors of financial worries, the thought of a secure permanent pensionable job is tempting. Determination is what will see you through these lows until you break through to success!

You should also consider your general state of health. Both the physical and mental stresses of running your own business can be very great. If you are driven to a state of collapse by the experience, you may leave your spouse and family much more exposed financially than would be the case if you were in a secure job with benefits attached.

You should be aware of the part your spouse and family will play in achieving your ambition of becoming an entrepreneur. Are they as committed as you are? Are they as willing to accept the lows as the highs? Without their support, you will find it difficult to start and develop your business. If they are actively pulling against you, quit now! Read *"My Family Doesn't Understand Me!"* (Yanky Fachler, Oak Tree Press) for an insight into the part that family can play in the success of your business and the strategies you need to use to make sure that they are truly on board.

Part of the experience of running your own business is learning to apply the appropriate personal resource at the right time. For example, deciding to become an exporter at a time when your resources – foreign language skills, contacts, finances – are not adequate is to misuse an opportunity that might lead to success in other circumstances. A touch of realism instead would have revealed the impracticality of your plan.

So the first thing you should do when thinking about starting a business is to conduct a rigorous self-assessment:

- What skills and experience do you have?
- What training do you need?
- What characteristics do you have that will help (or hinder) you?
- Why do you want to start a business?

Write down the answers – it's not as easy to fudge uncomfortable answers in writing.

Then write your own application for the position of managing director and general factotum of your proposed business. Give your application to a friend not noted for tact and wait for the laughs. You need to be able to see yourself as others see you.

Are your keyboard and literary skills really up to sending out customer letters and writing marketing blurbs? Perhaps you excel in production and technical innovation? Maybe you need to acquire other skills? If so, can you get by with a little training for yourself or should you buy in these skills on a freelance basis as and when required?

Will you need a management team, or are there family members who are sufficiently committed to help (and capable of doing so)? What will hiring all these people do to your costs? Salaries usually represent a high percentage of costs in a small business. You need to be realistic about how many people you need, and how many you can afford – and what you do about the difference.

In terms of your business skills, you should consider, in addition to management experience, actual contacts and sales leads, as these are the concrete beginnings of your trading. If you plan to supply other retailers or manufacturers, you will be hoping to establish several guaranteed sales contracts before you finally start trading. If you are leaving employment to set up this kind of business, check that your employment contract allows you to canvass business on your own account (and time) while still an employee.

You should read this chapter again in a year's time. Why? Because you will only begin to discover the extent of your personal resources as you go along. Starting your own business will not only lead you to find hidden resources within yourself, but will build up existing strengths. It may also, of course, identify unsuspected weaknesses, but recognising them is the first step towards correcting them.

Useful guides in the early stage of deciding whether you have what it takes are Yanky Fachler's classic, *Fire in the Belly: An Exploration of the Entrepreneurial Spirit* (Oak Tree Press, 2001) and *Could You Be Your Own Boss?* (Brian O'Kane, Oak Tree Press, 2009).

## START YOUR OWN BUSINESS COURSES

This book is designed to help you through the early stages of starting a business. Together with other books published by Oak Tree Press, it gives you an edge.

For further guidance, or for the comfort of meeting like-minded people who are about to embark on the same adventure as yourself, consider a Start Your Own Business course. These courses can be useful because they draw together all the aspects of running a business – it is often easy to ignore those tasks that bore you or for which you feel ill-equipped.

Another advantage of attending a course is that you get to know advisers who may be useful to contact later with queries. Many of the courses run by the County & City Enterprise Boards or similar organisations are particularly useful for steering participants towards further support, when it is needed.

### How Do You Choose the Right Course?

Before you book a place on a course, meet or talk to the organisers. Ask about the backgrounds of the presenters. Those who run their own business or who, like many accountants and other professionals, make their living from advising entrepreneurs are the best bet.

Ask about the success rate of the course in establishing new businesses. Ask about the success rate of those businesses after two or three years. Remember that the average failure rate of new businesses is very high – about 50 per cent of start-ups fail within the first three years. But this gloomy statistic need not apply to you, if you plan your start-up carefully.

Make an effort to find people who have completed any courses you are seriously considering, and talk to them. They are in the best position to know whether what they learnt on the course actually was of use in practice. Their answers will tell you whether you should take a place on the course.

### If You Can't Attend a Course

If you cannot participate in a Start Your Own Business course, try to attend some of the seminars on specific aspects of enterprise development and small business management presented from time to time by the banks and other organisations. These are aimed at reducing the fall-out rate of business start-ups and are usually open to the public (sometimes for a fee). Watch the newspapers for details.

Otherwise, read as widely as you can in the area of enterprise and business start-ups. There are plenty of good books and newspapers and magazines (for example, the *Sunday Business Post,* and *Business Plus* and *Owner Manager* magazines) regularly publish special features that give useful advice.

## INCUBATORS

Perhaps, instead of merely a training programme, what you need is a push-start. Here an 'incubator may help.

An incubator is a programme, usually focused on technology businesses, that encourages the faster development of a new business by providing a range of supports from workspace to finance to administrative assistance (and training, where necessary) in order to free up the entrepreneur to concentrate on the business alone.

Because of their success in reducing the failure rate of start-ups, dozens of these have sprung all over the country – **Enterprise Ireland** is active in funding the development of incubators in most of the **Institutes of Technology**, for example.

Sometimes, the term is used loosely to cover provision of workspace – if you're offered 'incubation workspace', check what is included.

Incubators include:

- **Bolton Trust.**
- **Business Innovation Centres** – see the *Directory* for a list.
- **Dún Laoire Enterprise Centre.**
- **Enterprise Acceleration Centre.**
- Enterprise Agencies (some, not all) that are members of **Enterprise Northern Ireland** – see the *Directory* for a list.
- **Enterprise Platform Programmes** – see the *Directory* for a list.
- **Flax Trust.**
- **Greenhouse Start-up Incubator.**
- **Growcorp Innovation Centre.**
- **Guinness Enterprise Centre.**
- **Institutes of Technology** – see the *Directory* for a list.
- **Liffey Trust.**
- **LINC Centre.**
- **NovaUCD.**
- **PDC.**
- **Shannon Development.**
- **SPADE Enterprise Centre.**
- **Synergy Centre.**
- **TCD Enterprise Centre.**
- **Terenure Enterprise Ltd.**
- **Údarás na Gaeltachta.**
- **Universities** – see the *Directory* for a list.

## START EARLY!

You're never too young to start thinking about enterprise and running your own business. Even if you're still in school or at college, there are programmes designed to attract you towards the notion of self-employment and to help you begin to gain the necessary skills. They include:

- **Choose Enterprise.com.**
- **Junior Achievement.**
- **Prince's Trust Northern Ireland.**
- Student Enterprise Awards (**Enterprise Ireland**).
- **Young Enterprise Northern Ireland.**
- **Young Entrepreneur Programme.**

## START-UP ALTERNATIVES

Of course, it's not always necessary to start a business from scratch. Brokers exist who will help you to identify and buy a suitable business, whose owner lacks the capital or enthusiasm to develop it further. Such brokers include:

- **Boylan & Dodd Corporate Services Ltd.**
- **Franchise Direct.**
- **Irish Business Sales & Corporate Finance Company.**

If you do go down this route, make sure that you take professional advice before making any financial or legal commitment. And continue to read the rest of this book, since you will still need to plan for the development of your business.

# 2: Researching Your Idea

After considering your own capacity to run a business, you need to ask yourself whether a market exists for your product or service. The market may be incredibly tough to break into but, as long as it exists, you can fight for your share of it. If there is no market at all for your product, it is clearly a non-starter.

You are not yet attempting to measure the size or location of the market, nor to distinguish its characteristics. What you want are the answers to the following questions:

- Do others already offer the same product or service as I intend to offer?
- Is my product / service an improvement on what already exists?
- What evidence is there that customers want to buy my improved product / service?

If your product / service is new to the market, you need to ask:

- What evidence is there that the market wants to buy this product / service?
- What evidence is there that the market is aware of its need for my product / service?

You may be able to find answers to these questions quite easily. For example, the market for ready-mixed concrete is quite visible but is dominated by a few big companies. So the question here quickly changes from whether a market exists to whether it is feasible to enter that market when there are already strong competitors in place.

On the other hand, the inventor of a solar-powered bicycle might have more difficulty assessing the existence of a market. All the Irish cyclists he talks to may tell him that they only cycle for the exercise value, since they cannot depend on sufficient sun to make any difference to the energy they must expend in cycling. They might have no interest in any source of power beyond their own muscles. Yet, in environmentally conscious (and sunnier) countries that encourage the use of a bicycle and / or solar power, the product could be greeted with cries of delight and massive demand. However, if the inventor does not know where to look, he or she may never get their business off the ground.

This quick feasibility review will tell you whether it's worth progressing to more formal market research, or whether you should go back to the drawing board to think of a new product or service.

## MARKET RESEARCH

Once you have provided yourself with proof – not just a gut feeling – of the existence of the market (see below, *Sources of Information*), you can move on to more detailed research. Analysing the nature of the market, competition and customer base will tell you whether your idea is feasible. The information you compile will allow you to develop your business plan in more detail.

Although a professional market research company will conduct research for you, at a price, you can often do your own research without too much difficulty, time or cost.

In collecting information during this research stage, remember that, as well as satisfying yourself, you may have to prove to outside investors that your figures and findings are valid. For this reason, independent proof is worth collecting wherever you can find it. Sources include:

- Talking to potential customers and even competitors.
- Questionnaires and surveys.
- Official government statistics or statistics compiled by trade associations and consumer bodies.

## MARKET RESEARCH

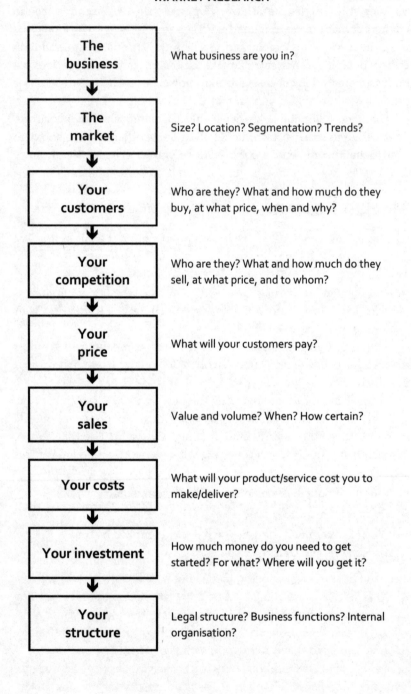

| | |
|---|---|
| **The business** | What business are you in? |
| **The market** | Size? Location? Segmentation? Trends? |
| **Your customers** | Who are they? What and how much do they buy, at what price, when and why? |
| **Your competition** | Who are they? What and how much do they sell, at what price, and to whom? |
| **Your price** | What will your customers pay? |
| **Your sales** | Value and volume? When? How certain? |
| **Your costs** | What will your product/service cost you to make/deliver? |
| **Your investment** | How much money do you need to get started? For what? Where will you get it? |
| **Your structure** | Legal structure? Business functions? Internal organisation? |

You need to sift carefully through the information you collect:

- To understand the business you are in.
- To work out the size and location of the market for your product / service.
- To build up a profile of your customers and their needs.
- To understand how competition operates in your market.
- To establish a reasonable price for your product / service – one at which your customers will buy.
- To forecast sales – both volume and value.
- To establish the cost of making your product or delivering your service – and how it will be done – the profit margins you can expect.
- To establish the investment needed to start your business.
- To decide what form your business must take.

### What Is Your Business?

This may seem an obvious question, one not worth asking, but setting it down in writing may provide a useful reference exercise.

For example, Waterford Crystal is not in the market of providing everyday glassware. Despite the fact that it produces glasses, bowls and vases, it does not compete with the producer of the everyday glass tumbler that you find in the supermarket or department store. Rather, it is in the international market for luxury goods and special occasion gifts. It will look to growth trends in these luxury markets, mainly overseas, rather than to growth in glassware sales generally.

In contrast, a contract carpet-cleaning business in Dublin is providing a very specific service in the city, or possibly even only in one area of the city.

Be aware that if you are a manufacturer, you are a manufacturer, not a retailer. You may sell your product to or through a dealer, but you are not a dealer, nor are you selling direct to the public. To try to be more than you are can spell doom for a small business, because your business may not have the resources and you may not have the necessary skills to take on your new ideas.

For example, a manufacturer of trailers in Mayo might wish to sell them to the end-customer himself (perhaps, in order to avoid losing a large share of the retail price to middlemen). But manufacturing and retailing are essentially two separate businesses. People in Cork are unlikely to travel to Mayo to buy a trailer, when there is probably a supplier of a range of comparable trailers already based in their own county. Even if the Mayo manufacturer sets up a shop in Cork, people may still be inclined to visit other retailers who offer a wider range of choice, or have local contacts. More sales will be achieved by sticking firmly to the core activity of manufacturing, and developing a distribution network through dealers around the country.

In time, your business may have the resources to expand its operation and become something else, but, initially, if you try to start two businesses, you will have to generate the cash flow and return for both, which is (at least) twice as difficult as generating them for one.

## Where Is Your Market?

Starting out, you are unlikely to be able to tackle the whole market for your product or service. You will instead look for a suitable segment of that market. That might be defined geographically – Cork, the North West counties, even a particular housing estate.

Alternatively, your segment might be defined as a product niche. For example, specialised stop-watches for use in sports, but not all sorts of watches or clocks.

However, even though you may decide only to tackle a small part of a market, you cannot afford to ignore what is happening in the whole market. For example, if you are opening the first small corner shop on a new housing estate, you should foresee that any one of several chains of supermarkets might open a shop nearby and become your main competition. Perhaps you could overcome this by becoming a franchisee of one of the chains yourself.

On the other hand, if your product will be manufactured and sold locally, for instance, in Dublin, but must compete against products from big international suppliers, you have to monitor what is going on in the international field as well as in the national market.

You need to look beyond your immediate market to see what the longer-term trends are:

- Is the size of your market growing or declining?
- Is it characterised by rapid innovation or evolution of products?
- Is it expanding geographically (as might be the case with an innovative product / service)?
- Is the number of competitors expanding or declining?
- Are prices rising or falling?

You need to end up with figures that show the size and growth potential of the total market – but these must be made relevant to your business proposal, in terms of the part of the market (the market segment) that you are targeting.

These concepts will help you to define your market:

- Wholesale or retail?
- One product or a range of products?
- A service?
- The luxury market?
- Necessities?

If your idea is very innovative and no market yet exists for it, it may be difficult to define what your market is likely to be. Obtaining hard information about the size and value of your market may be daunting. However, you must be able to provide this information in your business plan because it is a key element in establishing the existence of a market for your product and the cost structure that your business must attain in order to be competitive.

If you get this information wrong, other assumptions are likely to be invalid and your project may fail, perhaps at considerable loss to yourself. Equally, if bankers and other investors cannot find independent verification for the figures in your proposal, they will certainly have doubts regarding its overall viability, and are likely to refuse to finance you.

## Who Are Your Customers?

You must build as accurate a profile of your customers as you can. This depends on the type of business that you plan to start.

For a corner shop, the customers will be diverse in age, gender and requirements: everyone from children wanting sweets for a few pennies to adults wanting newspapers, grocery items and perhaps small gift items. On the other hand, an information technology company producing a single product, say an automated accounting package for bookmakers, has a very narrowly defined customer base.

Some useful questions to ask about your customers are:

- General public or business, or both?
- Public sector or private?
- Where do they live / operate?
- What and how much do they buy, at what price, when and why?

- What age are they?
- What gender?
- Are they spending for a necessity or a luxury; in other words, do they buy out of surplus income?
- Are they rich or poor?

For your product / service, are there criteria that define your customers, such as:

- A particular interest (for example, travel or sport)?
- Need for a particular service (for example, training to use accounting software)?

In terms of business customers, there may be other criteria to consider:

- Size of customer – will you supply only customers taking more than (or less than) a certain volume?
- Quality levels for the product (these may be imposed by certain wholesale purchasers, department / chain stores, etc.).
- Type of packaging preferred.

In considering who your customers are, you may also need to consider how easy it will be to deal with them. Larger organisations will have more decision-makers than small ones, and it may take longer to negotiate contracts and persuade them to take your product – although the resulting orders are likely to be bigger. To deal with the public sector, it is necessary to understand how it is structured, how decisions are made and who makes them.

Will your business deal only with one segment of the market, such as the public sector, or will you be tackling several segments? How much experience do you have in dealing with each segment? Do you have the resources to service more than one segment? Will you deal with them on the same terms? And, if not, how will you prevent sales 'leaking' from the segment that gets the most favourable terms?

## Who Is Your Competition?

Look hard at your own product / service. How does it differ from competing products / services? Very few businesses are genuinely innovative; most compete with existing businesses.

Why should a customer prefer your product / service?

- Better quality?

- Lower price?
- Higher profile?

What do your sales depend on?
- Price?
- Design?
- Advertising?
- Quality?
- Volume?
- After-sales service?
- Speed of delivery?
- Accessibility?

An important question is whether your product / service's differentiating feature is the one that makes the customer prefer it. Take the example of a Hermès scarf or a Rolls Royce car. It would be pointless to sell cheaper versions of either, since buyers value the image that the high price gives. Exclusive products are characterised by low-volume / high-margin sales. Their success depends on high marketing expenditure and careful selection and monitoring of distribution outlets.

If, on the other hand, your product / service's sale is characterised by high volumes and low margins, such as margarine or flour or fast food, your business needs to be structured very differently, with more emphasis on volume production, warehousing, constancy of supply and a good distribution network.

When looking at your competition, you may need to consider products / services that compete indirectly with yours, as well as those that compete directly. For example, if you produce frozen hamburgers, you compete not only against other frozen hamburger manufacturers, but against a variety of other cheap frozen food products, including fish fingers, vegetable burgers, pies and so on.

You need to find out:
- How many other companies supply products / services similar to yours?
- How will they react to your entry to the market place?
- Are all the companies in the market place the same size?
- Are they very much bigger than you?
- Have you the resources to equal their power in the market?

- Do new entrants normally start small and grow, or will you have to make a major commitment from the start?

## Price

The next piece of market information that you should research is the price that the market will pay for your product / service. How much will customers pay? Under what circumstances will they pay more?

You will generally be constrained by the market. You cannot charge more for your product / service than the going price for similar products / services unless it has something special to recommend it. Even then, a large number of customers may still choose the lower-priced option.

## Forecasting Sales

If you thought the earlier elements of your market research were hard, forecasting sales makes them look like child's play.

You need to have a good idea of likely sales (with some evidence to underpin your figures) in order to:

- Build your financial projections.
- Estimate the production capacity you require.
- Arrange for supply of materials.
- Hire staff.

Your requirements on each of these will vary depending on the sales volumes and values that you expect.

One way to do this is to start with a clean sheet of paper. Draw columns for each month and deep rows for each product or service (or variant thereof) that you expect to sell. Within each row, list the promotional and other activity that you plan to use to generate sales. (If you haven't planned any yet, it's time to start – products don't just sell on their own, they usually have to be sold).

Then, make some estimates month by month of the sales that will result from this activity. You may find it easier to forecast unit sales first and then to estimate sales value.

For example, if you intend to design and sell St Patrick's Day greetings cards, it's likely that most of your sales will happen in February and March – with perhaps a few early orders in January – but none after that, until the next year. So, in this case, your sales forecast exercise should naturally lead you into new product development – Easter cards, or cards for Mother's Day or Halloween and so on.

It's important to break down sales to the lowest level of product / service that you can manage without overwhelming yourself in detail. For example, if you were designing and selling greeting cards, it would be easy to overlook the potential for niche opportunities during the year, unless you specifically identified St Patrick's Day cards or the like.

Where you can, get forward orders or 'letters of comfort' from customers. These are better evidence in support of your forecasts than any market research – although your market research is still essential.

## Calculating Costs and Profit Margins

As part of your business planning (see *Chapter 4*), you will prepare financial projections for inclusion in your business plan.

However, even at this early stage, it is a good idea to estimate (even crudely) the minimum size or capacity at which you will make a profit – the break-even point – as well as the maximum operating capacity that you can afford to establish. To do this, you will need to work out what your costs of production will be – you already know the price the market will pay for your product, and how many units you expect to be able to sell.

You also need to identify the current market profit margins – how much your competitors are making. You may be prepared to accept a slimmer margin, but this may reduce your flexibility to deal with unexpected demands. It may also shorten the length of time your business can afford to wait to reach the break-even point. If you look for larger than average profit margins, without either reducing costs or convincing customers that your product is worth paying more for, you will quickly find yourself in difficulty.

Will your entry to the market place reduce profit margins generally? If you increase the total supply of product available, it may have the effect of reducing the price for which it sells. It may even trigger a price war, as existing suppliers try to kill off your business before it gets going by cutting their prices below the price you must get to stay in business.

You will most likely get a part of the market, not the whole. Yet, if you cannot meet the average costs achieved by your direct competitors, you may fail, even though your product / service may be better than theirs.

The income generated by sales must provide sufficient cash flow to enable your business to cover all costs. If money comes in too slowly, your business may choke to death while demand booms.     Cash flow – collecting money from customers as quickly as possible and getting the longest possible credit period from your suppliers – is often more important in the short term for a small business than profit. But, overall, you must make a profit to stay in business.

## Estimating Your Initial Investment

At this stage, you should draw up a list of what premises and equipment you absolutely must have (not what it would be nice to have).

You need to answer these questions:

- Will it be possible to keep overheads low by working from your garage or a spare room?
- Do you need retail premises in a good location?
- What about warehouse space?
- Do you need specialised equipment? How big is it?
- Will you have to make a large capital investment in equipment? Can you lease equipment instead? Can you buy it second-hand?

From this information, and your other market research, you will be able to estimate your initial investment – what you need to get started.

## Finding the Best Business Structure

Lastly, you need to decide what form your business organisation should take. When starting in business, you have a choice of five main types of business entity through which to conduct your enterprise:

- Sole trader.
- Partnership (and limited liability partnership in Northern Ireland).
- Unlimited company.
- Limited liability company.
- Co-operative.

Four things will decide which structure you choose:

- The kind of business you are starting. Some professional firms, for instance, can only be formed as sole traders or partnerships.
- The expectations of those with whom you plan to do business. Many business people expect to deal with limited companies and are wary of other forms of business entities as trading partners.
- Your attitude to risk – in particular, to risking those of your assets that you are not planning to commit to the business. A limited

liability company limits the risk of losing your capital if your enterprise is not successful.

- How you wish to organise your taxation affairs. Certain kinds of favourable tax treatment are only available to limited liability companies.

You are taking a risk in starting an enterprise. You are risking your money, time and reputation. You are entitled to protect those of your assets that you do not wish to commit to your enterprise. For this reason, and for your family's sake, you are strongly advised to form a limited liability company. Nonetheless, you should take professional advice for your accountant or solicitor in making your decision. If you do not yet have an accountant or solicitor, read the appropriate sections in *Chapter 9*.

Next, consider how your business will be organised. The main functional areas in any business are:

- Administration.
- Production.
- Marketing.
- Sales.
- Distribution.

What should be the balance between these functions within your company? Among the questions you need to ask yourself are:

- How will you get your product / service to the purchaser?
- Will you need large amounts of warehouse or office space?
- What are your costs of production?
- What are the overheads involved?

## SOURCES OF INFORMATION

There is no shortage of information available to help you in your market research – most entrepreneurs find that their main problem is too much information!

Consider all of these sources:

- Yourself.
- Professional advisers.

- Trade and professional associations.
- Libraries.
- Telephone directories.
- Other people.
- State and private sector enterprise support agencies.
- Professional researchers.
- The Internet.

## Yourself

Most people have started to research their idea long before they come to the formal planning stage. Often, the idea has grown out of a long period of personal interest and the 'research' is based on:

- Personal experience
- Talking to friends
- Talking to suppliers.

If you have an idea for a new type of light fitting, it is probably because over the years you have been driven mad by the failings of the many light fittings that you have used. So, immediately, you know what advantage your potential product offers above others in the market.

You may have to find out about the costs of making it, how it is distributed and who the competitors are before you can make an estimate of the size of the market and, most importantly, whether it is financially feasible to be a small manufacturer of light fittings only. You might discover that the machinery required is so expensive that you would have to make and sell a huge number of fittings in order to pay for it.

Many good business ideas provide an answer to a problem with existing products.

## Professional Advisers

Bank managers and accountants often have a good idea of how different types of businesses are faring, and what differentiates the successes from those that cannot pay the bills. Also, talking to your bank manager like this is a gentle introduction for him / her to your idea of starting your own business.

Banks and investment businesses often have specialists in a variety of industry sectors, who can be useful sources of market information and statistics. Approach your bank manager or the small business lending unit of your bank as a first step. They may be able to find the information for you, or direct you to someone in the corporate lending or investment divisions.

### Trade and Professional Associations

If a trade or professional association exists for the market sector in which you are interested, it may be an excellent source of information about the total size and value of your market. It may even have statistics broken down by region.

Some associations may only make this information available to members – and, if you are not yet in business, you may find it difficult to gain access to it. Other associations will make the information publicly available, though there is usually a charge involved as the organisation tries to recover some of its own costs.

Many associations have links to sister bodies internationally and thus can be a source of international statistics and information.

Most of these organisations provide training, networking and other services to their members so, if an association is relevant to your business, it's worth considering joining at the earliest possible opportunity.

### Libraries

Often overlooked, local libraries have a wealth of information available – either on the spot or available through inter-library loans. Make a friend of your local librarian – he or she has valuable research skills that you will spend a great deal of time to acquire yourself. And, increasingly, libraries provide access to the Internet (see below) for a modest charge.

Two excellent libraries are:
- **Belfast Business Library** at the Central Library, Royal Avenue.
- **Business Information Centre** at the ILAC Centre library.

### Telephone Directories

The *Golden Pages* or *Yellow Pages* – the classified part of the telephone directory – is a useful guide to the number of people doing what you want to do and their location. You want to be a carpenter? Look up carpenters in the phone book. If there are 15 in your locality, either it is a great place for carpenters or they are all very poor!

Another useful directory is the *Administration Yearbook & Diary*, published by the **Institute of Public Administration**.

## Other People in the Business

Talk to people already involved in the industry. Make use of their experience. Find them on **Smallbusinesscan.com**.

Trade and professional associations may be able to put you in contact with some of their members who may be willing to share their experience and expertise.

If yours is (or will be) a technology business, identify a 'Centre of Excellence' in your field. The **Institutes of Technology** and **Universities** have a wealth of information and experience at their disposal, much of which is available – though, usually, for a fee. Ask for the Technology Transfer Office or Industrial Liaison Office as a starting point.

## State and Private Sector Enterprise Support Agencies

There is a vast range of support available to entrepreneurs and those thinking of starting a business – much expanded since the first edition of this book. Much of it is provided by State or State-funded agencies; some of it is provided by the private sector.

**Chapters 5, 6** and **7** give details of State, private sector and European support for entrepreneurs and small business. **Chapter 8** provides this information for Northern Ireland. In addition, the comprehensive **Directory of Sources of Assistance** provides contact details for all organisations mentioned and this book's companion website, **www.startingabusinessinireland.com**, will keep you up-to-date, as well as providing you with additional information.

## Professional Researchers

If the market for your product is geographically extensive, or highly competitive, you might consider getting professional market researchers to prepare a report for you. Look in the *Golden Pages* classified telephone directory for contact details of market researchers in your area.

## The Internet

Another source of information – particularly on international trends – is the Internet. If you are not already connected to the Internet, ask a friend to show you or visit your local library or a 'cybercafé', where you can rent access by the hour.

Use search engines – Google, Yahoo or Bing, etc. – to help narrow your enquiries. Contact the companies whose websites you visit for more information.

Useful websites for start-ups include:

- **Amárach Consulting.**
- **BankofIrelandStartUpCourse.com.**
- **BASIS.ie.**
- **Bplans.ie.**
- **Business Plus.**
- **Central Statistics Office.**
- **ChooseEnterprise.com.**
- **CreativeIreland.com.**
- **Europa.**
- **Expertiseireland.com.**
- **First Tuesday.**
- **FranchiseDirect.**
- **Galway County and City Enterprise Board.**
- **Gov.ie.**
- **Irish Internet Association** – for its 'iia Internet resources' section.
- **Louth Craftmark.**
- **MovetoIreland.com.**
- **NIBusinessInfo.co.uk.**
- **Oak Tree Press.**
- **Revenue Commissioners.**
- **Smallbusinesscan.com.**
- **Webpayments.ie.**

## INTERPRETING RESEARCH RESULTS

Researching your proposed business is not just a matter of asking the right questions. Interpreting the results is equally important. You may be too close to your idea to see problems (or, less often, to see opportunities). Bringing in outsiders may be helpful. Consider friends whose business skills you respect. Ask your accountant, banker or other professional adviser – even if you have to pay for their opinion. It is important to arrive at an independently objective point of view, and it will be worth paying for if it saves you from disaster.

In addition to giving an independent view of your plans, a good accountant can help you draw up financial projections. In any case, you will probably need an accountant once you have begun trading. An accountant who is introduced at the planning stage will have a greater insight into the objectives of the business as well as the systems by which it functions. Your planning will benefit from the experience of your accountant, who, in turn, will be better placed to give you good service in future years.

## THE FINAL QUESTION

Now you are in a position to answer the question at the start of this chapter: Does a market for your product or service exist? Your answer will tell you whether to proceed to the next stage.

If not, don't despair. It's better to have found out that your idea won't work before you have invested much time and effort into it – and, if you're serious about starting your own business, there'll be plenty of other opportunities.

# 3: Writing a Business Plan

Once you have thoroughly done the necessary market research for your project and decided to go ahead and start your own business, your next step is to write a business plan that summarises the following points about your business:

- Where it has come from.
- Where it is now.
- Where it is going in the future.
- How it intends to get there.
- How much money it needs to fulfil its plans.
- What makes it likely to succeed.
- What threats or disadvantages must be overcome on the way.

The document can range in length from a few typed sheets of paper to several hundred pages. However, since professional readers of business plans – bankers, venture capitalists and enterprise officers – are offered more business plans than they can intelligently digest, the more concise your business plan, the more likely it is to be read.

## THE PURPOSE OF A BUSINESS PLAN

A business plan can have several purposes. The main ones usually are:

- To establish the fundamental viability of your project.
- To document your plan for the business.
- To act as a yardstick for measuring progress against plans.
- To communicate your plans for your business to outsiders, particularly those you want to invest in your business.

Although the business plan is most often used as a marketing document for raising finance, even if you do not need to raise finance you should still prepare one since it will:

- Focus your thoughts.
- Check your numbers.
- Provide a basis for monitoring results.
- Enable communication of your ideas.

Each of these purposes places its own demands on the format and contents of the business plan.

The focus of your business plan will vary, depending on the relative priorities that you assign to these purposes. Let's look at each in turn.

### Establishing the Viability of Your Project

There are many ways of researching whether your project will succeed. All, however, finally require an act of faith from the entrepreneur when the time comes to commit to the business. Before this point is reached, a great deal of planning and careful thought should have been completed.

A well-prepared business plan will assist immeasurably with that process, simply through the discipline it imposes. Too often, entrepreneurs are carried away with their own enthusiasm. They neglect the most cursory checks on the viability of their brainchild. Broad, and sometimes rash, assumptions are made about the market for the product, its cost of manufacture, distribution channels, acceptability to customers etc. But when a reasoned, written case must be made – even if only to oneself – it is less easy to overlook the unpalatable. At least, it is difficult to do so without being aware of it.

### Documenting the Plan

"The plan doesn't matter, it's the planning that counts", said Dwight D. Eisenhower, former US President. He was right. The quality of the planning you do for your business is critical to its success; how you document that planning process is less so. Nonetheless, a good business plan document actively aids the planning process by providing a structure. It forces you:

- To cover ground that you might otherwise, in your enthusiasm, skip over.
- To clarify your thinking — it is almost impossible to get your plan onto paper until you have formulated it clearly.

- To justify your arguments, since they will be written down for others to see.
- To focus on the risks and potential for loss in your plans as well as on the potential for profit and success.

Avoid unnecessary pessimism. Be realistic, but don't carry caution to extremes. If your proposal is realistic, have confidence in it.

## A Yardstick for Measuring Progress

Preparing any plan demands an objective. An objective assumes that you are going to make some effort to achieve it. Some objectives are quantifiable: if your aim is to sell 500 gadgets, sales of 480 is below target, while 510 units sold gives you reason to feel pleased with your performance. Other objectives cannot be quantified; all the more reason then to document them so that you can clearly establish whether or not you have achieved them.

Your business plan should contain the objectives, quantifiable and otherwise, that you have set for your business. Reading through your plan at regular intervals and comparing your performance to date with the objectives you set yourself one month, six months or two years earlier can help to focus your attention on the important things that need to be done if targets are to be achieved.

## Communicating Plans to Third Parties

Though they would readily acknowledge the importance of good planning, many businesses would not prepare a formal business plan document if it were not for the need to present their plans for the business to outsiders – usually to raise finance. But, if you wish to raise finance for your business to develop, you will have to prepare a plan.

Financiers, whether bankers, venture capitalists or private investors, need:

- A document they can study in their own time, and which makes its case independently of the promoters of the business.
- Evidence that the future of the business has been properly thought through and that all risks have been taken into account.
- Information about the business.

In addition, others may have reason to read your business plan – key employees or suppliers, for example. So it must communicate your message clearly.

No matter how good a writer you consider yourself to be, if you can't put your business proposition clearly and persuasively in writing, it suggests that you have more thinking to do. It doesn't mean that your project won't work. On the contrary, your business may be a resounding success – but you need to be able to communicate it!

## WHO SHOULD WRITE YOUR BUSINESS PLAN?

Very simply, you. No one else. You may receive offers from consultants, many of them highly reputable and professional in their work, to write your business plan for you. They will quote their extensive experience of business, of raising finance for start-up businesses, of presenting financial information – all valid points and, in many cases, true.

However, whatever experience consultants may have of business in general, and drafting business plans in particular, they lack one essential ingredient: your intimate relationship with your business. You are the one who has spent your waking hours – and many of your sleeping ones, too, probably – dreaming, planning and guiding your tender and frail creation to this point. You know what makes you tick; what makes your team tick; what will and will not work for you. Only you can assemble these thoughts.

Therefore, the first draft of the business plan is your responsibility. Do it yourself. Refine and redraft it – again, and again, if necessary – until it's finished.

Then, and only then, should you entrust it to someone who can put the right gloss on it. But let them do only that. Don't let them put *their* words on your pages.

## HOW LONG SHOULD YOUR BUSINESS PLAN BE?

How long is a piece of string? Your business plan should be as long as it needs to be – no longer and no shorter.

How long is that? No one can decide that except yourself. It depends on the purpose for which you are preparing the plan, the level of knowledge that likely readers will have of your business, and the complexity of your business.

Few businesses can be done justice to in less than, say, 10 A4 pages; equally, it will be a dedicated reader (or one who has spotted an outstandingly good business proposition) who will continue past the first hundred pages or so.

If a reader wants more information, they will ask for it. But make sure that they don't have to ask for information they should have had from the start – or, worse still (and sometimes fatal to your hopes of raising finance), that the absence of the information doesn't lead them to discard your plan altogether.

# FIGURES

Too many figures and your plan may become off-putting, but too few and your plans will simply be treated as ambitions without any underlying substance. Quantify as much as you can. Your plan is likely to be read by people whose currency is numbers. You help your cause by talking their language.

Make sure figures add up correctly. Nothing is more worrying to an investor than the suspicion that:

- You can't handle figures.
- There's a figure wrong or missing – or worse still, hidden.

You need to be able to show the existence of a market for your product, and some indication of its size, in a way that can be verified independently. You will also have to prove to the satisfaction of the bank manager or investor that adequate margins can be achieved to cover cash flow needs and meet repayment of debt or growth objectives.

Don't clog up the body of the business plan with detailed statistical analysis, although it must contain all the information a reader needs. For example, quote the proposed sales target, but show how you will achieve it at the back in an Appendix, and explain the underlying assumptions there also. The same applies to the CVs of key employees – mention crucial information where appropriate in the plan, but place the details in an Appendix.

## Business Models and Projected Figures

A financial model of the business is effectively a set of accounts, represented on computer spreadsheets or in a dedicated modelling package for ease of manipulation – for example, *Business Plan Pro* from **Palo Alto Software**.

While a financial model is useful for businesses of all sizes, for a business of any complexity it is essential. Your model should enable you to change certain variables, such as the number of units of product sold, or the price at which you sell them, or the cost of supplies, and discover what the effect will be on the business.

Your financial model should consist of:

- Profit and loss account.
- Cash flow statement.
- Balance sheet.

You may also create some management accounts that look in more detail at production and overhead costs and allow you to manipulate certain of those variables.

It is crucial that the figures you use in your model are as close to reality as can be. Your model must show what your breakeven point is likely to be in different circumstances, and allow you to estimate how long it will take to reach it. This calculation is very important when it comes to raising finance. If you will be able to repay borrowings in three to six months, you may be willing to risk a bigger initial loan than if your earliest estimated repayment date is a year away.

The rule is to be cautious and prudent, but realistic. If your figures are too optimistic, you could find that you cannot meet your repayment schedule, and the additional cost of borrowing over a longer time frame damages your business' growth prospects, if not its viability – and your credibility with your bank manager. Equally, if you are unnecessarily pessimistic about the length of time it will take to repay the loan, your calculations may indicate that the entire project should be dropped – which is exactly what your bank manager will do!

Some of the main reasons for using a financial model are to estimate:

- A breakeven point under different market conditions.
- How long it will take to reach a desired level of operation.
- The consequences of price changes.
- The consequences of undertaking expansion, R & D, and other special projects.

If you have no experience of financial modelling, you should seek help from your bank, **County & City Enterprise Board**, your accountant or one of the other organisations listed in the "Business Plans" section of the *Directory*.

Again, the details of the assumptions on which the model is based should go into an Appendix to the business plan, as should any detailed statistical analysis. Quote the important final figures in the body of the plan.

## A STANDARD BUSINESS PLAN FORMAT

Each business plan is unique. However, those whom you seek to convince to invest in your project have come to expect certain information in a broadly standard format that presents information in an easily-digested logical sequence.

For a very small or simple business, the following intuitive format (adapted from *Applying the Rules of Business, Steps to Entrepreneurship* series, Ron Immink & Brian O'Kane, Oak Tree Press) may be sufficient.

It sets out 10 key questions, the answers to which:

- Cover all the information that a reader of a business plan is likely to want to know in order to come to a decision on the plan.
- Ensure that you have fully thought through all aspects of your business.

For larger businesses, the second format shown two pages on, adapted from *Planning for Success, Steps to Entrepreneurship* series (Ron Immink & Brian O'Kane, Oak Tree Press) may be more appropriate.

This format is also closer to conventional business planning formats expected by banks and other financial institutions, a version of which (based on the template in *Starting Your Own Business: A Workbook*, Ron Immink & Brian O'Kane, Oak Tree Press) is available for download on **www.startingabusinessinireland.com**.

## SIMPLE BUSINESS PLAN OUTLINE

| | |
|---|---|
| **I am …** | Explain who you are, your education / work experience etc, especially insofar as it applies to your proposed business. |
| **My product is …** | Explain your product: What it is, what is does, how it works, how it is made, what makes it different / unique, etc. |
| **My customers are …** | Explain who your customers will be and what evidence you have to support this. |
| **My customers will buy my product because …** | Explain why your customers will buy your product and what evidence you have to support this. |
| **My customers will pay …** | Explain how much your customers will pay for each unit of your product and what evidence you have to support this. |
| **At this price, my customers will buy …** | Explain how many units of your product your customers will buy at the price set and what evidence you have to support this. |
| **I can make …** | Explain how many units of your product you can make in a given time period and what evidence you have to support this. |
| **To make each unit of product costs …** | Explain how much each unit of product costs you to make and what evidence you have to support this. |
| **The start-up investment I require is …** | Explain the start-up investment you need, what it will be used for and what evidence you have to support this. |
| **I have a viable business because …** | Explain why you believe you have a viable business and what evidence you have to support this. |
| **In summary …** | On a single page, list the main points of your plan, in bullet point form. This is the part of the business plan that will make the biggest impression on your reader – make sure it's easy to read and understand. Then put it at the front of your plan, where it will be seen! |

## PLANNING FOR SUCCESS BUSINESS PLAN OUTLINE

---

*1: Summary / Overview*

---

- **Founder(s).**
- **Business name.**
- **Contact details:** Address, telephone / fax, e-mail, website.
- **Status:** Sole trader, partnership or limited company.
- **Registered for:** VAT, PAYE, Corporation Tax.
- **Formed as:** Purchase of existing business / purchase of franchise / start-up / other.
- **Business Objective**
- **External Accountant:** Address, telephone / fax number, e-mail, contact name.
- **Product/Service Range:** Include descriptions and prices.
- **Staff:** Numbers employed in production, sales / promotion, administration, other duties.
- **Competitors:** Include estimates of competitors' turnover.
- **Investment and Financing:** Details of fixed assets, personal assets, current assets, long-term / medium-term assets, liquid assets, short-term finance, start-up costs, subsidies / grants, allowance for contingencies, total investment, total available finance.
- **Budgets:** Forecasts for turnover, gross profit, gross profit percentage, net profit, cash flow and personal expenses over first three years.
- **Other Information.**

---

*2: The Entrepreneur*
*(If there is more than one founder, each must complete this section.)*

---

- **Personal details:** Name, address, date of birth, etc.
- **Income**: Details of present income, source of income, benefits, income of spouse / partner, etc.
- **Education**: Details of post-primary education, including any courses that you are currently attending.

- **Practical Experience**: Details of your working history and experience and any other significant experience that could be useful for your business.

- **Motivation, Objectives and Goals**: Why do you want to start a business? What do you want to achieve with your business?

- **Personal Qualities**: What special qualities of yours are important for your business? List both your strong and your weak points. What are you going to do about your weak points?

---

### 3: Formal Requirements

- **Overall Description**: Give a general description of your proposed business.

- **Research**: List the organisations you have contacted to discuss your plans and summarise the outcome of these discussions.

- **Legal Status**: What legal status will your business take? What considerations led you to this choice?

- **Name and Location**: What is the name of the business? Have you checked that this name is available? Describe your location. How can customers reach your location? Is access for supply and removal of goods available? Is there enough parking for your customers' cars and for your own cars? How big are your office premises? Are there expansion possibilities at these premises? Are the premises leased or purchased? Give details of cost of lease / mortgage. Have the premises been professionally valued? Has a lease or purchase contract been prepared by a solicitor? (If so, give the name of the solicitor.) Is there any pollution in the ground at your premises?

- **Licences**: Do you fulfil all of the licensing and permit requirements for the field you will be working in? If so, which and on what grounds? If not, why not and what are you doing about it? Is your business registered at the Companies Registration Office? What other licences do you need? Are there any other legal applications required (for example, environmental concerns). If so, which?

- **Employer and Employees**: Initially, how will your staffing be organised? Have you drawn up clear job descriptions for your future employees? Do you plan to expand your employee numbers quickly? Who will replace you during any required absences?

- **Administration**: Who will do your accounting? Who will do your bookkeeping? Give names, addresses and contact numbers.

- **Insurance**: Are you insured against the normal risks? If so, what is insured and for how much?

- **Terms of Trade**: How is responsibility for product delivery arranged? Are product deliveries insured? If so, for how much? Summarise your terms of trade.

- **VAT**: Is your business registered for VAT? What is your VAT number? What rates of VAT apply to your business?

- **Start Date**: On what date do you want to start the business, or when did you start?

---

### 4: Marketing

- **Market**: Who are your target groups? What do you have to offer? What is your business objective in seven words?

- **Market Research**: Describe your market, future developments and your potential customers (local, county, national, and international). Describe the level of competition you face. What are the leading indicators in your market sector? Estimate the size of the Irish market for your product. What part of this market do you intend to service? Have you contacted future customers? What was their reaction? Have you obtained any forward orders? What comments did you receive with these orders?

- **Image**: What image will your business present? Formulate the core of your marketing plan based on your target groups, product assortment, price level, etc.

- **Product (Range)**: Describe briefly the product(s) you want to launch. Describe the primary and secondary functions of your product(s). What choices do you offer your customers? What extras do you offer compared to the competition?

- **Price**: What are customers prepared to pay? What are customers accustomed to paying? What are your competitors' prices? What is your price? How is your price made up? Will you offer discounts? If so, what will they be? Will you give special offers? If so, what will they be? Will cost calculations be monitored during operation? If so, how?

- **Place**: Explain your choice of location. Are there future developments that will change the attractiveness of your location? How did you allocate space for the various necessary functions?

- **Personnel**: Profile yourself as a business person. How many people will be involved in production, sales / promotion, administration, other duties? How are you going to make sure that your staff uphold the image of your business?

- **Presentation**: How are you going to present your business (layout, colours, music, atmosphere, correspondence, brochures, business cards, van signs)?

- **Promotion**: Rate those areas your customers are most interested in, and your relative strengths in those areas. How are you going to approach your customers and what buying motives are you going to emphasise? What marketing and promotion resources will you emphasise? Explain your promotion methods (how, where, frequency, etc.)

- **Competitors**: List your main competitors. Assess their strengths compared to your own. In what ways do your products / services differ from those of your competitors? Can you estimate the total turnover of your competitors? What are your strong points compared to those of your direct competitors? What are your weak points compared to those of your direct competitors?

- **Purchasing**: Have you contacted your future suppliers? If so, what are their terms of trade? Are there alternative suppliers? What advantages do these alternative suppliers offer you?

- **Production Process**: Are you involved with (or will you be using) new techniques or new products in your production processes? If so, are you receiving assistance from experts? If so, who are they and how are they involved? Describe your production process. What experience do you have with this process? What equipment do you use in the production process? List the equipment you intend to lease, buy new, or buy used. What guarantees / back-up do you have for this equipment in case of malfunction? Have you enough capacity to achieve the revenue for which you have budgeted? Have you checked your products and production processes for environmental considerations? If so, are there any environmental objections? If so, what are you planning to do about them?

---

### 5: Investment and Financing

- **Investment**: Describe the investment you will have to make to start your business, and to run it over the first three years (amounts exclusive of VAT).

- **Personal Assets**: What assets can you (and your business partner(s)) put up yourselves? How did you value your personal assets?

- **Other (Bank) Finance**: Details of long-term / medium-term finance, short-term finance, subsidies / grants; shortfall, surplus, etc.

- **Credit Assessment**: Can you support the required investment in fixed assets with quotations from suppliers? If not, how did you calculate your investment? Is your investment cost-effective? In your estimates, did you take seasonal business influences into account, and calculate based on your maximum requirements? How did you estimate your stock and work-in-progress levels? How did you estimate the value of your debtors? Do you have sufficient liquid assets to cope with disappointments and unexpected expenses? Did you approach a bank(s) about the financing of your plans? If yes, which bank(s), and who was your contact person? Did those contacts lead to any agreements? Did you approach other finance companies about your plans? If yes, with whom did you speak? Were any decisions reached, or arrangements made?

---

### 6: The Operating Budget

- **Turnover Forecast**: List your revenue sources, and project the amounts you expect from each in the first three years.

- **Costs**: Give details of costs for staff, production, premises, transport, sales and promotion, general expenses, finance and depreciation in each of the first three years.

- **Profits and Cash Flow**: Give detailed cash flow projections for the first three years.

- **Comments on the Budget**: Describe how you calculated and estimated your revenue (number of customers, average order per customer, turnaround). What expansion do you expect over the next few years? How did you calculate your purchase costs? How did you estimate salaries? What effect will any shortfall in turnover have on your business and how do you plan to handle it? What is your minimum required turnover?

---

### 7: Personal Expenses

---

- **Personal Expenses**: Fixed expenses; rent / interest and repayment gas, water, electricity; taxes / charges; insurance; study expenses; membership expenses / contributions; TV licence; private use of car; repayments (enclose loan details); household expenses, etc.

- **Home Equity**: Do you own your own home? If so, have you had it valued? What is its market value? How much equity do you have in your house?

- **Additional Debts**: What other debts do you have (personal / private loan or credit, car financing, study costs, etc.)?

- **Minimum Required Turnover**: What is the minimum required turnover for your business, including your personal expenses?

---

### 8: Cash Flow

---

- Detailed cash flow projections for each month / quarter, outlining all income and expenditure, together with the opening and closing bank balances each quarter over the first three years.

Sometimes the Summary / Overview is expanded with a narrative Executive Summary, a concise one- or two-page summary of the entire plan.

This Executive Summary is the last thing to be written, and the first to be read. It must persuade the reader that the idea is good, otherwise he or she may not read on. It summarises the company, its objectives, why it will be successful. It describes the products, the market, critical financial information and, finally, outlines what form of finance is required, how much, and when. It assumes that its reader is not expert in your industry and knows nothing about your business. And it does all this in as few words as possible!

You should avoid giving detailed personal reasons for wanting to be your own boss. It is very easy to confuse your personal ambitions with your objectives for the business. Bankers and other investors are primarily considering your prospects for success (getting them a good return), not your prospects for personal satisfaction. It is quite important to keep your focus, like theirs, on the business. Nonetheless, your character and skills will be of importance to them; these are the things to mention.

## HOW A FINANCIER READS A BUSINESS PLAN

How a financier reads a business plan depends on what kind of financier he, or increasingly she, is. There are two types of financier – the lender and the investor.

The lender is typically your bank manager. Lenders will invest money in your business, if they think it worth doing so by their criteria, in return for interest on the capital. The professional investor, on the other hand, will invest equity in your business and share in your risk as owner of the business. Professional investors will postpone their return for a period – typically, three to five years – but will look for an above-average return for the risk involved in doing so.

### The Lender

The average bank manager will be looking to see how you have handled, or propose to handle, the risks, particularly the financial risks, that your business is likely to encounter. Bank managers are concerned about the security of the bank's money – or more properly, the depositors' money – which you are seeking and for which they are responsible.

That is not to say that a bank manager will not back you. Most bank managers have discretion in the amounts they lend to businesses and will sometimes back their own hunches or gut feelings against the apparent odds. But do not bet on it. Turn the odds in your favour by writing your business plan and framing your request for finance in the best possible light.

Arnold S. Goldstein, American author of *Starting on a Shoestring* (John Wiley & Sons), suggests the following likely line of questioning from a bank manager:

- Why do you need the amount requested?
- What will you do with it?
- How do you know it's enough?
- How much less can you live with?
- Who else will you borrow from?
- How do you propose to repay it?
- How can you prove that you can?
- What collateral can you offer?

Unless you can answer these questions to your bank manager's satisfaction (especially the last two), it is unlikely that you will get the money you are looking for.

And don't wait for the interview with the manager for an opportunity to give the answers to these questions – that is far too late. The bank manager's mind will already be made up, more or less, before your meeting. Your plan will have been read thoroughly. The interview is intended to firm up the manager's decision. If you have not answered the relevant questions in the plan, you are not likely to have much chance to do so later.

You don't need to write your business plan in a style that asks the questions in the form above and then gives the answers. What you need to do is to ensure that the information that answers the questions is:

- Contained within the plan.
- Visible within the plan.
- Capable of being extracted by a reader from the plan.

Putting all this in another way, a bank manager will look for three things: character; collateral; and cash flow.

*Character* means you. A bank manager who has any reason to distrust or disbelieve you – from previous dealings or because of your reputation or because of errors or inconsistencies in your business plan – will not invest money with you.

*Collateral* means the backing that you can give as security for the loan. In some cases, collateral is not needed. But to the banker, who is responsible to the bank's depositors for their money, security is all. If you can offer collateral, it will certainly help your case.

*Cash flow* means your ability to repay the loan on time, out of the proceeds of the investment. The bank manager will prefer to see the loan repaid at regular monthly or quarterly intervals with interest paid on the due dates – anything else upsets the system. Unless you can show that the business will generate enough cash to make the payments the bank manager requires – or you have explained clearly in your business plan why this will not be possible for an initial period – you will not get the money that you ask for.

## Professional Investors

Professional investors – venture capitalists, for example – have a different viewpoint. They accept risk, though, like any prudent investor, they will avoid undue risk and seek to limit their exposure to unavoidable risk. David Silver, another American venture capitalist and author on enterprise, suggests that their questions will be along the lines of:

- How much can I make?
- How much can I lose?
- How do I get my money out?
- Who says this is any good?
- Who else is in it?

*How much can I make?* decides whether the project fits the profile of 30 to 50 per cent annual compound growth (well in excess of bank interest) usually required by such investors.

*How much can I lose?* identifies the downside risk. Although venture capitalists are used to investing in 10 projects for every one that succeeds, they cannot invest in projects that would jeopardise their own business of investment in the event of their failure.

*How do I get my money out?* is important since few venture capitalists invest for the long term. Most are happy to turn over their investments every three to five years. None will invest in a project unless they can see clearly an exit mechanism. There is no point in holding a 25 per cent share in a company valued at several millions if you cannot realise the shareholding when you want to.

*Who says this is any good?* Professional investors maintain networks of advisers, often on an informal basis. Venture capitalists will check out all that you say or include in your business plan. This is part of the 'due diligence' process. If you can supply a venture capitalist with evidence that people who ought to know support your plans, you will strengthen your case.

*Who else is in this?* panders to the investor's residual need for security. Even if investors know that they are going to take a risk, to place their faith and money in your hands, they like to know that others have come to the same conclusion. There is nothing like unanimity to convince people that they are right. Don't mock – particularly if you're trying to persuade someone to invest. Some venture capitalists have such a reputation for being right, for picking winners, that others try to follow their lead whenever they can.

Above all, in assessing the project itself, a professional investor will look at three key areas:

- The market – Is it large and growing rapidly?
- The product – Does it solve an important problem in the market, one that customers are prepared to pay for?
- Management – Are all the key functional areas on board and up to strength?

## WRITING THE BUSINESS PLAN

There are three stages in writing a business plan:

- Thinking.
- Writing.
- Editing.

Each is important but the most important is the first – thinking. Be prepared to spend at least 75 per cent of the time you have allocated to preparing your business plan in thinking. Time spent here will not be wasted. Use this time to talk through your business with anyone who will listen; read widely, especially about others in your area of business; and avoid finding reasons why things cannot be done.

Writing can be done fastest of all. Use a word-processor to give yourself the flexibility you will need to edit the document later.

If you find it difficult to start writing on a blank page or computer screen, talk instead. Buy, or borrow, a hand-held dictating machine. Talk to yourself about your business. Explain it to someone who knows nothing about it. Get the tape transcribed and your business plan will be on the way.

Editing is the last task. Editing is an art. Some people are better at it than others, but everyone can learn the basics. Essentially, it's about clear communication. Read through your draft business plan – aloud, if you find that helps. Does what you have written say what you want? Start deleting. You will find that quite a lot can come out without doing damage. When you are happy with your draft, put it aside for a day or two. Come back to it fresh and see whether it still makes sense. Edit again where it does not. And when it is right, leave it alone!

# 4: FINANCING YOUR START-UP

The 'Golden Rule' for financing a new business is: As little as possible, as cheaply as possible. Do not put money into the unnecessary. It is better to start off running your business from the attic without a loan than in a glossy, but unnecessary, high-street office with heavy bank borrowings.

On the other hand, do adopt a realistic position on the amount of money that you need to get going. Your financing must be sufficient to carry the business for a reasonable period before it reaches some kind of balance, where money coming in equals money going out. In addition to capital investment in plant, equipment and premises, your financing may have to supply most of the working capital until sales begin to generate sufficient income to give you an adequate cash flow.

You have two options in raising finance:

- Equity – capital invested in the business, usually not repayable.
- Debt – capital lent to the business, usually repayable at a specified date.

## EQUITY

For equity, the alternatives are:

- Your own equity – which leads to two questions: How much do you have? How much do you need?
- Other people's equity – which also leads to two questions: Are you prepared to allow other people to own part of your business? Can your business offer the sort of return that will attract outside investors?

Because equity means giving away part of your business, it's in your interest to minimise the amount held by outside investors. However, be sensible – it's better to own 70% (or even 30%) of a thriving and profitable business than 100% of a business going nowhere because it's starved for funds.

## Owners' Equity

In terms of the equity that you are able to put into the business, you must establish what assets you must retain as a fall-back position, and remove these from the equation. For example, you may not want to mortgage your house to raise finance for your business. Then consider what assets remain in the following terms:

- How easily can they be sold and how much will their sale raise?
- Are they mortgagable assets?
- Will they be acceptable as collateral?

Typical assets include: cash; shares; car; land; house; and boats, second / holiday homes, antiques, jewellery, paintings.

If you are considering mortgaging your family home for the sake of the business, you should be aware that this is a very serious step and professional advice should be obtained. The issues to be considered include:

- Ownership of the property.
- What would happen to the family home and your family should the business fail.
- The approach that the banks and the courts take in such circumstances.

Note that if you mortgage your home, or borrow personally, in order to invest equity into your business and the business fails, you still remain liable to repay the loan. There's a big difference between this and the situation where the bank lends directly to the business.

## Other Equity

For many small businesses, the option of raising equity capital is not a reality. Either the sums they need are too small to interest an investor, or the level of return, while adequate to pay a standard bank loan, is not sufficient to tempt the investor who is exposed to a greater risk. Most equity investors look to invest at least €500,000 in a company, arguing that amounts below this do not justify the amount of checking they need to do before making an investment. Thus, perversely perhaps, it is easier to raise €5,000,000 than it is to raise €50,000.

Fuelled by the 'Celtic Tiger' economy, the recent spectacular successes of some Irish technology companies and a growing awareness of the importance of private equity for business development, the number of venture capital funds in Ireland has increased significantly in the past few years. Some of these will consider investing seed capital (less than €250,000), although most prefer to invest venture (€250,000 to €1 million, for businesses at an early stage of development) or development (€1 million+) capital. Note that these amounts are arbitrary; some funds will invest in more than one category.

## Sources of Equity

Sources of equity in Ireland include:

- 4th Level Ventures.
- ACT Venture Capital.
- AIB Bank.
- AIB Seed Capital Fund.
- BOI Venture Capital.
- Clarendon Fund Managers.
- Corporate Finance Ireland.
- County & City Enterprise Boards.
- Crescent Capital.
- Cross Atlantic Capital Partners.
- Crucible Corporation.
- Delta Partners.
- Enterprise Equity Ltd.
- Enterprise Ireland.
- Executive Venture Partners.
- Fountain Healthcare Partners.
- Growcorp Innovation Centre.
- Halo Business Angel Partnership.
- Irish Film Board.
- Kernel Capital Partners.
- NCB Ventures.
- Novus Modus.
- Powerscourt Capital Partners.

- **Qubis.**
- **Seroba Kernel Life Sciences Ltd.**
- **Shannon Development**
- **Western Development Commission.**

Sources of information on equity and equity sources include:
- **BDO Simpson Xavier.**
- **EquityNetwork.**
- **Irish Venture Capital Association.**
- **PDC.**

In most cases – certainly where you require seed capital – you can approach the fund manager directly. A check on the fund's website to make sure that you meet the fund's criteria, a phone call to check the name of the person to whom you should send your business plan – then go for it!

Larger, technology-based projects requiring greater and more complex financing can choose whether to go directly to an appropriate fund or to work through a corporate finance house, which has specialist skills in fund-raising.

Whatever your route, remember that it's not just about money, as the growth of incubators shows. Depending on the strengths of your new business, supports may be as important as cash.

## Family equity

But, despite all the new funds, the best source of small-scale seed capital for most start-ups continues to be family or friends. If you do decide to involve family and friends as investors in your business, make sure both sides know – and agree on – the ground rules:

- Their investment is 'risk capital' – it may be lost and is not repayable (unless you agree otherwise).
- Equity investment does not automatically give a right to management involvement – even if it's clear that you cannot cope.
- Their investment may be diluted by other later investors, whose money is needed to continue the development of the business.

Put everything in writing – in a formal shareholders' agreement, if appropriate, or a simple letter of understanding signed by all parties.

### Business Angels

'Business Angels', a term adapted from the world of theatre where private investors ('angels') are often the source of finance for a new show on New York's Broadway or in London's West End, are private investors who take (usually) a minority stake in a business – sometimes with an active management role, too. They're hard to find and, since they're usually experienced businesspeople, often hard to convince.

Sources of business angels include:

- **EquityNetwork.**
- **FirstTuesday.**
- **Halo Business Angel Partnership.**

### Tax-based equity

While the **Revenue Commissioners** will not invest directly in your business, they provide a source of equity capital through the **Business Expansion Scheme** and the **Seed Capital Scheme**.

# DEBT

When considering financing your business with debt, consider:

- Fixed or floating.
- Long-term or short-term.

Fixed debt is a loan that is secured on a specific asset, for example, on premises. Floating debt is secured on assets that change regularly, for example, debtors. 'Secured' means that, in the event that the loan is not repaid, the lender can appoint a receiver to sell the asset on which the loan is secured in order to recover the amount due. Thus, giving security for a loan is not something to be done lightly.

Long-term for most lenders means five to seven years; short-term means one year or less.

Because you have to pay interest on debt, you should try to manage with as little as possible. However, few businesses get off the ground without putting some form of debt on the balance sheet. The issues are usually:

- What is the cheapest form of debt?
- What is the correct balance between debt and equity?
- How can you sensibly reduce the amount of borrowing required?

- To what extent must borrowing be backed by personal assets?

## Matching Loans and Assets

It is a good idea to try to match the term of the loan to the type of asset that you are acquiring:

- To avoid constant renewing or restructuring problems.
- To ensure that each loan is covered by the break-up value of the assets in case of disaster.

For example, a loan to buy premises should be a long-term loan, unless you can see clearly that you will have enough money within a short period to repay the loan. Taking out a short-term loan or overdraft to buy premises is a recipe for disaster. You may have to renegotiate it time and again – and, if your business runs into temporary difficulties, you run the risk of losing everything.

Short-term loans, or even overdrafts, are more suited to funding stock or debtors because you should be able to repay the loan once you have sold the goods or got the money in.

Short-term finance is also used to fund other forms of working capital and cash flow. It should always be repaid within the year – even if at the end of the period you still need to borrow more to fund future cash flow. In other words, your overdraft or short-term loan should be periodically cleared (or substantially reduced) by money coming in before you need to increase it again. If you have to borrow the same sum of money against the same asset for longer than a year at a time, you should be considering longer-term finance.

If disaster strikes and you have to repay the loan, it will be much easier to do so if the value of the assets is roughly equivalent to the outstanding value of the loan. Thus, for instance, you will hope to sell your premises for at least as much as you borrowed to buy them. Machinery may be more difficult, as the resale price is rarely comparable with the purchase price. For this reason, you may consider purchasing second-hand equipment for your start-up.

If you can, you should arrange your loans so that un-realisable assets are purchased out of your own equity, using borrowing only for realisable assets. If an asset is easily realisable, the bank is much more likely to accept it as security.

The main sources of loan finance (overdrafts, term loans and commercial mortgages) for start-ups are the banks:

- **AIB Bank.**
- **Bank of Ireland / Bank of Ireland Business Banking.**
- **Bank of Ireland Northern Ireland.**
- **Bank of Scotland (Ireland) Ltd.**
- **First Trust Bank.**
- **Lombard.**
- **National Irish Bank.**
- **Northern Bank.**
- **Permanent TSB.**
- **Rabobank Ireland plc.**
- **Ulster Bank.**

## Other Sources

Don't look only to banks for debt. Credit unions may consider a small loan to get your business off the ground, particularly if you have been a regular saver. Check the **Irish League of Credit Unions** website to find a credit union near you.

As well as dealing with banks, you may also find yourself dealing with finance companies. Finance companies exist to lend money and make a return on it. They sometimes are more willing to lend than a bank, as long as they can secure the loan with assets or personal guarantees. They are not often cheaper than banks, but may sometimes be prepared to lend when banks refuse. This is not always a good thing. While it may shore up your own confidence in your project, it does not of itself increase the chances of success.

If you are having trouble getting finance, it may be an indication that you should reappraise the project. Talk to those who have refused you finance about their reasons before proceeding to other financiers. You may end up increasing your chances of success, both in raising finance second time around and in the business itself.

Some finance companies specialise in certain types of finance, or special industry sectors. Because of their greater expertise and knowledge, they may be able to give you a better deal than the main retail banks because they understand your situation better.

When looking for finance, beware of 'specialists' who claim that they can find you money at favourable rates of interest if you pay an up-front fee. Don't pay anything until you have the money.

And don't forget the following as sources of loan finance – often as part of a support package (see *Chapter 5*):

- **Clann Credo.**
- **Clarendon Fund Managers.**
- **County & City Enterprise Boards** – see *Directory* for a list..
- Enterprise Agencies, members of **Enterprise Northern Ireland** (some, not all) – see *Directory* for a list.
- **First Step.**
- **Guinness Workers' Employment Fund Ltd.**
- **Irish Film Board.**
- **Prince's Trust Northern Ireland.**
- **Ulster Community Investment Trust.**
- **Western Development Commission.**

## Expanding Your Credit Line

When (or, preferably, before) you have exhausted the borrowing facilities that your bank is prepared to provide (your credit line), you should consider two other forms of financing: leasing and factoring.

Leasing is particularly attractive as a way of acquiring the use of fixed assets – for example, plant and machinery, cars, office equipment – with the minimum up-front cost. Instead, you pay a regular monthly or quarterly payment, which is usually allowable for tax purposes. At the end of the lease, depending on the terms of the particular lease, you may have the option to continue using the asset for a modest continuing payment or to buy it outright from the lessor. Most of the major banks provide leasing facilities.

Factoring, or invoice discounting, is a means of raising working capital, by 'selling' your debtors. The factoring company (usually a division or subsidiary of a bank) will pay you, say, 80 per cent of the face value of an invoice when it is issued. The balance, less charges, will be paid to you when the debt is settled. This form of financing is especially useful for the company that is rapidly expanding and in danger of being choked for lack of cash flow.

Sources of factoring / invoice discounting include:
- **Celtic Invoice Discounting plc.**
- **Clancy Business Finance.**
- **Ulster Factors.**

In addition, the major banks all offer invoice discounting, sometimes through specialist subsidiaries. Check with their small business unit.

### *Who to Approach?*

Who you approach for funds will depend on:

- How much finance you need.
- What you need finance for.
- Your company's risk profile.

Often, if you only need a small amount of money, the best way to raise it is still to approach a bank or credit union with which you have already built up some relationship, whether on a personal basis or in a business capacity. The larger borrower may feel it worthwhile to seek professional help to put together a more sophisticated finance package. Your accountant is the best person to give you advice in this area and may have contacts that will ease your path.

## DEALING WITH BANKS

Whatever the means of finance you adopt, you will almost certainly have to deal with a bank for your daily needs, if not for your whole financial package.

Banks are conservative institutions with fixed procedures. You will hopefully have laid a good foundation for your business relationship with the bank by the way in which you have handled your personal finances. In smaller towns, you may already be well-known to the bank manager.

However, the relationship that your business will have with the bank is likely to be different from any personal relationship that you had with them before. While you were employed by someone else, you probably had a regular, guaranteed income going into your personal account. You may have had an overdraft, a mortgage, or perhaps a personal loan, but unless you were careless with your finances, the risk of getting into serious financial difficulty was limited.

However, in dealing with you now as a business, some of the personal element disappears from the relationship and is replaced by an 'unknown risk' factor, which stems from the following facts:

- The business is (usually) a separate legal entity from yourself and has no previous relationship with the bank.
- The business has no guaranteed income (to the extent that your previous employment was secure, your personal income was

'guaranteed' – it no longer is, and don't be surprised if that changes your bank manager's attitude towards your personal account, too).
- A high proportion of new businesses fail or experience financial difficulty for a variety of reasons that are difficult to predict.
- The amount you have borrowed from the bank – for which the bank manager is ultimately responsible to shareholders – is likely to be much larger than any personal loan you have had in the past.

The more of the unknown risk that you are able to eliminate for the bank manager, the more the bank manager will be able to do for you, both in terms of providing the money you want and, in many cases, by giving you the benefit of their experience in commenting on your plans.

The sort of information you can supply includes:
- A business plan, and updates when necessary.
- Regular reports on the financial state of your business.
- Information on a timely basis about any emerging problems that are going to result in late repayments, choked cash flow or a need for additional funding. A problem many bankers mention is that clients do not tell the bank what is wrong until the situation has grown so terrible that it is too late to correct
- Encouraging your banker to visit on-site to see for themselves.

It is also true that too many bankers put a lot of effort into the initial analysis of a start-up loan, but fail to keep a close enough eye on their investment thereafter – hence, at least some of the losses on their small business lending the banks have experienced in recent years.

You can gain the maximum amount of assistance from your bank, not only by keeping the manager informed, but by asking occasionally for an opinion of the financial outcome of a certain course of action. You should certainly have a face-to-face chat with your banker at least twice a year, and once a quarter if you can arrange it.

## Other Points

If your business plan is approved and you are awarded your loan, overdraft etc.:
- Don't be afraid to negotiate for the best possible terms. Most entrepreneurs will haggle over the price of a computer but will accept a bank's terms like lambs.

- It may be a good idea to have an accountant or solicitor look at any loan agreement before you sign it. They may spot gaps, or unnecessary clauses, and their professional backing will give you added confidence in arguing your case.

- Make all payments on time and in the agreed manner. If, for some reason, you will be late with a repayment, at least warn the bank in advance and, if possible, discuss the reasons with your bank manager.

## Security

Providing security – pledging assets against a loan in case you are unable to repay it – is an ongoing issue (and a most vexatious one) between the small business community and the banks. Small business owners often feel it unjust that a large corporation can borrow a huge amount of money often without providing security, while they have to produce security for small loans.

Ideally, bankers will look for security in the business itself – premises, equipment or stock – but often small businesses rent their premises, lease their equipment and hold limited quantities of stock. Business machinery is not always suitable as security because it may have a low resale value, or may be built into the building where it is housed, making it difficult for the bank to sell it, if necessary, without incurring substantial additional costs. For this reason, the bank will often seek personal guarantees, that is, the pledge of personal assets against business loans.

Beware of personal guarantees. The bank may ask for them, although the major banks have repeatedly told the **Small Firms Association** and the **Irish Small & Medium Enterprises Association** that they do not ask for guarantees 'as a matter of course'.

A personal guarantee is exactly that. You are guaranteeing that, if the company cannot pay back the loan to the bank, you will do so. *How?* Think about it before you sign.

Try to avoid giving a personal guarantee. It is probably better to borrow less, or pay a higher rate of interest, or use leasing as a means of financing specific fixed assets, than to be saddled with a personal guarantee.

As a condition of a loan, you may be asked by the bank not to pay any dividends or repay any other loans (especially ones you have made personally to the company) until the bank has been repaid. Though this is less onerous than a personal guarantee, only agree if these conditions are reasonable.

Check that whatever legal document you sign agrees with what you agreed with your bank manager. And, if the condition is for a limited period of time or until the loan is repaid, don't be shy about asking to be released from it when you have done your part and repaid the bank.

## NON-EQUITY, NON-DEBT FINANCE

Although equity and debt represent the classic academic forms of financing, entrepreneurs are less concerned about such distinctions and are perfectly happy to consider sources of finance not listed in textbooks, for example:

- **Seed Capital Scheme** operated by the **Revenue Commissioners**, which can give you back some of your past five years' tax if you leave employment to start a new business
- Enterprise competition prizes, for example, the **Enterprise Ireland Student Enterprise Awards** or the **Seedcorn Business Plan Competition**.
- Grants from the organisations in *Chapters 5, 6* and *7* (*Chapter 8* for Northern Ireland).

# 5: State Support for Start-ups

There is no shortage of State support in Ireland at present for start-ups and small businesses. Instead, the very number of agencies, nationally and locally, that co-exist (and, on occasion, appear to compete for the entrepreneur pool) gives rise to confusion. This chapter aims to help you through the maze to find the agency that can help your fledgling business to get off the ground.

But, first, a note about the nature of State support. When *Starting a Business in Ireland* was first published, the expressed priority of Irish enterprise support agencies was the creation of sustainable jobs. "How many jobs?" was the benchmark used to assess projects. To be sure, other criteria were used too, but jobs over-rode everything else.

Today, with increasing numbers on the welfare rolls, and despite competitiveness and capability as watchwords, jobs are still the defining criterion for State small business support.

## Key State / Semi-State Agencies

Let's start with the basic geography of the landscape, as shown in the following diagrams.

## STATE SUPPORT FOR START-UPS (1)

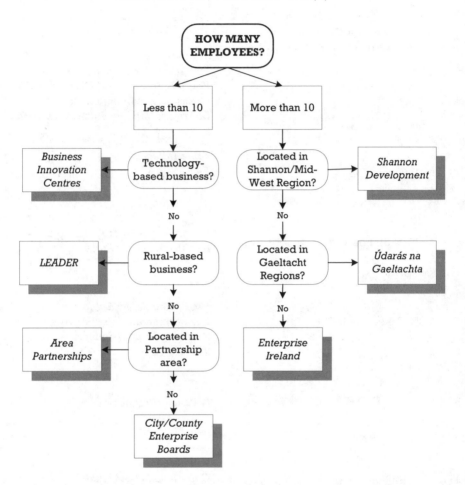

## STATE SUPPORT FOR START-UPS (2)

**Is the support/assistance
you require related to . . .**

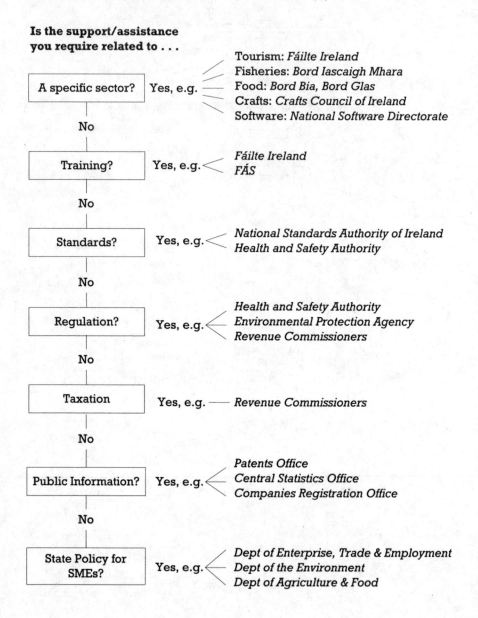

A specific sector? — Yes, e.g. —
Tourism: *Fáilte Ireland*
Fisheries: *Bord Iascaigh Mhara*
Food: *Bord Bia, Bord Glas*
Crafts: *Crafts Council of Ireland*
Software: *National Software Directorate*

No

Training? — Yes, e.g. —
*Fáilte Ireland*
*FÁS*

No

Standards? — Yes, e.g. —
*National Standards Authority of Ireland*
*Health and Safety Authority*

No

Regulation? — Yes, e.g. —
*Health and Safety Authority*
*Environmental Protection Agency*
*Revenue Commissioners*

No

Taxation — Yes, e.g. — *Revenue Commissioners*

No

Public Information? — Yes, e.g. —
*Patents Office*
*Central Statistics Office*
*Companies Registration Office*

No

State Policy for SMEs? — Yes, e.g. —
*Dept of Enterprise, Trade & Employment*
*Dept of the Environment*
*Dept of Agriculture & Food*

Overall responsibility for enterprise lies with the **Department of Enterprise, Trade & Employment**, which is responsible for promoting competitiveness in the economy and for creating a favourable climate for the creation of self-sustaining employment. It works to monitor and improve the environment for business by ensuring that the framework of law, regulation and Government policy promotes effective company performance and both public and business confidence.

Policy is determined by **Forfás**, which is the national Policy and Advisory Board for Enterprise, Trade, Science, Technology and Innovation. It reports to the Department of Enterprise, Trade and Employment.

The next layer consists of **IDA Ireland** and **Enterprise Ireland**, which both report to Forfás and implement policy set by it. IDA Ireland focuses on inwards investment – bringing foreign multinationals into Ireland – while Enterprise Ireland is tasked with supporting indigenous (local) businesses.

In the Mid-West, **Shannon Development** replaces Enterprise Ireland – likewise, **Údarás na Gaeltachta** in Gaeltacht (native Irish-speaking) areas.

Then, there is a range of specialist agencies, tasked with the development of a particular industry sector – **Fáilte Ireland**, for example, in relation to tourism – or specialist area – **FÁS**, for example, in relation to employment and training.

Some agencies have a regulatory role or monitoring role – for example, the **Environmental Protection Agency** or the **Food Safety Authority**. Not all the agencies report to the Department for Enterprise, Trade & Employment, but instead to the Government Department most closely associated with their work – for example, **Bord Bia** reports to the **Department of Agriculture, Fisheries & Food.**

The various State agencies all operate at a national level, although many have regional or local offices.

But, to ensure that local needs are met at local level, another range of agencies also exists. These include:

- Area Partnerships – many of which have little direct involvement in enterprise support and thus are not included in the *Directory*.
- **County & City Enterprise Boards.**
- **Community Groups** – many of which have little direct involvement in enterprise support and thus are not included in the *Directory*..
- **IRD (Integrated Rural Development) Companies.**
- **LEADER groups.**

And **County Development Boards** have been established in each county, and in the five cities, to ensure co-ordination of local resources towards enterprise development.

So, where should the potential entrepreneur begin to look for help? Indeed, what sort of help is available, and from whom?

Although there has been a shift away from a jobs focus among the enterprise support agencies, the first question that you must answer to decide where you should look for help still relates to the employment potential of your new business (see diagram: *State support for Start-ups (1)*).

If, within three years or so of start-up, you are likely still to employ under 10 people, you should make your way to the **County & City Enterprise Boards** and / or the other local support agencies.

Once you can show that you are likely to employ more than 10 people within three years or so of start-up (and meet some other criteria, including demonstrating export potential), **Enterprise Ireland** (or **Shannon Development / Údarás na Gaeltachta,** as appropriate, depending on your location) will classify your business as a 'high potential start-up' (HPSU) and take you under its wing.

So, let's start with Enterprise Ireland.

## Enterprise Ireland

The best source for information on Enterprise Ireland and how it helps small businesses is its own excellent website, www.enterprise-ireland.com.

Enterprise Ireland helps manufacturing and internationally-traded services businesses that employ more than 10 people to grow internationally. The agency is primarily focused on providing advice and support to companies in three areas: technology innovation, business development and internationalisation. Its aim is to work in partnership with these businesses to develop a sustainable competitive advantage that leads to a significant increase in profitable sales, exports and employment.

Key considerations in evaluating a project application include:

- Need for financial assistance.
- Value for money.
- Commercial considerations.
- Technical considerations.
- Financial track record.

Accordingly, a strong well-thought-through business plan is essential (see **Chapter 3**).

Enterprise Ireland's financial support is now usually a mix of non-repayable grants and equity investment (in the form of preference and ordinary shares), seeking to optimise the level of repayability. The argument behind this move is that, since Enterprise Ireland's resources are limited, they must be wisely invested in businesses that give the best return. In addition, a measure of repayability provides resources that can be recycled into other companies later on.

Once a financial package has been agreed between a business and its Enterprise Ireland Development Adviser, the adviser sends out a letter of offer, after which legal documentation is prepared for signature by both parties.

### Shannon Development

As noted earlier, in the Shannon Region, Shannon Development carries out many of the functions handled by **Enterprise Ireland** elsewhere and recently has been subsumed into Enterprise Ireland.

However, Shannon Development was promoting the Shannon Region, developing its infrastructure and sowing the seeds for the high-tech boom before enterprise development became fashionable. In partnership with the **University of Limerick**, it pioneered the **National Technology Park** as far back as 1980.

### Údarás na Gaeltachta

As noted earlier, in the Gaeltacht areas, Údarás na Gaeltachta carries out the functions handled by **Enterprise Ireland** elsewhere. In addition to its enterprise development role, Údarás has a mission to preserve and promote the Irish language. Its remit spreads across a wide geographical area – from Macroom in Co Cork through Connemara and into Donegal – which adds to the complexity of its task.

---

If your new business does not qualify for Enterprise Ireland support (and most don't), you should look to the **County & City Enterprise Boards** – and other local agencies – instead.

## County & City Enterprise Boards

County & City Enterprise Boards (CEBs) are arguably the most important source of assistance for a start-up business.

The 35 City and County Enterprise Boards (a list appears in the *Directory*) aim to encourage local initiative. Each is a company limited by guarantee, and has an executive staff, headed by a Chief Executive Officer. The 12 or 14 Board members are drawn from elected members of the local authority, the social partners, State agencies, ICTU, **IBEC**, the farming organisations, the county manager and community and other representatives.

Project promoters must demonstrate that:

- There is a market for the proposed product / service.
- Adequate overall finance will be available to fund the project.
- They possess the management and technical capacity to implement the proposed project.
- The projects will add value so as to generate income or supplement income for those involved, and will have the capacity to create new direct employment whether full-time, part-time or seasonal, or will, as a minimum, contribute directly to maintaining employment in existing small enterprises.
- They will comply with State policies on tax clearance, the certification of subcontractors, and related matters.

The CEBs do not fund projects that are contrary to public policy, nor do they duplicate support for projects that would be eligible for assistance from any existing sectoral or grant structure, or which involve primary agricultural production.

Assistance is not confined to grants, since the CEBs have authority to provide loans and loan guarantees and to take equity stakes in businesses. In addition, the CEBs act as a source of advice and information. Many provide training and mentoring services.

Since the activities of each CEB are tailored to the needs of its local community, you should check with your local CEB for the full range of assistance available.

You should contact your local CEB before taking your project much beyond an initial stage. An initial informal discussion will quickly determine whether:

- The CEB can support your project.
- A feasibility study grant may be available.

- You should make changes to your project to make it acceptable to the CEB for assistance.

Your application should be on an official application form, obtainable from your local CEB (in some cases, from the CEB's website). Read the notes with the application form carefully before completing.

Almost always, except in cases where very small amounts of money are involved, CEBs will require a Business Plan with your application. A feasibility study grant may help you to prepare one.

## Area Partnerships

The 38 Area Partnerships were set up under the Programme for Economic and Social Progress (PESP) in 1993. Most now operate the National Programme for Social Inclusion and / or the National Rural Development Programme – many have no direct involvement in enterprise support. Their funding is co-ordinated by **Pobal**.

Each Partnership is autonomous and agrees different work practices. Each works on an Area Action Plan for its own region. Practical measures are taken to discriminate in favour of the long-term unemployed and those who are socially excluded. There is variety in what each Partnership offers, and entrepreneurs should contact the Partnership in their area for further details.

## Community Groups

A third strand of local enterprise support are the Community Groups, established by **Pobal**, as part of its Local Development Programme. Their remit is more broadly focused on community development, although some have direct enterprise development activity. As each Community Group identifies and responds to needs within its own communities, its activities are unique to its own situation. Entrepreneurs seeking assistance should make contact with their local Community Group to see whether and what help is available.

## LEADER

LEADER is an EU initiative for rural development (part-funded by the Irish Government) that enables groups in rural areas to implement their own multi-sectoral integrated plans for the development of their areas. A list of LEADER groups appears in the *Directory*, under 'Irish LEADER Network'.

Again, as each LEADER Group identifies and responds to needs within its own communities, its activities are unique to its own situation. Because of this, entrepreneurs seeking assistance should make contact with their local LEADER Group to see whether and what help is available.

## Other State and Semi-State Agencies

As mentioned earlier, there are a wide range of these agencies, covering a variety of roles and responsibilities and reporting to appropriate Government Departments.

Regional, industry or sector-related bodies include:

- **Arts Council.**
- **Bord Bia.**
- **Bord Iascaigh Mhara.**
- **Borders, Midlands & Western Regional Assembly.**
- **Crafts Council of Ireland.**
- **Fáilte Ireland.**
- **FÁS.**
- **Marine Institute.**
- **Pobal.**
- **Southern & Eastern Regional Assembly.**
- **Sustainable Energy Ireland.**
- **Teagasc.**
- **Western Development Commission.**

Bodies that collect and disseminate information include:

- **Central Statistics Office.**
- **Companies Registration Office.**
- **Patents Office.**

Bodies with a regulatory or monitoring role include:

- **Data Protection Commissioner.**
- **Environmental Protection Agency.**
- **Food Safety Authority of Ireland.**
- **Health & Safety Authority.**
- **National Standards Authority of Ireland.**
- **Registry of Business Names.**
- **Registry of Friendly Societies.**

- **Revenue Commissioners.**

Details of all these bodies, their activities and links with other organisations are included in the *Directory*.

## Government Departments

Not all the State agencies that have a role in enterprise development or support report to the **Department of Enterprise, Trade & Employment**. Other Departments that support start-ups include:

- **Department of Agriculture, Fisheries & Food.**
- **Department of Justice, Equality & Law Reform.**
- **Department of Social & Family Affairs**
- **Department of the Environment, Heritage & Local Government.**

A useful website for information on Government Departments and their activities is:

- **www.gov.ie.**

In addition, **BASIS.ie** provides information on State support for business.

## Universities & Institutes of Technology

A final source of State support for enterprise are the **Universities** and **Institutes of Technology**. All have Industrial Liaison Officers, or Heads of External Services or Development, whose task it is to build links between the college and the business world. In many cases, this results in the college carrying out technical research for a local business or commercialising through a local business the fruits of their own research. The website, **www.expertiseireland.com**, provides a gateway to third-level expertise.

## Enterprise Link

And last, but definitely not least, **Enterprise Ireland** runs, on behalf of the Department for Enterprise, Trade and Employment, a service called **Enterprise Link** – a one-stop shop for information and direction – accessible on **1850 35 33 33**.

## SUPPORT BY CATEGORY

The *Directory of Sources of Assistance* is organised by categories. To make it easy to find the appropriate source of State assistance, this section lists State organisations by the type of support they offer. See *Chapter 6* for explanations of the categories.

### Business Plans

- Action Tallaght.
- Arklow Community Enterprise Ltd.
- Finglas Business Initiative.

### Community & Rural Development

- Arklow Community Enterprise Ltd.
- Ballyfermot / Chapelizod Partnership.
- Ballyhoura Community Partnership.
- Ballymun Whitehall Area Partnership.
- Blanchardstown Area Partnership.
- Bluebell, Inchicore, Islandbridge, Kilmainham and Rialto Partnership.
- Bray Partnership.
- Comhar Chathair Chorcaí / Cork City Partnership.
- CPLN Partnership.
- Department of Community, Rural & Gaeltacht Affairs.
- Dodder Valley Partnership.
- Drogheda Partnership Company.
- Dublin Employment Pact.
- Dublin Inner City Partnership.
- Dundalk Employment Partnership.
- Galway City Partnership.
- IRD Kiltimagh.
- LEADER – see *Directory* / 'Irish LEADER Network' for a list of LEADER groups.
- Meitheal Mhaigh Eo.
- Mountmellick Development Association.
- National University of Ireland, Galway
- Northside Partnership.
- Partas.

- Paul Partnership.
- Rathmines Pembroke Community Partnership.
- Southside Partnership.
- Tallaght Partnership.
- Tipperary Institute
- Tolka Area Partnership.
- West Offaly Partnership.
- Western Development Commission.
- Westmeath Employment Pact.

## Consulting

- Ashtown Food Centre.
- Centre for Co-operative Studies.
- Centre for Entrepreneurial Studies.
- Dairy Products Research Centre.
- Food Product Development Centre.
- Institutes of Technology – see *Directory* for a list.
- MAC.
- Marketing Centre for Small Business.
- Teagasc.
- Tyndall Institute.
- Universities – see *Directory* for a list.

## Co-operatives

- Centre for Co-operative Studies
- Registry of Friendly Societies.

## Cross-Border

- Centre for Cross-Border Studies.
- Louth County Enterprise Board.

## Grants

- Arklow Community Enterprise Ltd.
- Arts Council.
- Bord Bia.
- Bord Iascaigh Mhara.
- Cavan-Monaghan Rural Development Co-op Society Ltd.

- **County & City Enterprise Boards** – see *Directory* for a list.
- **Department of Social & Family Affairs.**
- **Enterprise Ireland.**
- **Finglas Business Initiative.**
- **LEADER groups** (some, not all) – see *Directory* / 'Irish LEADER Network' for a list.
- **Shannon Development.**
- **Údarás na Gaeltachta.**

## Information

- **BASIS.ie.**
- **Bord Bia.**
- **Bord Iascaigh Mhara.**
- **Business Information Centre.**
- **Central Statistics Office.**
- **Centre for Co-operative Studies.**
- **Centre for Cross-Border Studies.**
- **Centre for Entrepreneurial Studies.**
- **Companies Registration Office.**
- **County & City Enterprise Boards** – see *Directory* for a list..
- **Crafts Council of Ireland.**
- **Department of Social & Family Affairs.**
- **Drogheda Partnership Company.**
- **Dublin Inner City Partnership.**
- **Dundalk Employment Partnership.**
- **Enterprise Ireland.**
- **Enterprise Link.**
- **Environmental Protection Agency.**
- **ExpertiseIreland.com.**
- **Fáilte Ireland.**
- **Finglas Business Initiative.**
- **Food Safety Authority of Ireland.**
- **Galway City Partnership.**
- **Gov.ie.**
- **Government Publications.**
- **Health & Safety Authority.**
- **Institutes of Technology** – see *Directory* for a list.

- **LEADER groups** (some, not all) – see *Directory* / 'Irish Leader Network' for a list.
- **Louth Craftmark.**
- **Marine Institute.**
- **Meitheal Mhaigh Eo.**
- **National College of Ireland.**
- **National Standards Authority of Ireland.**
- **Northside Partnership.**
- **Patents Office.**
- **Paul Partnership Limerick.**
- **PDC.**
- **Registry of Business Names.**
- **Registry of Friendly Societies.**
- **Revenue Commissioners.**
- **Shannon Development.**
- **Southside Partnership.**
- **Sustainable Energy Ireland.**
- **Tallaght Partnership.**
- **Údarás na Gaeltachta.**
- **Universities** – see *Directory* for a list.

### Intellectual Property

- NovaUCD.
- **Patents Office.**

### Inwards Investment

- **IDA Ireland.**

### Marketing

- **Arklow Community Enterprise Ltd.**
- **Bord Bia.**
- **Bord Iascaigh Mhara.**
- **Crafts Council of Ireland.**
- **Fáilte Ireland.**
- **Marketing Centre for Small Business.**

## Mentoring

- County & City Enterprise Boards – see *Directory* for a list.
- Enterprise Ireland.
- Enterprise Platform Programmes – see *Directory* for a list.
- Finglas Business Initiative.
- Shannon Development.
- Tipperary Institute.

## Policy

- Borders, Midlands & Western Regional Assembly.
- Centre for Cross-Border Studies.
- County Development Boards.
- Department of Agriculture, Fisheries & Food.
- Department of Community, Rural & Gaeltacht Affairs.
- Department of Enterprise, Trade & Employment.
- Department of Justice, Equality & Law Reform.
- Department of the Environment, Heritage & Local Government.
- Forfás.
- Western Development Commission.

## Publications

- Central Statistics Office.
- County & City Enterprise Boards (some, not all) – see *Directory* for a list.
- Crafts Council of Ireland.
- Government Publications.
- Institute of Public Administration.
- Revenue Commissioners.

## R & D

- Ashtown Food Centre.
- Dairy Products Research Centre.
- Food Product Development Centre.
- Institutes of Technology – see *Directory* for a list.
- MAC.
- Marine Institute.
- Tyndall Institute.

- Universities – see *Directory* for a list.

## Regulator & Standards

- Bord Bia.
- Bord Iascaigh Mhara.
- Companies Registration Office.
- Data Protection Commissioner.
- Environmental Protection Agency.
- Food Safety Authority of Ireland.
- Health & Safety Authority.
- National Standards Authority of Ireland.
- Registry of Business Names.
- Registry of Friendly Societies.
- Revenue Commissioners.

## Social Economy

- Galway City Partnership.
- Partas.
- Southside Partnership.

## Tourism Development

- Ballyhoura Community Partnership.
- Cavan-Monaghan Rural Development Co-op Society Ltd.
- Fáilte Ireland.

## Training

- Arklow Community Enterprise Ltd.
- Ashtown Food Centre.
- Bord Iascaigh Mhara.
- Cavan-Monaghan Rural Development Co-op Society Ltd.
- Centre for Co-operative Studies.
- Centre for Entrepreneurial Studies.
- City of Dublin Vocational Education Committee.
- County & City Enterprise Boards – see *Directory* for a list.
- Crafts Council of Ireland.
- Drogheda Partnership Company.
- Dublin Inner City Partnership.

- Dundalk Employment Partnership.
- Enterprise Acceleration Centre.
- Enterprise Platform Programmes – see *Directory* for a list.
- Fáilte Ireland.
- FÁS.
- Food Product Development Centre.
- Galway City Partnership.
- Institutes of Technology – see *Directory* for a list.
- LEADER groups (some, not all) – see *Directory* / 'Irish LEADER Network' for a list.
- LINC Centre.
- Louth Craftmark.
- Meitheal Mhaigh Eo.
- Northside Partnership.
- Partas.
- Paul Partnership Limerick.
- PDC.
- Shannon Development.
- Southside Partnership.
- Sustainable Energy Ireland.
- Synergy Centre.
- Tallaght Partnership.
- TCD Enterprise Centre.
- Teagasc.
- Tyndall Institute.
- Údarás na Gaeltachta.
- Universities – see *Directory* for a list.

## Women

- County & City Enterprise Boards (some, not all) – see *Directory* for a list.
- Dundalk Employment Partnership.

## Workspace

- Digital Hub.
- Dundalk Employment Partnership.
- Institutes of Technology – see *Directory* for a list.

- National Technology Park.
- Northside Partnership.
- Partas.
- Shannon Development.

# 6: PRIVATE SECTOR SUPPORT FOR START-UPS

If confusion exists in the State sector due to the number of organisations that provide support for enterprise, it's nothing compared to the private sector, where the range of organisations – and the breadth of their activities – is even greater and lacks any form of co-ordination.

## SUPPORT BY CATEGORY

The simplest way through this maze is to identify the main private sector enterprise support organisations by the type of support they provide (clearly, some fit into more than one category).

The *Directory of Sources of Assistance* provides details on each of the organisations included. This chapter explains what the organisations within each category do in broad terms.

The chapter should be read with the other chapters for a full understanding of the sources of assistance available.

The website, **www.startingabusinessinirelandcom**, includes updates to the information in the *Directory*, as well as other sources of support known to me.

### Accountants

Accountants provide a variety of services to start-ups. They can assist and advise you on:

- The legal structure, taxation and accounting systems suitable for your business.
- Business planning (though you should not let your accountant write your business plan – after all, it's your plan, not theirs!).

- Fund-raising and/or funding applications to banks, venture capitalists and grant-giving organisations.

Accountants are usually members of one or other of a small number of professional bodies, which include:

- **Association of Chartered Certified Accountants.**
- **Chartered Accountants Ireland.**
- **Chartered Institute of Management Accountants.**
- **Institute of Certified Public Accountants in Ireland.**

These bodies will help you find a suitable accountant from among their members.

Accounting firms with particular expertise in small business issues include:

- **BDO Simpson Xavier.**
- **Crowleys DFK.**
- **Deloitte & Touche.**
- **Ernst & Young.**
- **FGS.**
- **Gahan & Co.**
- **KPMG.**
- **Mazars.**
- **OSK Accountants & Business Consultants.**
- **PKF O'Connor, Leddy & Holmes.**
- **PricewaterhouseCoopers.**

Providers of accounting software for small businesses include:

- **AccountsIQ.**
- **Aisling Software.**
- **Big Red Book.**
- **Mamut.**
- **Sage Ireland.**

## Business Plans

As *Chapter 3* makes clear, a business plan is essential for every start-up, regardless of its size, potential or the background of the promoters.

The *Directory* lists organisations, in addition to accountants, that assist entrepreneurs, directly or indirectly, with developing a business plan or an application (to themselves or a third party) for finance. (The *caveats* already expressed about doing it yourself apply.) These organisations include:

- **Action Tallaght.**
- **Bplans.ie.**
- **Dublin Business Innovation Centre.**
- **Invest-Tech.**
- **Liffey Trust.**
- **Palo Alto Software UK.**
- **South East Business Innovation Centre.**
- **Terenure Enterprise Ltd.**

Many of the enterprise support agencies provide grants or other support for feasibility studies – a good test-bed for a business plan.

## Community & Rural Development

A sizeable element of the support for enterprise in Ireland comes from efforts towards community development, particularly where these are aimed at replacing industries that have closed down or relocated (or reducing dependence on them in advance).

The *Directory* lists organisations active in this area, as well as those active more generally in rural development, including:

- **Ardee Community Development Company Ltd.**
- **Clann Credo.**
- **Institute for Minority Entrepreneurship.**
- **Terenure Enterprise Ltd.**

Guidance in business planning in this increasingly important area is provided in *Community Enterprise: A Business Planning Workbook for the Social Economy* (Ron Immink & Pat Kearney, Oak Tree Press).

## Consulting

As the *Directory* shows, there are dozens – even hundreds – of consultants with a bewildering array of expertise, available to help you to develop your start-up business and help it grow.

Use consultants carefully. Know what you want them to do, when, and at what cost to you. Make sure they deliver before you sign off and pay their fees. Look for the consultant who thinks long-term – and is prepared to invest in you and your future success. But recognise that consultants must eat too – if you want work done, you must be prepared to pay for it. Free advice will not take you far!

Consultants with experience of value to start-ups include:

- **Action Tallaght.**
- **Amárach Consulting.**
- **Aspire! Marketing Consultants.**
- **Century Management Ltd.**
- **Chartered Institute of Management Accountants.**
- **Crowleys DFK.**
- **Darlington Consulting.**
- **Deloitte & Touche.**
- **Ernst & Young.**
- **FGS.**
- **Innovation Partners.**
- **Innovator.**
- **Institute of Management Consultants & Advisers.**
- **Invest-tech.**
- **KPMG.**
- **Liffey Trust.**
- **Mazars.**
- **Optimum Results.**
- **OSK Accountants & Business Consultants.**
- **PricewaterhouseCoopers.**
- **Profiles Ireland.**
- **Xanthal Ltd.**

## Co-operatives

As **Chapter 9** explains, there are a variety of legal structures that you can choose when establishing your new business. One of these is the co-operative, for a democratically-controlled business.

The *Directory* identifies organisations that promote the co-operative concept and / or assist in their formation, including:

- **Co-operative Development Society Ltd.**
- **Irish Co-operative Society Ltd.**
- **Irish League of Credit Unions.**
- **National Association of Building Co-operatives Ltd**

## Cross-Border

A growing number of organisations are active in this area – good news for entrepreneurs and for the Border regions generally. If you live in the Border regions, or are willing to relocate there, check with these organisations about the support they offer:

- **Centre for Cross-Border Studies.**
- **Equity Network.**
- **InterTradeIreland.**
- **Legal-Island.**
- **PLATO.**

## E-Businesss

The bloom has definitely faded from the e-business 'gold rush' that marked the end of the millennium. A sad, but harsh truth was learnt by the early e-entrepreneurs (and their investors) – that you have to make a profit to stay in business and that profits require a business model that works (back to planning!).

Nonetheless, technology is changing the way we live and do business. The *Directory* lists initiatives and sources of advice or assistance in this area. Many of these are aimed at providing small businesses with the tools and techniques to succeed in this new age, including:

- **IE Domain Registry Ltd.**
- **Irish Internet Association.**
- **Webpayments.ie**

## Enterprise Support

A 'catch-all' category for organisations whose activities cannot be captured elsewhere, including:

- **Bolton Trust.**
- **Pobal.**

## Franchises

Organisations active in the franchise area include:

- **FranchiseDirect.**
- **Irish Franchise Association**
- **Ulster Bank.**

## Information

Information is critical to a good business plan and a well-planned and managed start-up. Many potential sources of market research information were identified in **Chapters 2** and **5**. The *Directory* expands on these, giving you a headstart in finding out what you need to know. The organisations listed include:

- **Action Tallaght.**
- **AIB Bank.**
- **Amárach Consulting.**
- **Ardee Community Development Company Ltd.**
- **BankofIrelandStartUpCourse.com.**
- **BASE Centre.**
- **Bplans.ie.**
- **Business Plus.**
- **Chambers Ireland.**
- **Chartered Institute of Personnel and Development.**
- **Company Formations International Ltd.**
- **Co-operative Development Society Ltd.**
- **CreativeIreland.com.**
- **Data Ireland.**
- **Excellence Ireland Quality Association.**
- **Franchise Direct.**
- **IBEC.**
- **Institute of Directors in Ireland.**
- **Institute of Management Consultants & Advisers.**
- **Invest-Tech.**
- **Irish Co-operative Society Ltd.**
- **Irish Countrywomen's Association.**
- **Irish Direct Marketing Association.**
- **Irish Exporters Association.**
- **Irish Franchise Association.**
- **Irish Institute for Training & Development.**
- **Irish Internet Association.**
- **Irish League of Credit Unions.**
- **Irish Management Institute.**
- **Irish Organic Farmers & Growers Association.**
- **Irish Small & Medium Enterprises Association.**

- Irish Software Association.
- Irish Wind Energy Association.
- Legal-Island.
- Marketing Institute of Ireland.
- MovetoIreland.com.
- National Association of Building Co-operatives Ltd.
- National Guild of Master Craftsmen.
- Network Ireland.
- Oak Tree Press.
- Public Relations Consultants Association.
- Public Relations Institute of Ireland.
- Sales Institute of Ireland.
- Small Firms Association.
- Smallbusinesscan.com.
- Terenure Enterprise Ltd.

Recognise that some of these organisations are member-based and restrict their services to members only, or charge fees to non-members. Most of the organisations listed are key players in their own industries, with a good finger on what's happening – it may be well worth your while paying for their specialist insight.

## Intellectual Property

Intellectual property is a catch-all phrase used to describe the various rights conferred by patents, trade marks, copyright, etc. Under Irish, UK and EU law, you can protect your 'rights' in inventions and so on (but not in ideas alone).

You can then exploit these rights yourself or license or sell them to others – this is called 'technology transfer'. Often technology transfer works on an inwards basis, with Irish businesses acquiring rights to use technologies developed elsewhere. It's a specialist area in which you should take advice and proceed with caution.

Organisations that can assist you here include:
- Cruickshank & Co.
- FR Kelly & Co.
- MacLachlan & Donaldson.
- Tomkins.

## Inwards Investment

This is primarily a State responsibility. However, a number of organisations provide information of general use, including:

- MovetoIreland.com.

## Legal

Legal advice can be critical for a start-up. Sources include:

- Action Tallaght.
- Law Society of Ireland.
- Legal-Island.

## Marketing

A consistent failing of Irish business has been – and still is, sadly – its lack of emphasis on, and commitment to, marketing. That this is changing is shown by the number of organisations committed to helping small businesses succeed at marketing. Here the *Directory* lists both consultants and support agencies with programmes to support small businesses' own marketing efforts, including:

- Action Tallaght.
- Aspire! Marketing Consultants.
- Century Management Ltd.
- Company Formations International Ltd.
- Data Ireland.
- Dublin Business Innovation Centre.
- Guaranteed Irish
- Irish Direct Marketing Association.
- Liffey Trust.
- Marketing Institute of Ireland.
- Sales Institute of Ireland.
- Xanthal Ltd.

## Networking

The Directory identifies a large number of organisations that provide networking opportunities or facilitate them – sometimes for members only, since many of these are the same key industry player organisations that were a source of market research and other information earlier.

If you're not out and about meeting people for some part of your time, you're probably missing opportunities to meet potential customers, to find out what competitors are up to, or to spot new business leads.

Networking opportunities include:

- **Chambers Ireland.**
- **CreativeIreland.com.**
- **First Tuesday.**
- **Institute of Directors in Ireland.**
- **Irish Countrywomen's Association.**
- **Irish Exporters Association.**
- **Irish Institute for Training & Development.**
- **Irish Internet Association.**
- **Irish Management Institute.**
- **Irish Small & Medium Enterprises Association.**
- **Irish Software Association.**
- **Irish Wind Energy Association.**
- **Network Ireland.**
- **PLATO.**
- **Sales Institute of Ireland.**
- **Small Firms Association.**
- **Smallbusinesscan.com.**

## Publications

As a writer and publisher, publications of all types are always of interest to me personally. But they should be of interest to you too – as a source of information, a replacement for training (some, not all), and as a means of developing yourself.

The *Directory* identifies those relevant to the Irish enterprise situation, including:

- **Amárach Consulting.**
- **Business Plus.**
- **Century Management Ltd.**
- **Data Ireland.**
- **Irish Small & Medium Enterprises Association.**
- **Oak Tree Press.**
- **Small Firms Association.**
- **Sunday Business Post.**

Even allowing for an obvious bias here, it's fair to say that **Oak Tree Press** has a special focus on publications and resources of value and interest to the owner / managers of micro and small businesses – all available from **www.oaktreepress.com**.

## R & D

Critical to the development of most small businesses, even if not always identified as such. Support is available from a range of organisations, including:

- **Innovation Partners.**
- **Innovator.**

## Regulator & Standards

Neither is the most popular of subjects, but both are equally necessary. In Ireland, by and large, both regulators and standards-setters are approachable and informative – even the Revenue Commissioners provide early assistance and encouragement towards developing the habit of compliance rather than merely enforcing it by rule of law subsequently. The Directory identifies key regulatory and standards-setting bodies of interest and relevance to start-ups and small businesses, including:

- **Excellence Ireland Quality Association.**
- **Guaranteed Irish Ltd.**
- **IE Domain Registry Ltd.**
- **National Guild of Master Craftsmen.**

## Social Economy

The Directory identifies organisations that support 'social economy' or 'third economy' approaches to enterprise, including:

- **Clann Credo.**

## Training

It's not enough to start a business – in some ways, that's actually the easy bit! – you also have to keep it going. And as you do, you will discover that you need new skills or to develop existing skills further – you need training on an on-going basis.

Most professional bodies have long since identified this requirement and have made some quantum of continuing training a condition of membership. You could do worse than adopt the same high standards for your new profession of entrepreneur. And the *Directory* will help with some useful sources, depending on your own specific needs and circumstances.

Training organisations include:

- **Action Clondalkin Enterprise.**
- **Aisling Software.**
- **Ardee Community Development Company Ltd.**
- **BankofIrelandStartUpCourse.com**
- **Century Management Ltd.**
- **Chartered Institute of Personnel & Development.**
- **Cork Business Innovation Centre.**
- **Darlington Consulting.**
- **Dublin Business Innovation Centre.**
- **Enterprise Acceleration Centre.**
- **Gahan & Co.**
- **Greenhouse Start-up Incubator.**
- **Innovation Partners.**
- **Innovator.**
- **Institute for Minority Entrepreneurship.**
- **Institute of Directors in Ireland.**
- **Irish Countrywomen's Association.**
- **Irish Direct Marketing Association.**
- **Irish Exporters Association.**
- **Irish Institute for Training & Development.**
- **Irish Management Institute.**
- **Irish Small & Medium Enterprises Association.**
- **Liffey Trust.**
- **LINC Centre.**
- **Marketing Institute of Ireland.**
- **Network Ireland.**
- **Oak Tree Press.**
- **Optimum Results Ltd.**
- **Organic College.**
- **PLATO.**
- **Sales Institute of Ireland.**
- **Small Firms Association.**
- **Synergy Centre.**
- **Terenure Enterprise Ltd.**

- WestBIC.
- Western Management Centre.

## Women

Surprisingly, or perhaps not depending on your point of view, the research identified relatively few organisations that specifically catered for the needs of women entrepreneurs. Those that were identified are listed in the *Directory*, including:

- **County & City Enterprise Boards** (most) – see *Directory* for a list.
- **Irish Countrywomen's Association.**
- **Network Ireland.**

## Workspace

A number of organisations provide (often as part of a support package) workspace tailored to the needs of a start-up. These include:

- **Action Clondalkin Enterprise.**
- **Ardee Community Development Company Ltd.**
- **BASE Centre.**
- **Dún Laoire Enterprise Centre**
- **Galway Technology Centre.**
- **Guinness Enterprise Centre.**
- **Limerick Enterprise Development Partnership.**
- **National Software Centre.**
- **Premier Business Centres.**
- **SPADE Enterprise Centre.**

# 7: EU SUPPORT FOR START-UPS

Support from the European Union for start-ups and small businesses in Ireland comes in three forms:

- EU Institutions.
- Direct.
- Indirect.

## EU INSTITUTIONS

Some EU institutions provide assistance direct to Irish start-up entrepreneurs – mainly in the form of information or policy. These institutions include:

- Enterprise DG.
- **Europa website**.
- European Commission.

## DIRECT ASSISTANCE

This is usually in the form of information and guidance through EU-funded agencies such as:

- **Business Innovation Centres** – part-funded by the EU – see *Directory* for a list.
- **Enterprise Europe Network** – see *Directory* for a list.
- **Europe Direct.ie** – see *Directory* for a list.
- **LEADER groups** – see *Directory* / "Irish LEADER Network" for a list.

### Business Innovation Centres

The five Business Innovation Centres in Ireland (a list appears in the *Directory*) are part of an EU-funded, EU-wide network. They are primarily targeted at technology-based businesses. They encourage and foster innovation in new or existing businesses, through services directed at the development of new ideas and their conversion into real business projects. As BIC support services may vary between centres, entrepreneurs seeking assistance should make contact with their local BIC to see whether and what help is available.

### LEADER Groups

LEADER is an EU initiative for rural development (part-funded by the Irish Government) that enables groups in rural areas to implement their own multi-sectoral integrated plans for the development of their areas. A list of LEADER groups appears in the *Directory* under "Irish LEADER Network".

As each LEADER Group identifies and responds to needs within its own communities, its activities are unique to its own situation. Because of this, entrepreneurs seeking assistance should make contact with their local LEADER Group to see whether and what help is available.

## INDIRECT ASSISTANCE

This is delivered indirectly through State and other agencies, for example:

- The Global Loan Facility for SMEs from the European Investment Bank, which cannot be accessed by businesses directly but is made available through the major banks.
- The European Investment Fund, which has invested in a number of Irish venture capital funds.
- EU Structural Funds, which support Government spending.

Full information on the European Union and its support for enterprise is available on the **Europa** website.

## SUPPORT BY CATEGORY

EU support by category for start-ups and small businesses in Ireland includes:

### Business Plans

- Business Innovation Centres – see *Directory* for a list.

### Community & Rural Development

- LEADER groups – see *Directory* / "Irish LEADER Network" for a list.

### EU Information

- **Enterprise Europe Network** – see *Directory* for a list.
- **Europe Direct.ie** – see *Directory* for a list.
- **Europa.**

### Marketing

- **Business Innovation Centres** – see *Directory* for a list.

### Training

- **Business Innovation Centres** – see *Directory* for a list.

# 8: Supports for Start-ups in Northern Ireland

This chapter identifies the organisations and agencies involved in supporting start-ups and small businesses in Northern Ireland. Read *Chapter 6* for information on the various categories and earlier chapters, as indicated, for additional entries in some categories.

## Government Support

The Government Department responsible for enterprise in Northern Ireland is the **Department of Enterprise, Trade & Investment.** As with the **Department of Enterprise, Trade & Employment** in the Republic, much of DETI's work is in creating an environment in which enterprise can flourish. Implementation is handled primarily by **Invest Northern Ireland**.

### Other Government Support

Other Government support in Northern Ireland is provided by:
- **Companies Registry.**
- **Department of Agriculture & Rural Development.**
- **Health & Safety Executive for Northern Ireland.**
- **HM Revenue & Customs.**
- **Invest Northern Ireland.**
- **NIBusinessInfo.co.uk.**
- **Northern Ireland Statistics & Research Agency.**
- **Northern Ireland Tourist Board.**
- **Rural Development Council.**
- **Social Economy Agency.**

## SUPPORT BY CATEGORY

### Business Plans

- NORIBIC.
- Palo Alto Software UK.

### Community & Rural Development

- ARC North West Ltd.
- Creggan Enterprises Ltd.
- Department of Agriculture & Rural Development.
- Down Rural Area Partnership.
- Flax Trust.
- Glenwood Enterprise Ltd.
- GROW South Antrim.
- Lagan Rural Partnership.
- North East Rural Development Programme.
- Rural Community Network.
- Rural Development Council.
- Social Economy Agency.
- South West Action for Rural Development.
- Southern Organisation for Action in Rural Areas.
- Tyrone Donegal Partnership.
- Ulster Community Investment Trust.
- Workspace.

### Consulting

- Acorn Business Centre.
- Banbridge District Enterprises Ld.
- Causeway Enterprise Agency.
- Lisburn Enterprise Organisation.
- Mallusk Enterprise Park.
- North West Marketing.
- ORTUS.
- Queen's University of Belfast.
- University of Ulster.

### Co-operatives

- Social Economy Agency.

### Cross-Border

- Centre for Cross-Border Studies.
- Equity Network.
- InterTradeIreland.
- Legal-Island.
- Newry & Mourne Enterprise Agency
- Tyrone Donegal Partnership.
- Ulster Community Investment Trust.

### Franchises

- Ulster Bank.

### Grants

- Arts Council of Northern Ireland.
- Business Innovation Link.
- InterTradeIreland.
- Invest Northern Ireland.
- NORIBIC.
- Northern Ireland Tourist Board.
- Prince's Trust Northern Ireland.

### Information

- Argyle Business Centre Ltd.
- Belfast Business Library.
- Centre for Cross-Border Studies.
- ChooseEnterprise.com.
- Companies Registry.
- Enterprise Agencies, members of **Enterprise Northern Ireland** – see *Directory* for a list.
- Equity Network.
- Health & Safety Executive for Northern Ireland.
- InterTradeIreland.
- Invest Northern Ireland.
- Legal-Island.

- Momentum.
- NIBusinessInfo.co.uk.
- NORIBIC.
- Northern Ireland Centre for Entrepreneurship.
- Northern Ireland Chamber of Commerce & Industry.
- Northern Ireland Food & Drink Association.
- Northern Ireland Statistics & Research Agency.
- Northern Ireland Tourist Board.
- North West Marketing.
- Rural Community Network.
- Social Economy Agency.

### Inwards Investment

- Invest Northern Ireland

### Legal

- Law Society of Northern Ireland.
- Legal-Island.

### Marketing

- NORIBIC.
- Northern Ireland Food & Drink Association
- Northern Ireland Tourist Board.
- North West Marketing.

### Mentoring

- Prince's Trust Northern Ireland.

### Networking

- Momentum.
- Northern Ireland Chamber of Commerce & Industry.
- Northern Ireland Food & Drink Association.
- PLATO.
- Rural Community Network.

### Policy

- Centre for Cross-Border Studies.

- Department for Employment & Learning.
- Department of Agriculture & Rural Development.
- Department of Enterprise, Trade & Investment.
- InterTradeIreland.

## R & D

- Business Innovation Link.
- Northern Ireland Science Park.
- QUBIS.
- Queen's University Belfast.
- University of Ulster.

## Regulator & Standards

- Companies Registry.
- Health & Safety Executive for Northern Ireland.
- HM Revenue & Customs.

## Social Economy

- Antrim Enterprise Agency Ltd.
- Creggan Enterprises Ltd.
- Glenwood Enterprises Ltd.
- Larne Enterprise Development Company Ltd.
- North West Marketing.
- Social Economy Agency.
- Ulster Community Investment Trust Ltd.
- Work West.
- Workspace.

## Tourism Development

- Northern Ireland Tourism Board.

## Training

- Department for Employment & Learning.
- Enterprise Agencies, members of **Enterprise Northern Ireland** – see *Directory* for a list.
- NORIBIC.
- Northern Ireland Centre for Entrepreneurship.

- Northern Ireland Food & Drink Association.
- North West Marketing.
- PLATO.
- Prince's Trust for Northern Ireland.
- Social Economy Agency.
- Tyrone Donegal Partnership.
- Ulster Community Investment Trust Ltd.

### Workspace

- Argyle Business Centre.
- Enterprise Agencies, members of **Enterprise Northern Ireland** – see *Directory* for a list.
- Flax Trust.
- Northern Ireland Science Park.

### Young Enterprise

- ChooseEnterprise.com.
- Young Enterprise Northern Ireland.

# 9: IMPLEMENTATION

OK! So you're ready to go – market research done, business plan drafted, finance and supports in place. But there are a few small hurdles that could still trip you.

You ought to consider each of the following and build them into your business plan:

- Bank account.
- Legal structure.
- Tax registration.
- Advisers.
- Accountants.
- Solicitors.
- Company administration.
- Accounting systems.
- Quality certification.
- Premises.

## BANK ACCOUNT

At least one bank account is an essential for any business, however small. Don't be tempted to run your business through your own personal bank account 'until it gets off the ground'. That is a recipe for disaster. Open a separate bank account for your business as soon as (or before) you begin to trade.

A limited company needs to pass a resolution of the Board of Directors to open a bank account. The steps involved are:

- Ask your bank manager for a copy of the form of resolution that they require. This is called a Bank Mandate because it mandates (that is, authorises) the bank to carry out the instructions of the directors regarding the operation of the account.

- Hold a meeting of the directors of the company.
- Decide what instructions you want to give the bank regarding who is authorised to sign cheques on behalf of the company, and how often you want to receive statements.
- Propose the resolution in the form required by the bank – see the mandate form for the wording – and have it adopted by the directors at a formal Board meeting.
- Complete the mandate form. Usually this is in the format of a request to the bank to open an account, and certifies that the resolution, in the prescribed wording, was passed at a meeting of the directors held on the date noted.
- Get sample signatures from each of the people authorised to sign cheques on behalf of the company.
- Return the mandate form and sample signatures to your bank manager.
- Give the bank manager a copy of your company's Memorandum of Association and Articles of Association. These will be kept for the manager's files.
- Show the original of the company's Certificate of Incorporation to your bank manager. A copy of this will be taken for the manager's files and on the copy will be marked the fact that the original has been seen by the manager. You will not be asked for, and you should not give the bank manager, the original Certificate of Incorporation. (The only exception to this is in the larger city branches where the documents needed to open your bank account go to the Securities department for checking. In this case, your bank manager should give you a receipt for the certificate and give you a date when you can return to collect it.)
- Have available some money to lodge to the new account.
- Decide the name in which you want the account to be opened. You can use only the registered name of the company, unless you are trading under a registered business name – that is, trading as *West Cork Forest Advisory Services* even though the company is registered in your own name as *Frank Kelly Ltd*. In this case, you will also need to show the bank manager the Certificate of Registration of Business Name for the company (note that it is no longer possible or necessary to register 'business names' in Northern Ireland).

Depending on the bank and branch, it may take a few days or a few weeks to clear all the paperwork associated with opening your company's bank account. Allow for this in your planning.

If you need immediate access to the funds you are lodging, your bank manager can usually arrange for temporary cheques to be made available while a chequebook is being printed.

## LEGAL STRUCTURE

You have most likely already made a choice as to your legal structure (see *Chapter 2*). Now you need to implement it.

### Setting Up as a Sole Trader

You automatically become a sole trader by starting up a business. Setting up as a sole trader needs almost nothing by way of legal formality. A further advantage of being a sole trader is that apart from normal tax returns, which every business must make, a sole trader is not required to make public any information on the business.

However, if you plan to run your business under a name other than your own, you must register with the *Registry of Business Names* (except in Northern Ireland, where registration of business names is not possible).

### Setting Up as a Partnership

A partnership, essentially, is an agreement between two or more people to go into business together. It may be no more formal than a handshake or may run to a multi-page legal document. Whichever route you take, build the following points into your planning:

- In a partnership, each partner is liable for all the liabilities of the business. If the business fails, and your partner(s) abandon(s) you, you could be left to pay for everything out of your own pocket. Before entering a partnership, decide whether you trust your partner(s)-to-be with everything you own – because that's what you will be doing.
- If you write down nothing else, write down and have all the partners sign a document setting out how the business is to be financed, how profits and losses are to be shared, and what will happen if one of the partners decides to leave. These are important points. Failure to agree on them at an early stage can lead to difficulty later.

In Northern Ireland, it is possible to form a 'limited partnership'. Full details of the procedures involved, and implications of this, are available from the **Companies Registry**.

## Forming an Unlimited Company

An unlimited company is formed in much the same way as a limited liability company. The principal difference is that the company's Memorandum of Association (part of the company's constitution) states that the liability of members is unlimited. Again, like sole traders and partnerships, this exposes your total assets in the event of the failure of the company. There seems little advantage in going through the formation requirements of a company without benefiting from limited liability.

## Forming a Limited Liability Company

A limited liability company is a legal entity separate from its share-holders. The shareholders are only liable, in the event of the business becoming unable to pay its debts, for any amount outstanding on their subscribed shareholdings.

The steps involved in forming a limited company are:

* Decide on a name for your company.
* Define the purpose for which the company is being formed. This will make up the company's Objects clause.
* Prepare the Memorandum of Association, which states what the company has been set up to do, who the initial share-holders are and how much they have subscribed.
* Prepare the Articles of Association, which details the rules governing internal procedures of the company.
* Submit the appropriate forms, together with the Memorandum and Articles of Association and a cheque or draft for the formation fees, to the **Companies Registration Office** or **Companies Registry**.

The cost of forming a limited company depends on whether you do the work yourself or ask an accountant, solicitor, or company formation agent to do it for you. Typically, using a professional adds considerably to the cost.

If your application to form a company is accepted, the Registrar will issue a Certificate of Incorporation. Only after its issue, and the first meeting of the Board of Directors of the company, may the company begin to trade.

### Forming a Co-operative

A worker co-operative is where a team comes together to form and run a business according to a set of values that includes self-help, self-responsibility, democracy, equality and solidarity. The business is jointly owned and democratically controlled. Co-operative members believe in the ethical values of honesty, openness, social responsibility and caring for others. The Co-operative Principles provide guidelines on how the business should conduct itself.

Co-operatives can be registered as an Industrial & Provident Society, a company limited by guarantee or a company limited by shares.

## TAX REGISTRATION (REPUBLIC OF IRELAND)

The **Revenue Commissioners** now use a single form to register a business for the many taxes to which it is liable. Form TR1 applies to individuals and Form TR2 to companies.

Your business's PAYE / PRSI registration number, its VAT registration number and its Corporation Tax number should be the same, though this number has nothing to do with the company's Registered Number, which is issued by the **Companies Registration Office** when the company is formed.

As a first step, download the Revenue's *Starting in Business* guide (reference IT 48) and *VAT for Small Businesses* (IT 49) from its website.

### Employers

Employers must register for PAYE when they pay remuneration exceeding a rate of €8 a week (€36 a month) to a full-time employee or €2 a week (€9 a month) to an individual with other employment – in other words, **all** employees.

When you take on an employee, you should first obtain from them a form P45 or tax-free allowance certificate. Then you must notify the tax office in respect of the new employee's former employment that you have employed them.

If neither a P45 nor a current year's tax-free allowance certificate is available (for example, in the case of an employee in first-time employment), you must complete form P46 (ring the tax office for a copy) and send it to the tax office. In those circumstances, PAYE / PRSI should be operated on the 'emergency basis' until a tax-free allowance certificate is received. Details on how to do this are available from the tax office.

An employer must:

- Maintain PAYE / PRSI records.
- Deduct tax, levies and the employee's share of PRSI and keep records of the amounts deducted.
- Submit a monthly return on form P30 between the 5th and 14th of the month, detailing the tax payable and PRSI (including employer's share).
- Submit a cheque for the total amount due with each monthly return.
- Submit yearly returns on forms P35 and P35L to the Collector General after the end of the tax year.
- Give to each employee working on 31 December each year a completed form P60 showing details of earnings and deductions for the income tax year ended on that date.
- Advise the Inspector of Taxes of any employee commencing or ceasing employment.

You should consider using the Revenue Online Service to submit your returns electronically.

### Your Own Position as an Employee

If you are a director of a limited company, then you must send in a P45 or P46 to the tax office in order to become a registered employee. Thereafter, with the exception of PRSI rates, which are lower for owner-directors, you will be treated on a day-to-day basis like any other PAYE employee.

However, directors are now subject to self-assessment (which means you must make an annual return of income), even though their income from the company already is subject to PAYE. Directors will be liable to a surcharge where they fail to make a return of income by the appropriate date. You should discuss your own situation with your accountant.

If you are self-employed, write to your local tax office explaining your situation. You are not liable for tax payments until after the first year of trading. Two months before the first year of trading ends, you will be sent a preliminary tax notice that informs you when your first tax payment is due.

## Registering for VAT

You must register your business for Value Added Tax as soon as its taxable supplies (that is, your business transactions that are liable to VAT) exceed or become likely to exceed the limits for registration. The current limits are:

- €75,000, where the supplies are of goods.
- €37,500, where the supplies are of services.

Your registration for VAT is notified to you on Form VAT 2. This will tell you:

- The date from which your business is registered for VAT. From this date onwards, you will have to charge VAT to all your customers and account to the Revenue Commissioners for it.
- Your VAT number, which you will have to quote on all invoices, statements, credit notes, etc.

In certain circumstances, you may register for VAT before you begin to trade or while your turnover is below the limits for registration. Doing so allows you to reclaim VAT paid on purchases of goods and may be of advantage to you. However, voluntary registration for VAT should not be done without professional advice. Consult your accountant and / or local tax office for further information.

## Registering for Corporation Tax

Once your new company has been registered, and you have submitted Form TR2, it will be registered for Corporation Tax, which is payable in two instalments following the end of your accounting year. Consult your accountant and / or local tax office for further information.

Note that start-up companies, which commenced trading on or after 1 January 2009, and whose tax liability for each year does not exceed €40,000, are exempt from Corporation Tax (including capital gains tax) in each of the first three years of trading.

# TAX REGISTRATION (NORTHERN IRELAND)

Businesses in the Northern Ireland, which is part of the UK, are subject to:

- **Income Tax** – Sole traders and partnerships on their profits.
- **Corporation Tax** – Limited companies on their profits.
- **Value Added Tax (VAT)** – All businesses with turnover over £68,000.
- **National Insurance Contributions (NIC)** – All businesses with employees (including owner/directors).

## Registration for tax

It is your obligation to notify **HM Revenue & Customs** through your local tax office of the establishment of your business and to provide them with the information required to register your business for the relevant taxes.

Your starting point is to contact Business Link on 08459 15 45 15 or www.businesslink.gov.uk/taxhelp to get a copy of the booklet, *Giving Yourself the Best Start with Tax*. Then call HM Revenue & Customs' helpline for the newly self-employed on 0845 915 4515, or contact your local tax office (check the telephone directory), to register for tax. If you are setting up a limited liability company, HMRC will send you an introductory pack with all the forms and explanations you need.

## Corporation Tax

Limited liability companies pay Corporation Tax on the company's total profits, including any capital gains, for an accounting period – normally the period for which the company's accounts are prepared, though an accounting period cannot exceed 12 months.

A self-assessment system applies to companies. The company assesses its own liability to tax and pays it no later than nine months after the end of the accounting period. Payments can be made by cheque, GIRO, or electronically through the BACS or CHAPS systems. Interest will be charged if payments are made after their due date. The company will also complete a company tax return and send it to the Inland Revenue with its accounts for the period. The company's self-assessment is then complete, unless changes are made to the return by the company or HMRC query it. HMRC queries some returns to check that they are correct or to understand better the figures in them.

The rates of Corporation Tax are:

- **Main Rate** – 28%, on profits over £1,500,000.
- **Small Companies' Rate** – 21% on  profits up to £300,000.

Marginal relief, which applies less than the full rate of the next tax band, applies to profits between £300,001 and £1,500,000.

## Income Tax

Income tax is payable by self-employed individuals on income earned in the tax year – that is, on annual profits or gains from an individual's trade, profession or vocation and on other income, such as investment income, rental income etc.

As soon as you start business as a self-employed person, you must complete Form CWF1, *Notification of Self-employment* and send it to the HMRC National Insurance Contributions Office. This office will then tell:

- Your local tax office.
- HMRC (if your turnover is more than £68,000 in a 12-month period, you must register for VAT – see below).
- Your Job Centre, if you are registered with one.

Your tax office requires a return of your business income and expenses in a standard format. You do not need to prepare separate accounts, although you may find that your bank wants to see formal accounts anyway.

Income tax is calculated on a 12-month basis, for a year running from 6 April to the following 5 April.

In April, you will receive a tax return, asking you for the information needed to calculate your tax bill for the year. If you can calculate the bill yourself (the return explains how), you must send back the return by 31 January following. Alternatively, you can ask the HMRC to calculate the tax bill, based on the information on your return. In this case, you must send back your return before 30 September.

In your second and later years in business, you must make two payments on account against your tax bill each year. These payments are due on 31 January (during the relevant tax year to 5 April) and 31 July (just after its end). The final payment of your tax bill must be made by 31 January following the end of the tax year.

## Calculating taxable profits

Taxable profits are calculated by deducting allowable business expenses from turnover. Turnover is the gross amount of income earned by a business before deducting any business expenses – the total amounts from sale of goods or provision of services. If a business is registered for VAT, the turnover figure should exclude VAT.

Business expenses are normally referred to as revenue expenditure, which covers day-to-day running costs (exclusive of VAT, if the business is registered for VAT), including:

- Purchase of goods for resale.
- Wages, rent, rates, repairs, lighting, heating, etc.
- Running costs of vehicles or machinery used in the business.
- Accountancy and audit fees.
- Interest paid on any monies borrowed to finance business expenses / items.
- Lease payments on vehicles or machinery used in the business.

Some expenses cannot be claimed as revenue expenditure, including:

- Any expense, not wholly and exclusively paid for the purposes of the trade or profession.
- Any private or domestic expenditure.
- Business entertainment expenditure – the provision of accommodation, food, drink or any other form of hospitality.
- Expenditure of a capital nature.

For expenditure relating to both business and private use, only that part relating to the business will be allowed.

Expenditure is regarded as 'capital' if it has been spent on acquiring or altering assets that are of lasting use in the business – for example, buying or altering business premises. Capital expenditure cannot be deducted in arriving at the taxable profit. However, capital allowances may be claimed on capital expenditure incurred on items such as office equipment, business plant and machinery, to take account of wear and tear on these items.

To arrive at the correct taxable income, the net profit should be calculated and any allowances and relief entitlements deducted.

## Self-employed National Insurance Contributions

Self-employed people pay National Insurance Contributions in two classes: Class 2 and Class 4 (on profits above a certain level).

## PAYE & National Insurance Contributions

When you employ someone in your business, you should immediately tell your local tax office. They will send you a *New Employer's Starter Pack* and tell the local Business Support Team, which provides payroll support to employers in their area.

The Pay As You Earn (PAYE) system operates on the basis that an employer deducts tax at a specified rate from an employee's pay. The system is designed so that, as far as is possible, the correct amount of tax is deducted from an employee's pay to meet his / her tax liability for the year. To achieve this, PAYE is normally computed on a cumulative basis, from the beginning of the tax year to the date on which a payment is being made.

In addition to deducting PAYE, employers are also obliged to deduct National Insurance Contributions (NIC) from employees.

You must:

- Work out employees' PAYE and NIC each pay-day.
- Pay this amount to HMRC monthly.
- Tell your local tax office at the end of each tax year how much each employee has earned and what PAYE and NIC you have deducted.

Your local HMRC Business Support Team will advise you on the details.

## Value Added Tax

Value Added Tax (VAT) is a consumer tax collected by VAT-registered traders on their supplies of taxable goods and services in the course of business and HMRC on imports from outside the EU.

Each trader pays VAT on goods and services acquired for the business and charges VAT on goods and services supplied by the business. The amount by which VAT charged exceeds VAT paid must be paid to HMRC.

If the amount of VAT paid exceeds the VAT charged, you will get a refund. This ensures that VAT is paid by the ultimate customer and not by the business.

You must register for VAT if your turnover for a 12-month period exceeds £68,000 (this amount is reviewed annually). Traders whose turnover is below this limit are not obliged to register for VAT but may do so if they wish. You should only do so on your accountant's advice.

The current rate of VAT is 17.5%, though some goods and services are zero-rated or taxed at a reduced rate of 5%.

The Annual Accounting Scheme allows you to pay monthly direct debits and send in a single VAT return at the end of the year. The Cash Accounting Scheme lets you account for VAT on the basis of cash paid and received, rather than invoices issued and received. You should take advice from your accountant before registering for either of these schemes. Both schemes are subject to maximum turnover limits.

### Record-keeping

HMRC requires all businesses to keep 'sufficient' records of transactions to allow the correct tax to be calculated. You must keep:

- Details of all receipts and expenses incurred in the course of your business and of what they relate to.
- Details of all sales and purchases made in the course of the trade, if you deal in goods.
- All other supporting documents.

HMRC publishes a number of guides (available on its website) that provide guidance in this area. Most businesses set up as a limited liability company will be required by law to keep certain records in order to prepare accounts. In most cases, the Companies Acts requirements are the same as HMRC's – except that HMRC requires records to be kept for six years, while the Companies Acts only requires private limited companies to keep records for three years. Note that alternatives to the original documents – for example, optical images, etc – are usually acceptable.

### Returns

For each of the taxes, you are required to supply HMRC with specific information on or by specific dates. These are called 'returns' and there are severe penalties for late submission or not submitting returns at all.

### Information and assistance

Comprehensive guides to all aspects of business taxation may be obtained from any tax office or HMRC's website (www.hmrc.gov.uk). Your accountant will also provide advice.

### On-line Services

HMRC is increasingly moving on-line. Not only are all forms and publications available on their website but, increasingly, taxpayers can make returns and payments online too.

### Talk to an accountant

Because tax regulations are becoming increasingly complicated, it is worth talking to an accountant about your specific situation and needs.

## ADVISERS

As you start in business, you need two key advisers: an accountant and a solicitor. In the pressures of setting up your new business, there will be a temptation to avoid finding either of these two. Not doing so saves you time and possibly money, both of which are important in a start-up situation. But it could cost you dearly later on.

The reasons for choosing a financial and a legal adviser at the start are:

- Their experience and expertise in dealing with other start-ups may save you hours of time and hundreds, or even thousands, of pounds. If they are the right advisers for you, they will be prepared to assist your enterprise with timely and constructive advice – take it and use it!

- With luck, you will never find yourself in a situation where you need to be bailed out of difficulty, but if you do, it's better to have your advisers on your team already than have to start looking for them with the millstone of your problem around your neck.

In choosing advisers, look for:

- Membership of the appropriate professional body. This is your guarantee of quality of work and source of redress, should the need ever arise (hopefully not!).

- Experience in the type of business or at least in the business area in which you intend to operate. You want to learn from your advisers' experience, not spend your time teaching them about your business.

- Adequate resources to meet your needs. What is adequate will depend on you, but don't choose a one-man band if you expect a limitless range of expertise. There is only so much one person can be expert in. Ask about the advisers' hours of business (actual hours, not published hours). Can you telephone them at 7 p.m. on a Sunday night? What happens when they go on holidays?

- People you can trust and work easily with. If you can't trust your advisers with your most confidential information, you shouldn't have them on your team. Find someone else.

## Choosing an Accountant

If your business is set up as a limited company, your accountant will have one primary task: to carry out the annual audit (note that an audit is not required where the company's turnover is below €1.5 million – £6.5 million in Northern Ireland – and certain other conditions are met). This is a statutory inspection of the company's accounting records, which results in a formal set of accounts and an audit report.

This report is to the members (that is, the shareholders) of the company and gives the auditor's (the accountant's) opinion on:

- Whether the accounts give a true and fair view.
- Whether proper books of account have been kept.
- Whether a meeting as specified under the Companies (Amendment) Act, 1986 needs to be called (this would arise where the share capital of the company amounts to less than half the net assets of the company).
- Whether all the explanations and information considered necessary for the purposes of the audit were received.

and, as a matter of fact:

- Whether the accounts agree with the books.
- Whether proper returns were received from branches (if any) not visited by the auditor.

If you do not know a suitable accountant, check the *Golden Pages* or *Yellow Pages* or contact one of the following:

- **Association of Chartered Certified Accountants.**
- **Chartered Accountants Ireland.**
- **Institute of Certified Public Accountants in Ireland.**

Many accountants provide advice and assistance in taking a business concept from viability assessment through to the production stage and also in obtaining assistance from State and other support organisations.

An initial meeting between a potential entrepreneur and the accountant is usually free and is used to gather information about the promoter and the business proposal. Based on the information available, appropriate action to advance the project will be agreed. Where further information is required, a structured feasibility study is carried out, embracing key aspects such as products, markets, competitors, technology, funding etc. A fee should be agreed before work starts. If the proposal is viable, the accountant will assist in the preparation of a comprehensive business plan, at a further agreed cost. They will make application for grants appropriate to the project and assist in raising finance from banks or private investors. They may also help to obtain commercial partners.

### Choosing a Solicitor

Unlike an accountant, a solicitor has no statutory duties in relation to a company. You will, however, need a solicitor for the following:

- To sign a statutory declaration when you are forming your company.
- To check out the lease of any premises you decide to buy or rent.
- To prepare employment contracts for you and your staff.
- To draft or review contracts that you enter into with customers or suppliers.

In addition, from time to time, you may require advice on legal issues.

If you do not know a suitable solicitor, look in the *Golden Pages* or *Yellow Pages* or contact the **Law Society of Ireland** or **Law Society of Northern Ireland**.


## ACCOUNTING SYSTEMS

Accounts systems provide a record of all the income and outgoings of a business and produce the basic information for the end-of-year accounts and for management information.

In a manual system, you may need some or all of the following (in varying levels of detail, depending on the size and complexity of your business – your accountant will advise):

- Cash book.
- Petty-cash book.
- Purchase day book.

- Purchase ledger.
- Sales day book.
- Sales ledger.
- Control accounts.
- Wages book / deduction sheets.
- Register of fixed assets.
- Nominal ledger.
- System for ordering goods / dealing with purchase invoices.
- System for dealing with customers' orders / sales invoices.
- Credit control procedures.
- Control of workforce and hours worked.
- Stock control procedures.
- System for regular management information.
- Adequate control procedures by management over employees.

You can also use a computerised accounting system or, indeed, an online accounting system, to be fully up-to-date – again, your accountant will advise.

Your accountant will also advise you on a system for filing and retrieving documents. You also need to consider the flow of documents and information around the business – for example, how a customer order is processed so that the goods are sent out, an invoice generated and payment received.

Whether manual or computerised, there are three simple aids that you should use to help you in the financial control of your business:

- Bank balance book.
- Still-to-be-received file.
- Still-to-be-paid file.

The 'bank balance book' does exactly what its name suggests – it tells you what your bank balance is. You need five columns – for the date, for the transaction detail (cheque or lodgement will do), for lodgements, for cheques and other withdrawals, and for the balance. If every transaction with your bank is written into this book *when it happens,* you will always know your correct bank balance. The little effort that it takes to keep this book up-to-date will be more than repaid as it keeps you out of trouble.

Cash flow is important for any business. If you sell goods on credit, you will probably find that you spend a great deal of time chasing debtors, trying to collect money. A 'still-to-be-received' file helps you by providing all the information you need on outstanding debts. Just put a copy of every invoice into the file when you issue it, and take the copy out when it is paid – then every invoice in the file represents an unpaid debt, money due to you. You can list them out, total them up, cry over them – whatever takes your fancy – but you have accurate information on which to do so.

The 'still-to-be-paid' file works in the opposite way – it reminds you of money you owe. Put a copy of every invoice you receive into it and take it out when you pay it (send the copy with your cheque so that your creditor knows which invoice you are paying!) – and what's left in the file is what you owe. So, when you get a telephone call saying that such and such an invoice is due for payment or overdue, you can check it out immediately.

## QUALITY CERTIFICATION

For some businesses in particular, and increasingly for all businesses, some form of quality certification is becoming essential. Schemes such as ISO 9000 are the norm among high-tech companies and are a minimum requirement to supply many of the foreign-owned multinationals operating in Ireland. ISO 9000 is the best known of such schemes, though the Q-Mark, awarded by **Excellence Ireland Quality Association** is important in some sectors.

ISO 9000 is a standard for quality management systems, covering every stage of the production process – procurement, incoming materials, production performance, final inspection, and delivery. To implement ISO 9000 (or any quality standard):

- Management has to define clearly what is needed.
- The message must reach staff so that everybody knows what they have to do and how to do it.
- The right equipment, processes and tools must be there to do the job.
- The right information must reach the right people at the right time.
- There must be a system of management and control.

For further information, read *ISO 9000*, by Brian Rothery (2nd edition, Gower).

Even if your business's involvement in quality certification stems purely from a supplier-imposed requirement, keep two things in mind:

- Quality is an attitude of mind, a way of working, not just mindless compliance with written procedures. Most quality schemes involve the recording of operational procedures, together with systems to audit compliance. Beware that compliance with the system does not become the end, rather than quality itself.

- Quality involves a cost and any investment in quality systems must be justified like any other business expense. Investing in quality for its own sake may be very noble, but it's not good business.

## PREMISES

In the property business, they say that only three things matter: location, location, location. For certain kinds of business – shops, hotels, restaurants – location can make or break the business. But in all cases, the right working environment is important.

For workshops and factories, you need to check lay-out, logistics, transport, weight of machinery, health and safety regulations, environmental issues, availability of three-phase electricity, etc. Draw out your ideal space before starting to look for accommodation.

If you are looking for offices, and you expect to be working on your own for a while, consider somewhere like **Premier Business Centres** that offers secretarial support (for example, telephone answering, message-taking, fax, photocopying, reception, etc.) It will save you hiring a secretary until the workload justifies it. And you save the capital cost of little-used but essential equipment and meeting facilities – instead, you pay only as you need them.

A 'virtual office', where you only pay for the facilities as you use them, can be the ideal way to combine working from home with having top-class facilities when you need to meet visitors – or just to provide yourself with flexibility while you assess your needs.

Wherever you locate, you need to consider insurance premiums, compliance with food hygiene and health and safety regulations, planning permission, lighting, heating, alarms, signs, locks, insurance, toilets, interior decor, fittings. And get a solicitor (see earlier) to check any lease before you sign.

# DIRECTORY OF SOURCES OF ASSISTANCE

The aims of this directory are:

- To highlight the many sources of assistance available to start-up and small / medium-sized enterprises in Ireland
- To direct readers to sources appropriate to their needs.

The directory is arranged alphabetically by organisation, with full contact details (address, telephone, fax, e-mail, website and contact name) for each, where possible. Note that dialling codes are those applicable locally – readers may need to amend the code when making cross-border calls or sending faxes.

Each entry summarises the assistance provided by the organisation.

All the information has been checked before publication but, of course, it is subject to change. See this book's companion website, **www.startingabusinessinireland.com**, or contact the organisations directly for the most up-to-date position.

---

## 4TH LEVEL VENTURES LTD

75 St Stephen's Green, Dublin 2  T: (01) 633 3603  F: (01) 633 3889
E: info@4thlevelventures.ie  W: www.4thlevelventures.ie  C: Ronan Reid
**Categories:** Equity

4th Level Ventures is a €20 million venture capital fund managed by Dolmen Securities. It is focused on investing in companies whose intellectual property arises from third level education institutional research, working on campus with university commercialisation teams.

## ACCOUNTS IQ

Visor Ltd, Sand House, Bath Place, Blackrock, Co Dublin  T: (01) 707
4400  F: (01) 12 1000  E: sales@accountsiq.com  W: www.accountsiq.com
**Categories:** Accountants

The flagship product of Visor Ltd, accountsIQ is a hosted online
accounting package, designed by accountants and IT specialists, to
provide simultaneous real time access to accounting information and
business documents as well as productive collaboration online, any
time and anywhere.

## ACORN BUSINESS CENTRE

2 Riada Avenue, Garryduff Road, Ballymoney, Co Antrim BT53 7LH
T: (028) 2766 6133  F: (028) 2766 5019
E: lyndamoore@acornbusiness.co.uk  W: www.acornbusiness.co.uk
C: Lynda Moore
**Categories:** Consulting; Information; Training; Workspace

Acorn Business Centre is a member of Enterprise Northern Ireland and
offers workspace, training, premises and consultancy.

## ACT VENTURE CAPITAL LTD

Richview Office Park, Clonskea, Dublin 14  T: (01) 260 0966  F: (01) 260
0538  E: info@actvc.ie  W: www.actventure.com  C: Niall Carroll
**Categories:** Equity

ACT Venture Capital provides capital to growth-oriented private
companies in the range of €750K to €15 million. Larger sums can be
provided in syndication with institutional investors.

## ACTION CLONDALKIN ENTERPRISE

Clondalkin Enterprise Centre, Neilstown Road, Clondalkin, Dublin 22
T: (01) 457 8115  F: (01) 457 8121  E: dbyrne@aceenterprise.ie
C: David Byrne
**Categories:** Training; Workspace

Action Clondalkin Enterprise provides support to people starting
businesses, including training and workspace in the Bawnogue
Enterprise Centre.

# From Concept, Through Innovation, To Growth

Synergy Centre puts you at the heart of a vibrant entrepreneurial community.

> MENTORING

> TRAINING

> NETWORKING

> OFFICE SPACE

> CAFÉ

> RESEARCH LINKS

> FUNDING LINKS

35 tenant companies

High funding success rates

Seedcorn Prize Winner

www.synergycentre.ie
E-mail: Innovate@synergycentre.ie
Tel. 01 4042083

synergy
centre
at ITT Dublin

## ACTION TALLAGHT

Brookfield Enterprise Centre, Brookfield, Tallaght, Dublin 24
T: (01) 462 3222  F: (01) 462 3433  C: Olive Whelan
**Categories:** Business Plans; Consulting; Information; Legal; Marketing

Action Tallaght was formed in 1992 as the umbrella body for five community enterprise groups in Tallaght. It provides integrated support — sales and marketing advice, business consultancy, accountancy and legal advice, financial management and feasibility studies, business plans and funding applications — to people from Tallaght who intend to establish a business.

## AIB BANK

Bankcentre, Ballsbridge, Dublin 4  T: (01) 660 0311  W: www.aib.ie
**Categories:** Debt; Equity; Information

AIB Bank is Ireland's largest bank. It provides a full range of banking services to business customers. AIB operates in Northern Ireland as First Trust Bank.

## AIB SEED CAPITAL FUND

Dublin Business Innovation Centre, The Tower, TCD Enterprise Centre, Pearse Street, Dublin 2  T: (01) 671 3111  F: (01) 671 3330  E: bif@dbic.ie
W: www.dbic.ie  C: Alex Hobbs
**Categories:** Equity

This fund has €30m under management, with AIB and Enterprise Ireland both committing €15m. It is managed by experienced managers, who are empowered to make seed investments of up to €500,000.

## AISLING SOFTWARE

12 Castle Park, Park Road, Killarney, Co Kerry  T: (064) 32112
E: info@sortmybooks.ie  W: www.sortmybooks.com  C: Aileen Hannan
**Categories:** Accountants; Training

Aisling Software is an Irish software company, specialising in accounting packages for small businesses and owner / managers. Its products include SortMyBooks, a book-keeping software designed with the small business in mind, which produces the Irish VAT return. Aisling also offers training in book-keeping, using its software, as well as information evenings.

# AMÁRACH CONSULTING

37 Northumberland Road, Dublin 4  T: (01) 660 5506  F: (01) 660 5508
E: info@amarach.com  W: www.amarach.com  C: Gerard O'Neill
**Categories:** Consulting; Information; Publications; Website

Amárach (Irish for 'tomorrow') specialises in predictive market research and business forecasting. It focuses on understanding the changes taking place in Irish markets and on linking these insights to effective business strategies designed to profit from anticipated change, using a multi-disciplinary approach that draws on economics, demographics, social psychology and technological forecasting. Many of Amárach's reports are published on its website.

# ANTRIM ENTERPRISE AGENCY LTD

58 Greystone Road, Antrim BT41 1JZ  T: (028) 9446 7774  F: (028) 9446 7292  E: admin@antrimenterprise.com  W: www.antrimenterprise.com
C: Jennifer McWilliams
**Categories:** Debt; Information; Social Economy; Training; Workspace

Antrim Enterprise Agency is a member of Enterprise Northern Ireland. It offers workspace, start-up and ongoing training and loans.

# ARC NORTH WEST

1 Market Street, Omagh, Co Tyrone BT78 1EE  T: (028) 8225 0202
F: (028) 8225 0265  W: www.arcnorthwest.com  C: Claudine McGuigan,
Rural Development Programme Manager
**Categories:** Community & Rural Development

ARC North West is responsible for Axis 3 of the Northern Ireland Rural Development Programme 2007-2013 for the North West Cluster, comprising Derry City Council, Limavady Borough Council, Omagh District Council and Strabane District Council. It aims 'to improve the quality, cohesiveness and sustainability of local social and economic life in the rural North West by supporting development work taken forward by the private, community, voluntary and public sectors'.

## ARDEE COMMUNITY DEVELOPMENT CO. LTD

Hale Street, Ardee, Co Louth  T: (041) 685 7680  F: (041) 685 7681
E: ardbuspark@eircom.net  W: www.ardeebusinesspark.ie
**Categories:** Community & Rural Development; Information; Training;
Workspace

Ardee Community Development Co. Ltd. is a community-owned project, serving local entrepreneurs and businesses whose primary objective is to assist local enterprises to boost employment in the region. It operates the Ardee Business Park.

## ARDS BUSINESS CENTRE LTD

Sketrick House, Jubilee Road, Newtownards, Co Down BT23 4YH
T: (028) 9181 9787  F: (028) 9182 0625  E: postbox@ardsbusiness.com
W: www.ardsbusiness.com  C: Leslie Ross , Chief Executive
**Categories:** Information; Training; Workspace

Ards Business Centre is a member of Enterprise Northern Ireland. It is the local enterprise agency for the Ards Borough Council area and has been providing support to businesses for over 20 years, through advice to those forming and growing their businesses and through the provision of reasonably priced property to address changing market needs.

## ARGYLE BUSINESS CENTRE LTD

39 North Howard Street, Belfast BT13 2AP  T: (028) 9181 9787
F: (028) 9182 0625  E: frank.hamill@abc-ni.co.uk  W: www.abc-ni.co.uk
C: Frank Hamill
**Categories:** Information; Workspace

One of several Enterprise Agencies / Centres in Belfast.

## ARKLOW COMMUNITY ENTERPRISE LTD

8 St. Mary's Terrace, Arklow, Co Wicklow  T: (0402) 91092
F: (0402) 91091  E: arklowace@eircom.net
W: www.arklow.ie/chamber/aceContact.asp  C: Ann Byrne, Manager
**Categories:** Business Plans; Community & Rural Development; Grants;
Marketing; Training

ACE offers new and small businesses in the Arklow area: advice on creating a business plan; advertising and marketing; customer service; grants (subject to conditions); and training.

## ARMAGH BUSINESS CENTRE LTD

2 Loughgall Road, Armagh BT61 7NH  T: (028) 3752 5050
F: (028) 3752 6717  E: info@abcarmagh.com  W: www.abcarmagh.com
C: Anna Logan, Manager
**Categories:** Debt; Information; Training; Workspace

Armagh Business Centre is a member of Enterprise Northern Ireland. Its mission is 'to stimulate economic and social regeneration in Armagh City and District Council area by positively encouraging the formation, development and subsequent growth of small and medium enterprises through extensive business and technical expertise'.

## ARTS COUNCIL

70 Merrion Square, Dublin 2  T: (01) 618 0200  F: (01) 676 1302
E: paul@artscouncil.ie W: www.artscouncil.ie
C: Paul Johnson, Artists Services Manager
**Categories:** Grants

The Arts Council is the development agency for the arts in Ireland and the primary source of support for the individual creative and interpretative artist. Its role is to provide advice to government and non-governmental bodies, individuals and arts organisations on artistic matters, and support and financial assistance for artistic purposes to individuals and organisations.

## ARTS COUNCIL OF NORTHERN IRELAND

77 Malone Road, Belfast BT9 6AQ  T: (028) 9038 5200  F: (028) 9066 1715
E: info@artscouncil-ni.org  W: www.artscouncil-ni.org
**Categories:** Grants

The Arts Council of Northern Ireland is the lead development agency for the arts in Northern Ireland. Its website gives details of the funding available – and information on application procedures.

## ASHTOWN FOOD CENTRE

Ashtown, Dublin 15  T: (01) 805 9500  F: (01) 805 9550
E: declan.troy@teagasc.ie  W: www.teagasc.ie
C: Declan Troy, Head of Centre
**Categories:** Consulting; R & D; Training

The Ashtown Food Centre is a division of Teagasc. Its mission is to provide leadership and excellence in research, consultancy and training to the food sector, thereby encouraging product innovation and enhanced food safety and quality.

## ASPIRE! MARKETING CONSULTANTS

Schull, Co Cork  T: (01) 633 5149  E: simon.okeeffe@aspire.ie
W: www.aspire.ie  C: Simon O'Keeffe
**Categories:** Consulting; Marketing

aspire! provides marketing strategy and branding expertise and works with clients to support them in executing the strategies and plans it develops with them.

## ASSOCIATION OF CHARTERED CERTIFIED ACCOUNTANTS

9 Leeson Park, Dublin 6  T: (01) 498 8900  F: (01) 496 3615
E: kevin.kernan@ie.accaglobal.com  W: www.accaglobal.com
C: Kevin Kernan
**Categories:** Accountants

ACCA is one of the accountancy bodies whose members are permitted to audit company accounts. It has nearly 10,000 members and students throughout the island of Ireland. If you're looking for an accountant, ACCA can direct you to one of its members.

## ATHLONE INSTITUTE OF TECHNOLOGY

Dublin Road, Athlone, Co Westmeath  T: (0906) 424400 F: (0906) 424417
E: hfitzsimons@ait.ie  W: www.ait.ie  C: External Services Manager
**Categories:** Consulting; Incubator; R & D; Training

AIT's External Services Unit acts as a central contact point for companies and community organisations to the Institute's range of industrial services, including: consultancy / business expertise, customised training programmes and opportunities for the development of collaborative research projects in the manufacturing, services, life sciences, physical sciences and information technology sectors. AIT also offers the Midlands Enterprise Platform Programme and operates the Midlands Innovation & Research Centre.

## AVONDHU / BLACKWATER PARTNERSHIP

The Showgrounds, Fermoy, Co. Cork T: (025) 33411  F: (025) 33422
5/6 Park West, Mallow, Co. Cork  T: (022) 43553  F: (022) 43681
E: valerie@avondhublackwater.com  W: www.avondhublackwater.com
C: Valerie Murphy, CEO
**Categories:** Community & Rural Development

Formed from the strategic integration of Blackwater Resource Development and Avondhu Development Group, Avondhu / Blackwater Partnership is supported under the Local Development Social Inclusion Programme and LEADER in achieving local development through the promotion of sustainable enterprise.

## BALLYFERMOT / CHAPELIZOD PARTNERSHIP

4 Drumfinn Park, Ballyfermot, Dublin 10  T: (01) 623 5612
F: (01) 623 0922  E: info@ballyfermotpartnership.ie
W: www.ballyfermotpartnership.ie  C: Justin Purcell
**Categories:** Community & Rural Development

Ballyfermot / Chapelizod Partnership is supported under the Local Development Social Inclusion Programme in achieving local development through the promotion of sustainable enterprise.

## BALLYHOURA COMMUNITY PARTNERSHIP

Ballyhoura Centre, Kilfinane, Co Limerick  T: (063) 91300  F: (063) 91330
E: localdev@ballyhoura.org  W: www.ballyhouracountry.com
C: Carmel Fox, Chief Executive

**Categories:** Community & Rural Development; Tourism Development

Ballyhoura Community Partnership is supported under LEADER and the Local Development Social Inclusion Programme in achieving local development through the promotion of sustainable enterprise.

## BALLYMENA BUSINESS DEVELOPMENT CENTRE LTD

62 Fenaghy Road, Galgorm Industrial Estate, Ballymena BT42 1FL
T: (028) 2565 8616  F: (028) 2563 0830
E: info@ballymenabusiness.co.uk  W: www.ballymenabusiness.co.uk
C: Melanie Christie, Centre Manager

**Categories:** Information; Training; Workspace

Ballymena Business Development Centre is a member of Enterprise Northern Ireland and provides a range of business support services.

## BALLYMUN WHITEHALL AREA PARTNERSHIP LTD

North Mall, Ballymun Town Centre, Dublin 11  T: (01) 842 3612
E: declandunne@ballymun.org  C: Declan Dunne, Manager

**Categories:** Community & Rural Development

Ballymun Whitehall Area Partnership is supported under the Local Development Social Inclusion Programme in achieving local development through the promotion of sustainable enterprise.

## BANBRIDGE DISTRICT ENTERPRISES LTD

Scarva Road Industrial Estate, Scarva Road, Banbridge, Co Down BT32 3QD  T: (028) 4066 2260  F: (028) 4066 2325  E: info@bdelonline.com
W: www.bdelonline.com  C: Ciaran Cunningham

**Categories:** Consulting; Information; Training; Workspace

Banbridge District Enterprises is a member of Enterprise Northern Ireland. It is dedicated to the generation and development of the local economic wealth in its area and beyond.

## BANK OF IRELAND

Head Office, Lower Baggot Street, Dublin 2  T: (01) 661 5933
W: www.boi.ie
**Categories:** Debt

Bank of Ireland is one of the largest banks in Ireland, providing a range of banking services to business customers. Bank of Ireland has invested in the Bank of Ireland Kernel Private Equity Fund. It operates in Northern Ireland as Bank of Ireland Northern Ireland.

## BANK OF IRELAND BUSINESS BANKING

40 Mespil Road, Dublin 4  T: (01) 665 3438  F: (01) 665 3480
E: damian.young@boimail.com  W: www.bankofireland.ie
C: Damian Young, Head of Small Business
**Categories:** Debt

In addition to the full range of banking facilities, Bank of Ireland Business Banking offers a special start-up package with free current account banking for two years and a range of offers from its partners. It also offers a free online start-up training course.

## BANK OF IRELAND NORTHERN IRELAND

54 Donegall Place, Belfast BT1 5BX  T: (028) 9023 4334  F: (028) 9023 4388
W: www.bankofireland.co.uk
**Categories:** Debt

Bank of Ireland in Northern Ireland employs 1,100 staff across its various units and Province-wide retail branch network and offers a full range of banking services to start-ups and small businesses.

## BANKOFIRELANDSTARTUPCOURSE.COM

W: www.bankofirelandstartupcourse.com
**Categories:** Information; Training; Website

Bank of Ireland offers a free online start-up course, developed by Oak Tree Press and Fix-IT.

# BANK OF SCOTLAND (IRELAND) LTD

Bank of Scotland House, 124-127 St Stephen's Green, Dublin 2
T: (01) 267 4000 F: (01) 267 4010  W: www.bankofscotland.ie
**Categories:** Debt

Bank of Scotland's services include commercial lending and SME banking, asset finance, treasury and trade finance.

# BASE CENTRE

Patrickstown House, Ladyswell Road, Mulhuddart, Dublin 15
T: (01) 820 3020  F: (01) 820 9469  E: info@base-centre.com
W: www.base-centre.com  C: Ken Germaine
**Categories:** Information; Workspace

The BASE (Blanchardstown Area Small Enterprises) Centre is an Enterprise Centre that serves the Dublin 15 area. It offers incubation units and supports to SMEs.

# BASIS.IE

BASIS Project, Department of Enterprise, Trade & Employment, 4th Floor, Earlsfort Centre, Lower Hatch Street, Dublin 2  T: (01) 631 2787 / (01) 631 2788  F: (01) 631 2563  E: basis@entemp.ie  W: www.basis.ie
**Categories:** Information; Website

BASIS stands for 'Business Access to State Information Services'. It aims to provide information about State services and regulations to all businesses with Web access.

# BDO SIMPSON XAVIER

Beaux Lane House, Mercer Street Lower, Dublin 2  T: (01) 470 0000
F: (01) 477 0000  E: info@bdosx.ie  W: www.bdosx.ie  C: Colm Nagle
**Categories:** Accountants; Equity

Accountants and advisers to entrepreneurial and growing owner-managed businesses, BDO Simpson Xavier provides a useful online checklist for start-ups on its website. The firm also assists in raising Business Expansion Scheme funding for small businesses.

## BELFAST BUSINESS LIBRARY

Central Library, Royal Avenue, Belfast BT1 1EA  T: (028) 9050 9150
F: (028) 9033 2819  E: info@libraries.belfast-elb.gov.uk
C: Stephen McFarlane, Librarian
**Categories:** Information

The Library provides a reference, lending and information service, including: books on accountancy, computing, HR management, legislation and management; over 250 current periodicals and market research reports; company financial and background information; general and specialised trade directories; HMSO and selected non-governmental statistics; and UK & Northern Ireland legislation.

## BIG RED BOOK

Rathdown Hall, Upper Glenageary Road, Glenageary, Co Dublin
T: (01) 204 8300  F: (01) 204 8324  E: info@bigredbook.com
W: www.bigredbook.com
**Categories:** Accountants

Designed by professional accountants, Big Red Book is an easy-to-use, computerised bookkeeping package ideal for small businesses.

## BLANCHARDSTOWN AREA PARTNERSHIP

Dillon House, Unit 106, Coolmine Industrial Estate, Dublin 15
T: (01) 820 9550  E: lcurran@bap.ie  C: Linda Curran, Manager
**Categories:** Community & Rural Development

BAP is supported under the Local Development Social Inclusion Programme in achieving local development through the promotion of sustainable enterprise.

## BLUEBELL, INCHICORE, ISLANDBRIDGE, KILMAINHAM & RIALTO PARTNERSHIP

2nd floor, Oblate View, Tyrconnell Road, Inchicore, Dublin 8  T: (01) 473
2196  E: kennybj@canalpartnership.com  C: Brian Kenny, Manager
**Categories:** Community & Rural Development

Bluebell, Inchicore, Islandbridge, Kilmainham & Rialto Partnership is supported under the Local Development Social Inclusion Programme in achieving local development through the promotion of sustainable enterprise.

## BOI VENTURE CAPITAL LTD

43 Pearse Street, Dublin 2  T: (01) 604 1752  F: (01) 677 5588
E: margaret.broderick@boimail.com  C: Margaret Broderick
**Categories:** Equity

A €19 million fund, targeting high growth manufacturing and information, communication and technology (ICT) businesses throughout Ireland, with typical investments ranging between €350k and €2 million.

## BOLTON TRUST

128-130 East Wall Road, Dublin 3  T: (01) 240 1300  F: (01) 240 1310
E: info@boltontrust.com  W: www.boltontrust.com
C: Michael Drennan, Estate Manager
**Categories:** Enterprise Support; Incubator

The Bolton Trust encourages and promotes new business enterprise in Ireland. It is an independent voluntary trust, established in 1986 by staff of the Dublin Institute of Technology, and actively committed to assisting people create sustainable business. The Trust's centre-piece is the Docklands Innovation Park, from which it operates the DIT Hothouse programme.

## BORD BIA

Clanwilliam Court, Lower Mount Street, Dublin 2  T: (01) 668 5155
F: (01) 668 7521 E: info@bordbia.ie  W: www.bordbia.ie
C: Eileen Bentley, Manager, Small Business
**Categories:** Grants; Information; Marketing; Regulator & Standards

Bord Bia (The Irish Food Board) is the Irish government agency charged with the promotion, trade development and marketing of the Irish food, drink and horticulture industry. It operates programmes to develop and foster contact between buyers and Irish companies, including participation under the 'Ireland' umbrella brand at international trade exhibitions, and co-coordination of inward buying visits.

# BORD IASCAIGH MHARA

PO Box 12, Crofton Road, Dún Laoire, Co Dublin  T: (01) 214 4100
F: (01) 284 1123  E: info@bim.ie  W: www.bim.ie  C: Imelda Bradley
**Categories:** Grants; Information; Marketing; Regulator & Standards;
Training

BIM provides a wide range of financial, technical, educational, business innovation and trade development services for fishermen, processors, fish-farmers, retailers and exporters, organised through five divisions: Aquaculture, Business Development and Innovation, Fisheries Development, Marine Services and Secretariat.

# BORDERS, MIDLANDS & WESTERN REGIONAL ASSEMBLY

The Square, Ballaghaderreen, Co Roscommon T: (0907) 62970
F: (0907) 62973  E: info@bmwassembly.ie  W: www.bmwassembly.ie
**Categories:** Policy

The Borders, Midland & Western Regional Assembly covers counties Cavan, Donegal, Galway, Laois, Leitrim, Longford, Louth, Mayo, Monaghan, Offaly, Roscommon, Sligo, Westmeath. Its role is to: manage the BMW Regional Operational Programme under the National Development Plan; monitor the impact of the EU programme under the NDP / Community Support Framework; and promote the co-ordination of public services. The BMW Assembly does not provide direct funding to individuals or organisations but funds through 'Implementing Bodies'.

# BOYLAN & DODD CORPORATE SERVICES LTD

41 Percy Place, Dublin 4  T: (01) 660 7166  F: (01) 660 7193
E: mailto@businessireland.net  W: www.businessireland.net
C: James Gormley, Donal Boylan, Chris Dodd
**Categories:** Business Sales / Purchases

Boylan & Dodd offer a range of corporate finance services, including assistance with the purchase or sale of businesses.

## BPLANS.IE

W: www.bplans.ie
**Categories:** Business Plans; Information; Website

Bplans.ie contains the largest single collection of free sample business plans online. In addition, Bplans.ie includes practical advice on planning. See also Palo Alto Software.

## BRAY PARTNERSHIP

4 Prince of Wales Terrace, Quinsboro Road, Bray, Co Wicklow
T: (01) 286 8266  F: (01) 286 8700  E: info@braypartnership.org
C: Peter Brennan, Manager
**Categories:** Community & Rural Development

Bray Partnership is supported under the Local Development Social Inclusion Programme in achieving local development through the promotion of sustainable enterprise.

## BREFFNI INTEGRATED COMPANY

Unit 6a, Corlurgan Business Park, Ballinagh Road, Cavan
T: (049) 473 2196  F: (049) 432 7280  E: cavpart.ie@iol.ie
C: Terry Hyland, Enterprise Officer; Brendan Reilly, CEO
**Categories:** Community & Rural Development

Breffni Integrated is supported under LEADER and the Local Development Social Inclusion Programme in achieving local development through the promotion of sustainable enterprise.

## BUSINESS EXPANSION SCHEME

Office of the Revenue Commissioners, Dublin Castle, Dublin 2
T: (01) 702 4107  E: cillbyrn@revenue.ie  W: www.revenue.ie
C: Cillian Byrnes
**Categories:** Equity

BES is intended to help smaller businesses and certain R&D projects to raise funds. Subject to conditions, relief from income tax is available as a deduction from income to individuals who invest long-term risk capital in companies that are incorporated and resident in Ireland, not quoted on the Stock Exchange, and engaged in a 'qualifying trade'. An explanatory guide is available on the Revenue's website.

## BUSINESS INFORMATION CENTRE

Dublin City Public Library, ILAC Shopping Centre, Henry Street,
Dublin 1 T: (01) 873 4333 F: (01) 872 1451
E: businesslibrary@dublincity.ie
W: www.dublincitypubliclibraries.ie C: Anne Collins
**Categories:** Information

A reference service specialising in company and market research information. It stocks books, reports, directories, journals / periodicals, databases, newspapers / press cuttings (from the late 1970s) on Irish companies and organisations and a wide range of business-related subjects.

## BUSINESS INNOVATION CENTRES

See individual entries for: Cork Business Innovation Centre; Dublin Business Innovation Centre; NORIBIC (Business Innovation Centre, Derry); South-East Business Innovation Centre; WestBIC (Business Innovation Centre, Galway).

## BUSINESS INNOVATION LINK

PO Box 1140, Belfast BT1 9GT T: (028) 9041 9970 F: (028) 9041 9970
E: bil-manager@www.bil-ni.co.uk W: www.bil-ni.co.uk
**Categories:** Grants; R & D

The Business Innovation Link (BIL) provides Northern Ireland's inventors and innovators with financial support and assistance for new product ideas. If an idea is of patentable quality and capable of commercialisation with real market potential, BIL may provide assistance with development.

## BUSINESS PLUS

30 Morehampton Road, Dublin 4 T: (01) 660 8400 F: (01) 660 4540
E: info@businessplus.ie W: www.bizplus.ie C: Nick Mulcahy, Editor
**Categories:** Information; Publications; Website

Good business magazine, with strong focus on e-business / e-commerce issues, and a useful website. The magazine is available at newsagents or on subscription.

## CARLOW COUNTY DEVELOPMENT PARTNERSHIP LTD

Main Street, Bagenalstown, Co. Carlow  T: (059) 972 0733
E: carlowleader@eircom.net  C: Mary Walsh, CEO
**Categories:** Community & Rural Development

Carlow County Development Partnership is supported under LEADER and the Local Development Social Inclusion Programme in achieving local development through the promotion of sustainable enterprise.

## CARLOW COUNTY ENTERPRISE BOARD

Enterprise House, O'Brien Street, Carlow  T: (059) 913 0880  F: (059) 913 0717  E: enterprise@carlow-ceb.com  W: www.carlow-ceb.com
C: Michael P. Kelly, CEO
**Categories:** Debt; Equity; Grants; Information; Mentoring; Training

Carlow CEB provides a support network for small business in Co Carlow and provides a single point of contact at local level for small and micro-enterprises.

## CARRICKFERGUS ENTERPRISE AGENCY LTD

8 Meadowbank Road, Carrickfergus BT38 8YF  T: (028) 9336 9528
F: (028) 9336 997  E: info@ceal.co.uk  W: www.ceal.co.uk
**Categories:** Information; Training; Workspace

CEAL is a member of Enterprise Northern Ireland and offers workspace, start-up and ongoing training.

## CASTLEREAGH ENTERPRISES LTD

Dundonald Enterprise Park, Enterprise Drive, Carrowreagh Road,
Dundonald BT16 1QT  T: (028) 9055 7557  F: (028) 9055 7558
E: enterprise@castlereagh.com  W: www.castlereagh.com
C: Jack McComiskey, Chief Executive
**Categories:** Information; Training; Workspace

Castlereagh Enterprises is a member of Enterprise Northern Ireland. It aims to promote economic development and job creation in the Castlereagh Borough Council Area.

# Managing your farm cashflow?

## Working Capital Finance.

AIB can provide you with a credit line to manage
seasonal and short term funding requirements.

Talk to us today or click on www.aib.ie/farming

be with

## CAUSEWAY ENTERPRISE AGENCY

Loughanhill Industrial Estate, Coleraine BT52 2NR T: (028) 7035 6318
F: (028) 7035 5464 E: info@causeway-enterprise.co.uk
W: www.causeway-enterprise.co.uk C: Jayne Taggart, Chief Executive
**Categories:** Consulting; Information; Training; Workspace

A member of Enterprise Northern Ireland, Causeway Enterprise Agency
is an independent, business support organisation dedicated to building a
strong and sustainable local economy by helping new and established
small businesses in the Coleraine area to maximise their potential.

## CAVAN COUNTY ENTERPRISE BOARD

Cavan Innovation & Technology Centre, Dublin Road, Cavan
T: (049) 437 7200 F: (049) 437 7250 E: info@cceb.ie
W: www.cavanenterprise.ie C: Vincent Reynolds, CEO
**Categories:** Debt; Equity; Grants; Information; Mentoring; Training

Cavan CEB provides a range of services to support micro-enterprises in
its region, including the Cavan Innovation & Technology Centre.

## CAVAN-MONAGHAN RURAL DEVELOPMENT
## CO-OP SOCIETY LTD

Agricultural College, Ballyhaise, Co Cavan  T: (049) 433 8477  F: (049)
433 8189  E: info@cmrd.ie  W: www.cmrd.ie  C: Elaine Heatherton
**Categories:** Community & Rural Development; Grants; Tourism
Development; Training

A LEADER company, CMRD empowers individuals and communities
to work towards the sustainable economic, social, environmental,
cultural and heritage development of their areas.

## CÉIM ENTERPRISE DEVELOPMENT PROGRAMME

Letterkenny Institute of Technology, Port Road, Letterkenny, Co
Donegal  T: (074) 918 6070  E: ultan.faherty@lyit.ie  W: www.ceim.ie
C: Ultan Faherty
**Categories:** Incubator; Mentoring; Training

Céim is an enterprise development and training programme offered by
Letterkenny and Sligo ITs, supported by Enterprise Ireland and Údarás
na Gaeltachta, and delivered by WestBIC. It is targeted at graduates
with innovative business ideas.

## CELTIC INVOICE DISCOUNTING PLC

54 Mulgrave Street, Dún Laoire, Co Dublin  T: (01) 230 0866
F: (01) 230 1121  E: pkerrigan@celtic-id.com  W: www.celtic-id.com
C: Peter Kerrigan, MD
**Categories:** Debt

Celtic Invoice Discounting is the largest, independent provider of invoice discounting, specialising in SMEs and start-ups.

## CENTRAL STATISTICS OFFICE

Skehard Road, Mahon, Cork  T: (021) 453 5000  F: (021) 453 5555
E: information@cso.ie  W: www.cso.ie
**Categories:** Information; Publications; Website

The CSO collects, compiles, analyses and disseminates statistical information relating to the economic and social life of Ireland. It is a key source of market research information. Many of its publications are available from the Government Publications sales office.

## CENTRE FOR CO-OPERATIVE STUDIES

O'Rahilly Building, University College Cork, Cork  T: (021) 490 2570
F: (021) 490 3358  E: ccs@ucc.ie  W: www.ucc.ie/en/ccs/
C: Michael Ward
**Categories:** Consulting; Co-operatives; Information; Training

CCS is a university research centre that promotes education and training and independent research and consultancy in all aspects of co-operative organisation.

## CENTRE FOR CROSS-BORDER STUDIES

39 Abbey Street, Armagh BT61 7EB  T: (028) 3751 1550
F: (028) 3751 1721  E: a.pollak@qub.ac.uk W: www.crossborder.ie
C: Andy Pollak, Director
**Categories:** Cross-Border; Information; Policy

The Centre is a policy research and development institute, whose purpose is to commission and publish research on issues related to opportunities for, and obstacles to, cross-border co-operation in all fields of society and economy.

## CENTRE FOR ENTREPRENEURIAL STUDIES

Department of Management & Marketing, Kemmy Business School,
University of Limerick, Plassey, Limerick  E: naomi.birdthistle@ul.ie
W: www.ul.ie  C: Dr Naomi Birdthistle
**Categories:** Consulting; Information; Training

The Centre for Entrepreneurial Studies at University of Limerick
undertakes teaching, research and outreach activities in
entrepreneurship and the SME sector.

## CENTURY MANAGEMENT LTD

Century House, Newlands Business Park, Newlands Cross, Clondalkin,
Dublin 22  T: (01) 459 5950  F: (01) 459 5949
E: centmgmt@century-management.ie
W: www.century-management.ie  C: John Butler, Managing Director
**Categories:** Consulting; Marketing; Publications; Training

Century Management works with a wide range of Irish companies on
strategic thinking and planning, organisational development, leadership
issues, internal and customer audits, transforming cultures, attitude
management and sales / marketing initiatives.

## CHAMBERS IRELAND

17 Merrion Square, Dublin 2  T: (01) 661 2888  F: (01) 661 2811
E: info@chambers.ie  W: www.chambers.ie  C: James Kiernan
**Categories:** Information; Networking

Chambers Ireland is Ireland's largest business network with 13,000
member companies drawn from all sectors of the Irish economy. There
are 59 chambers in Ireland, affiliated to Chambers Ireland. Each
Chamber strives for local economic development, representation of its
members' interests, and the provision of market-led services to the local
business community.

## CHARTERED ACCOUNTANTS IRELAND

Chartered Accountants House, 47-49 Pearse Street, Dublin 2
T: (01) 637 7200   F: (01) 668 0842   E: ca@charteredaccountants.ie
W: www.charteredaccountants.ie   C: Conal Kennedy, Practice Advisory
Executive
**Categories:** Accountants

Chartered Accountants Ireland is one of the accountancy bodies whose members are permitted to audit company accounts. It has 10,000+ members throughout the island of Ireland. If you're looking for an accountant, Chartered Accountants Ireland can direct you to one of its members.

## CHARTERED INSTITUTE OF MANAGEMENT ACCOUNTANTS

45-47 Pembroke Road, Dublin 4   T: (01) 643 0400   F: (01) 643 0401
E: dublin@cimaglobal.com   W: www.cimaglobal.com
**Categories:** Accountants; Consulting

Chartered Management Accountants assist SMEs in a wide variety of ways, although CIMA members do not audit limited companies' accounts. If you are looking for a Chartered Management Accountant, see: www.cimaglobal.com/main/resources/services/consultants.

## CHARTERED INSTITUTE OF PERSONNEL & DEVELOPMENT

Marine House, Clanwilliam Place, Dún Laoire, Co Dublin   T: (01) 653
0400   F: (01) 653 0500   E: info@cipd.ie   W: branchwebs.cipd.co.uk/ireland
C: Michael McDonnell, Director
**Categories:** Information; Training

CIPD Ireland is the professional membership body for those involved in the management and development of people. It offers training and other supports to its members, while providing research and reports more widely.

# CHOOSEENTERPRISE.COM

W: www.chooseenterprise.com
**Categories:** Information; Website; Young Enterprise

A website for young people thinking about setting up their own business.

# CILL DARA AR AGHAIDH TEO

Woods House, Clane, Co. Kildare  T: (045) 861 973  E: justin@kelt.ie
W: www.thekcp.ie  C: Justin Larkin, CEO
**Categories:** Community & Rural Development

Formed from the merger of KELT, the Kildare Community Partnership and OAK Partnership, Cill Dara Ar Aghaidh Teo is supported under the Local Development Social Inclusion Programme and LEADER in achieving local development through the promotion of sustainable enterprise.

# CITY OF DUBLIN VOCATIONAL EDUCATIONAL COMMITTEE

Town Hall, Merrion Road, Ballsbridge, Dublin 4  T: (01) 668 0614
F: (01) 668 0710  E: jim.boland@cdvec.ie  W: www.cdvec.ie
C: Jim Boland, Management Services; Jacinta Stewart, CEO
**Categories:** Training

CDVEC is the local education authority for Dublin City and its inner suburbs. It offers courses for career-improvement, leisure, and self-development, including 'Start Your Own Business' courses – check with your local college.

# CLANCY BUSINESS FINANCE LTD

33 Carysfort Avenue, Blackrock, Co Dublin  T: (01) 438 6462  F: (01) 438
6463  E: lucinda@clancybusiness.com  W: www.clancybusiness.com
C: Lucinda Clancy, Managing Director
**Categories:** Debt

Clancy Business Finance is an independent broker, experienced in invoice discounting and trade finance for start-up and growing companies.

## CLANN CREDO, THE SOCIAL INVESTMENT FUND

Irish Social Finance Centre, 10 Grattan Crescent, Inchicore, Dublin 8
T: (01) 453 1861  F: (01) 453 1862  E: info@clanncredo.ie
W: www.clanncredo.ie  C: Paul O'Sullivan, Chief Executive
**Categories:** Community & Rural Development; Debt; Social Economy

Clann Credo is a leading provider of social finance to community organisations.

## CLARE COUNTY ENTERPRISE BOARD

Enterprise House, Mill Road, Ennis, Co Clare  T: (065) 684 1922
F: (065) 684 1887  E:clareceb@clareceb.ie  W: www.clare-ceb.ie
C: Eamonn Kelly, CEO
**Categories:** Debt; Equity; Grants; Information; Mentoring; Training

Clare CEB provides a range of services to support micro-enterprises in its region.

## CLARE LOCAL DEVELOPMENT COMPANY

Westgate Business Park, Kilrush Road, Ennis, Co. Clare  T: (065) 686
6800  E: info@cldc.ie  W: www.cldc.ie  C: Doírín Graham, CEO
**Categories:** Community & Rural Development

Clare Local Development is supported under LEADER and the Local Development Social Inclusion Programme in achieving local development through the promotion of sustainable enterprise.

## CLARENDON FUND MANAGERS LTD

12 Cromac Place, Belfast BT7 2JB  T: (028) 9032 6465  F: (028) 9032 6473
E: info@clarendon-fm.co.uk  W: www.clarendon-fm.co.uk
C: Jim Curran, Alan Mawson, Neil Simms
**Categories:** Debt; Equity

Clarendon Fund Managers Limited is a venture capital fund manager based in Belfast, authorised and regulated by the Financial Services Authority. Clarendon has £13.5 million of funds under management, with an investment focus on innovative SMEs based in Northern Ireland.

## COMHAIR CHATHAIR CHORCAÍ : CORK CITY PARTNERSHIP

Heron House, Blackpool Park, Cork  T: (021) 430 2310  F: (021) 430 2081
E: info@partnershipcork.ie  C: Ann O'Sullivan
**Categories:** Community & Rural Development

Cork City Partnership is supported under the Local Development Social Inclusion Programme in achieving local development through the promotion of sustainable enterprise.

## COMHAR NA OILEÁIN TEO

Inis Oírr, Árainn, Cuan na Gaillimhe  T: (099) 75096  F: (099) 75103
E: comhdhail.oileain@indigo.ie  W: www.oileain.ie  C: Mairéad O'Reilly
**Categories:** Community & Rural Development; Grants

Comhar na Oileáin is supported under LEADER and the Local Development Social Inclusion Programme in achieving local development through the promotion of sustainable enterprise.

## COMPANIES REGISTRATION OFFICE

Parnell House, 14 Parnell Square, Dublin 1 / O'Brien Road, Carlow
(postal submissions only)  T: (01) 804 5200  F: (01) 804 5222
E: info@cro.ie  W: www.cro.ie
**Categories:** Information; Regulator & Standards

The CRO is the authority for the incorporation of new companies and the registration of business names in the Republic of Ireland. It is also responsible for the receipt and registration of post-incorporation documents, for enforcement of the filing requirements of companies and for the provision of information to the public. Almost all of the information filed with the CRO is available for public inspection, usually for a small fee.

## COMPANIES REGISTRY

W: companieshouse.gov.uk
**Categories:** Information; Regulator & Standards

With effect from 1 October 2009, the work of Companies Registry for Northern Ireland has been transferred to Companies House in Cardiff.

## COMPANY FORMATIONS INTERNATIONAL LTD

22 Northumberland Road, Ballsbridge, Dublin 4  T: (01) 664 1111
F: (01) 664 1100  E: cfi@formations.ie  W: www.formations.ie
C: Marc O'Connor, Chief Executive
**Categories:** Information; Marketing

CFI is a specialist in company formation and secretarial and business information.

## COOKSTOWN ENTERPRISE CENTRE LTD

Derryloran Industrial Estate, Sandholes Road, Cookstown,
Co Tyrone BT80 9LU  T: (028) 8676 3660  F: (028) 8676 3160
E: info@cookstownenterprise.com  W: www.cookstownenterprise.com
C: Ciaran Higgins, Manager
**Categories:** Information; Training; Workspace

Cookstown Enterprise Centre is a member of Enterprise Northern Ireland. It is the leading provider of business start-up and development assistance for businesses setting up or developing in its area.

## CO-OPERATIVE DEVELOPMENT SOCIETY LTD

Dominick Court, 41 Lower Dominick Street, Dublin 1
T: (01) 873 3199  F: (01) 873 3612  E: coopsoc@tinet.ie
W: www.ablaze.ie/cds  C: Dermot McKenna
**Categories:** Co-operatives; Information

One of the organisations that provides Model Rules for the formation of worker and community co-operatives.

## CORK BUSINESS INNOVATION CENTRE

NSC Campus, Mahon, Cork  T: (021) 230 7005  F: (021) 230 7020
E: postmaster@corkbic.com  W: www.corkbic.com
C: Michael O'Connor, Chief Executive
**Categories:** Business Plans; Incubator; Marketing; Training

CORKBIC is a leading interdisciplinary venture consultancy in the South West of Ireland, providing an integrated process for incubating and growing high potential technology-driven companies. CORKBIC identifies, selects and develops about 12 higher potential start-ups each year and works as a hands-on catalyst or project developer in infrastructure gap initiatives.

## CORK CITY ENTERPRISE BOARD

1-2 Bruach na Laoi, Union Quay, Cork  T: (021) 496 1828  F: (021) 496
1869  E: info@corkceb.ie  W: www.corkceb.ie  C: Dave Cody, CEO
**Categories:** Debt; Equity; Grants; Information; Mentoring; Training

Cork City Enterprise Board offers direct grant aid and other supports to
manufacturing industry, internationally-traded services and, in certain
circumstances, the service sector.

## CORK INSTITUTE OF TECHNOLOGY

Rossa Avenue, Bishopstown, Cork  T: (021) 432 6100  F: (021) 454 5343
E: jsomullane@cit.ie  W: www.cit.ie
C: Josette O'Mullane, Industrial Liaison Officer
**Categories:** Consulting; Incubator; R&D; Training

CIT provides Research & Development and services to industry and
operates a number of Technology Centres. It also operates the Genesis
Enterprise Platform Programme from the Rubicon Centre.

## CORK NORTH COUNTY ENTERPRISE BOARD

The Enterprise Office, 26 Davis Street, Mallow, Co Cork  T: (022) 43235
F: (022) 43247  E: corknent@iol.ie  W: www.theenterpriseoffice.com
C: Rochie Holohan
**Categories:** Debt; Equity; Grants; Information; Mentoring; Training

Cork North CEB offers a full range of supports for micro-enterprises in
its region.

## CORPORATE FINANCE IRELAND

CFI House, 133 Strand Road, Sandymount, Dublin 4  T: (01) 283 7144
F: (01) 283 7256  E: info@cfi.ie  W: www.cfi.ie  C: James McCarthy
**Categories:** Equity

Corporate Finance Ireland is an independent corporate finance, financial
and fundraising adviser to SMEs.

## COUNTY & CITY ENTERPRISE BOARDS

W: www.enterpriseboards.ie

See individual entries for: Carlow; Cavan; Clare; Cork City; Cork North County; Donegal; Dublin City; Dún Laoire Rathdown; Fingal (Dublin North); Galway County and City; Kerry; Kildare; Kilkenny; Laois; Leitrim; Limerick City; Limerick County; Longford; Louth; Mayo; Meath; Monaghan; Offaly; Roscommon; Sligo; South Cork; South Dublin; Tipperary North; Tipperary South Riding; Waterford City; Waterford County; West Cork; Westmeath; Wexford; and Wicklow.

## COUNTY DEVELOPMENT BOARDS

W: www.cdb.ie
**Categories:** Policy

County Development Boards (CDBs) have been established in all county councils and in the five major city corporations. In each CDB, local government, local development, social partners (including the community / voluntary sector) and the relevant State agencies active at local level work together for the area's economic, social and cultural development and success. For more information, contact the Director of Community & Enterprise at your County Council or City Corporation.

## COUNTY KILKENNY LEADER PARTNERSHIP COMPANY LTD

42 Parliament Street, Kilkenny City, Co. Kilkenny  T: (056) 775 2111
E: declan.rice@cklp.ie  W: www.cklp.ie  C: Declan Rice, CEO
**Categories:** Community & Rural Development

County Kilkenny Leader Partnership is supported under the Local Development Social Inclusion Programme and LEADER in achieving local development through the promotion of sustainable enterprise.

## COUNTY WICKLOW PARTNERSHIP

Saville House, Saville's Cross, Rathdrum, Co. Wicklow  T: (0404) 46977
F: (0404) 46978  E: bkehoe@wicklowleader.ie
W: www.wicklowleader.ie  C: Brian Kehoe, CEO
**Categories:** Community & Rural Development

County Wicklow Partnership is supported under the Local
Development Social Inclusion Programme and LEADER in achieving
local development through the promotion of sustainable enterprise.

## CPLN AREA PARTNERSHIP

Unit D, Nangor Road Business Park, Nangor Road, Clondalkin, Dublin
22  T: (01) 450 8788  F: (01) 450 8748  E: reception@cpln.ie
W: www.cpln.ie  C: Aileen O'Donoghue, CEO
**Categories:** Community & Rural Development

CPLN Area Partnership is supported under the Local Development
Social Inclusion Programme in achieving local development through the
promotion of sustainable enterprise.

## CRAFTS COUNCIL OF IRELAND

Castle Yard, Kilkenny  T: (056) 776 1804  F: (056) 776 3754
E: info@ccoi.ie  W: www.ccoi.ie  C: Emer Ferran
**Categories:** Information; Marketing; Publications; Training

The CCOI is the national design and economic development agency for
the craft industry in the Republic of Ireland, offering a range of services
in support of its mission.

## CRAIGAVON INDUSTRIAL DEVELOPMENT
## ORGANISATION LTD

CIDO Innovation Centre, 73 Charlestown Road, Portadown, Craigavon
BT63 5RH  T: (028) 3833 3393  F: (028) 3835 0390
E: info@cido.co.uk  W: www.cido.co.uk  C: Jim Smith, Chief Executive
**Categories:** Debt; Incubator; Information; Training; Workspace

CIDO is a member of Enterprise Northern Ireland. It acts as a first-stop-
shop for potential entrepreneurs, providing managed workspace,
business start-up and development training, loans, incubation and
workspace.

## CREATE

Development Office, IADT, Kill Avenue, Dún Laoire, Co Dublin  T: (01) 214 4644  F: (01) 214 4714  E: frederic.herrera@iadt.ie  W: www.create.ie
C: Frederic Herrera, Programme Manager
**Categories:** Incubator; Mentoring; Training

Create is a 12-month incubation programme, run by IADT, that trains entrepreneurs in starting new digital media companies in the fast-evolving market of digital media (images, audio, video, design) and their related business models.

## CREATIVEIRELAND.COM

E: editor@creativeireland.com  W: www.creativeireland.com
**Categories:** Information; Networking; Website

Creative Ireland is the online home for the Irish creative design community. It provides news, a directory of designers, a jobs desk, for those looking for work or designers, and a gateway to essential design resources on the Internet.

## CREGGAN ENTERPRISES LTD

Ráth Mór Business & Community Enterprise Centre, Bligh's Lane,
Derry BT48 0LZ  T: (028) 7137 3170  F: (028) 7137 3004
E: info@rathmor.com  W: www.rathmor.com/cel_intro.html
C: Conal McFeely, Chairperson
**Categories:** Community & Rural Development; Social Economy

Creggan Enterprises Ltd (CEL) works to address the social and economic needs of the local community. CEL has created the successful Ráth Mór Business and Community Enterprise Centre.

## CRESCENT CAPITAL

7 Upper Crescent, Belfast BT7 1NT  T: (028) 9023 3633  F: (028) 9032 9525
E: mail@crescentcapital.co.uk  W: www.crescentcapital.co.uk
C: Colin Walsh, Managing director
**Categories:** Equity

A Belfast-based venture capital fund manager, specialising in early-stage to MBO Northern Ireland investments in IT, life sciences and manufacturing.

## CROSS ATLANTIC CAPITAL PARTNERS

Alexandra House, The Sweepstakes, Ballsbridge, Dublin 4
T: (01) 664 1721  F: (01) 664 1806 E: info@xacp.com
W: www.xacp.com  C: Paul Sutton, Managing director
**Categories:** Equity

Cross Atlantic Capital Partners is a venture capital firm whose investment focus is on commercialisation of patented and specialised know-how in early to mid-stage companies.

## CROWLEYS DFK

16-17 College Green, Dublin 2  T: (01) 679 0800  F: (01) 679 0805
C: James O'Connor / 5th Floor, 5 Lapps Quay, Cork  T: (021) 427 2900
F: (021) 427 7621  C: Jack Crowley  E: info@crowleysdfk.ie
W: www.crowleysdfk.ie
**Categories:** Accountants; Consulting

A firm of chartered accountants and business advisers, experts in advising small to medium-sized businesses.

## CRUCIBLE CORPORATION

13 Richview Office Park, Clonskea, Dublin 14  T: (01) 218 2200
F: (01) 218 2230  E: info@cruciblecorp.com  W: www.cruciblecorp.com
C: Kevin Magee
**Categories:** Equity

Crucible is an early-stage investment company concentrating on the technology sector. Its mission is to help Irish entrepreneurs develop innovative business concepts into transatlantic business operations.

## CRUICKSHANK & CO

8a Sandyford Business Centre, Sandyford, Dublin 18  T: (01) 299 2222
F: (01) 299 2289  E: post@cruickshank.ie  W: www.cruickshank.ie
C: Donal O'Connor
**Categories:** Intellectual Property

Cruickshank & Co is a multidisciplinary patent and trade mark practice.

## DAIRY PRODUCTS RESEARCH CENTRE

Moorepark, Fermoy, Co Cork  T: (025) 42222  F: (025) 42340
E: eileen.lehane@teagasc.ie
W: www.teagasc.org/research/research_centres.htm
C: Dr WJ Donnelly, Head of Centre
**Categories:** Consulting; R & D

The Dairy Products Research Centre (DPC) undertakes scientific research and provides technological services to the dairy processing and food ingredients sectors.

## DARLINGTON CONSULTING

3 Waterville, Enniscrone, Co. Sligo T: 096 37608
E: info@darlington.ie  W: www.darlington.ie  C: Mary Darlington
**Categories:** Consulting; Training

Darlington Consulting are safety and HR trainers and consultants to companies nationwide on health and safety issues.

## DATA IRELAND

3rd Floor, Chapel House, 21 - 26 Parnell Street Dublin 1   T: (01) 858 4800
F: (01) 858 4801  E: info@dataireland.ie  W: www.dataireland.ie
**Categories:** Information; Marketing; Publications

Data Ireland is owned by An Post, and incorporates both Precision Marketing Information and Kompass. It provides mailing lists for over 80 business sectors from a pool of over 200,000 updated Irish business contacts, which can be tailored by location, size, sector, named contact, as well as over 2 million consumer records.

## DATA PROTECTION COMMISSIONER

Canal House, Station Road, Portarlington, Co Laois  T: (057) 868 4800
F: (057) 868 4757  E: info@dataprotection.ie  W: www.dataprotection.ie
**Categories:** Regulator & Standards

If you keep information about people on computer, the law says you must: obtain it fairly; keep it accurate and up-to-date; use it and disclose it only in accordance with the purposes for which you obtained it; keep it no longer than necessary; give a copy to the individual concerned if he or she requests it. The Data Protection Commissioner's website sets out your rights as an individual and your responsibilities as a 'data controller'.

## DELOITTE & TOUCHE

Deloitte & Touche House, Earlsfort Terrace, Dublin 2  T: (01) 417 2200
F: (01) 417 2300  W: www.deloitte.ie
**Categories:** Accountants; Consulting

Deloitte & Touche is a leading professional services firm, which offers assurance and advisory, tax, and consulting services through 500 people in offices in four Irish locations.

## DELTA PARTNERS

South County Business Park, Leopardstown, Dublin 18  T: (01) 294 0870
F: (01) 294 0877  E: frank@delta.ie  W: www.delta.ie  C: Frank Kenny
**Categories:** Equity

Delta Partners is a venture capital firm investing in Ireland and the United Kingdom, with €230 million under management. It has a strong focus on investing in early stage technology companies, and the team has made over 50 investments in the following sectors: information technology, communications and healthcare.

## DEPARTMENT FOR EMPLOYMENT & LEARNING

Adelaide House, 39-49 Adelaide Street, Belfast BT2 8FD  T: 028 9025
7777  F: 028 9025 7778  E: del@nics.gov.uk  W: www.delni.gov.uk
**Categories:** Policy; Training

The Department for Employment & Learning is responsible for third level education, training and employment measures across Northern Ireland.

## DEPARTMENT OF AGRICULTURE, FISHERIES & FOOD

Agriculture House, Kildare Street, Dublin 2  T: (01) 607 2000 (LoCall
1890 200 510)  E: info@agriculture.gov.ie  W: www.agriculture.gov.ie
**Categories:** Policy

The Department's mission is 'to lead the sustainable development of a competitive, consumer-focussed agri-food sector and to contribute to a vibrant rural economy and society'.

# DEPARTMENT OF AGRICULTURE & RURAL DEVELOPMENT

Dundonald House, Upper Newtownards Road, Belfast BT4 3SB
T: (028) 9052 4999  F: (028) 9052 5003
E: dardhelpline@dardni.gov.uk  W: www.dardni.gov.uk
**Categories:** Community & Rural Development; Policy

The Department of Agriculture and Rural Development (DARD) aims to promote sustainable economic growth and the development of the countryside in Northern Ireland. The Department assists the competitive development of the agri-food, fishing and forestry sectors of the Northern Ireland economy, having regard for the need of the consumers, the welfare of animals and the conservation and enhancement of the environment.

# DEPARTMENT OF COMMUNITY, RURAL & GAELTACHT AFFAIRS

Dún Aimhirgin, 43-49 Mespil Road, Dublin 4  T: (01) 647 3000
F: (01) 647 3051  E: eolas@pobail.ie  W: www.pobail.ie
**Categories:** Community & Rural Development; Policy

The Department of Community, Rural & Gaeltacht Affairs has responsibility for a wide range of policies and programmes in respect of community and rural development, volunteering, the Gaeltacht, Irish language and the islands. The Department's mission is 'to promote and support the development of communities and to advance the use of the Irish language'.

# DEPARTMENT OF ENTERPRISE, TRADE & INVESTMENT

Netherleigh, Massey Avenue, Belfast BT4 2JP  T: (028) 9052 9900
E: information@detini.gov.uk  W: www.detini.gov.uk
**Categories:** Policy

DETI's goal is 'to grow a dynamic, innovative economy'. It plays a crucial role in formulating and delivering economic development policy in terms of enterprise, social economy, innovation, energy, telecoms, and tourism in Northern Ireland. In addition, the Department has responsibility for ensuring a modern regulatory framework to support business and protect consumers.

# DEPARTMENT OF ENTERPRISE, TRADE & EMPLOYMENT

Head Office, Kildare Street, Dublin 2  T: (01) 631 2121  F: (01) 631 2827
W: www.entemp.ie  C: Information Section
**Categories:** Policy

The Department's mandate is to implement Government policy in: the development of enterprise; employment promotion; trade development; protection of workers; regulation of businesses. Agencies reporting to the Department include: Companies Registration Office; Registry of Friendly Societies; Patents Office. The Department also has policy responsibility for a number of bodies, including: County & City Enterprise Boards; Enterprise Ireland; FÁS; Forfás; Health & Safety Authority; IDA Ireland; InterTradeIreland; National Standards Authority of Ireland; Shannon Development. Assistance to individual small businesses is **not** undertaken directly by the Department.

# DEPARTMENT OF JUSTICE, EQUALITY & LAW REFORM

72–76 St. Stephens Green, Dublin 2  T: (01) 602 8202  F: (01) 661 5461
E: info@justice.ie  W: www.justice.ie
**Categories:** Policy

The Department of Justice, Equality & Law Reform implements policy on the admission of persons who wish to visit, immigrate to, or seek refuge in the State in line with the best international practice and standards and in the case of persons wishing to become Irish citizens. Work permit applications by employers on behalf of non EEA-nationals are handled by the Department of Enterprise, Trade & Employment.

# DEPARTMENT OF SOCIAL & FAMILY AFFAIRS

Information Services, College Road, Sligo  T: (1890) 66 22 44
E: info@welfare.ie  W: www.welfare.ie
**Categories:** Grants; Information

In addition to providing information on PRSI for employers, the Department operates the Back to Work Allowance (Enterprise), which encourages unemployed people, lone parents and people getting Disability Allowance or Blind Person's Pension to become self-employed. Full details are available in the *Guide to Social Welfare Services* (downloadable from the Department's website).

# DEPARTMENT OF THE ENVIRONMENT, HERITAGE & LOCAL GOVERNMENT

Custom House, Dublin 1  T: (01) 888 2000  F: (01) 888 2888
E: press-office@environ.irlgov.ie  W: www.environ.ie
**Categories:** Policy

The Department services the public directly on issues such as environmental information and awareness, anti-litter legislation, the planning system, noise pollution, construction, local government reform and urban renewal.

# DIGITAL HUB DEVELOPMENT AGENCY

Digital Exchange, Crane Street, Dublin 8  T: (01) 480 6200
F: (01) 480 6201  E: info@thedigitalhub.com  W: www.digitalhub.com
**Categories:** Workspace

The Digital Hub is a Government initiative to create an international centre of excellence for knowledge, innovation and creativity, focused on digital content and technology enterprises. It provides facilities for early-stage, fast-growth and established companies in OneFiveSeven and Digital Depot.

# DIT HOTHOUSE

Docklands Innovation Park, 128-130 East Wall Road, Dublin 3
T: (01) 240 1300  F: (01) 240 1310  E: hothouse@dit.ie
W: www.dit.ie/hothouse  C: Bernadette O'Reilly
**Categories:** Incubator; Mentoring; Training

HotHouse is a year-long programme that helps entrepreneurs of knowledge-intensive businesses to start-up and build firms with global potential. It comprises: practical workshops; strategic business counselling; 'buddy counselling' from experienced entrepreneurs; office space and facilities; access to funding.

## DODDER VALLEY PARTNERSHIP

Killinarden Enterprise Centre, Killinarden, Tallaght, Dublin 24
T: (01) 466 4280  E: anna.lee@doddervalley.ie  C: Anna Lee, Manager
**Categories:** Community & Rural Development

Dodder Valley Partnership is supported under the Local Development
Social Inclusion Programme in achieving local development through the
promotion of sustainable enterprise.

## DONEGAL COUNTY ENTERPRISE BOARD

Enterprise Fund Business Centre, Ballyraine, Letterkenny, Co Donegal
T: (074) 916 0735  F: (074) 916 0783  E: info@donegalenterprise.ie
W: www.donegalenterprise.ie  C: Michael Tunney, CEO
**Categories:** Debt; Equity; Grants; Information; Mentoring; Training

Donegal County Enterprise Board provides direct supports (capital,
employment or feasibility grant aid) and indirect supports (mentoring,
management development, or other capacity building programmes).

## DONEGAL LOCAL DEVELOPMENT COMPANY

1 Millennium Court, Pearse Road, Letterkenny, Co Donegal
T: (091) 27056  F: (091) 21527  E: info@dldc.org  W: www.dldc.org
C: Caoimhín Mac Aoidh, CEO
**Categories:** Community & Rural Development

Donegal Local Development Company is supported under the Local
Development Social Inclusion Programme and LEADER in achieving
local development through the promotion of sustainable enterprise.

## DOWN BUSINESS CENTRE

46 Belfast Road, Downpatrick, Co Down BT30 9UP  T: (028) 4461 6416
F: (028) 4461 6419  E: reception@downbc.co.uk  W: www.downbc.co.uk
**Categories:** Information; Training; Workspace

Down Business Centre is a member of Enterprise Northern Ireland. It
provides training, support and workspace for start-up and existing
businesses.

## DOWN RURAL AREA PARTNERSHIP

Ards Business Centre, Sketrick House, Jubilee Road, Newtownards,
Co Down, BT23 4YH  T: (028) 9182 0748  F: (028) 9181 1339
E: info@downrualareapartnership.com
W: www.downruralareapartnership.com
C: Marguerite Osborne, Rural Development Programme Manager
**Categories:** Community & Rural Development

Down Rural Area Partnership administers funds under Axis 3 of the
Northern Ireland Rural Development Programme 2007-2013. The
programme aims to 'improve the quality of life in rural areas and
encouraging diversification of economic activity in rural areas by
supporting a wide range of projects under six measures including:
diversification into non-agricultural activities; support for business
creation and development; encouragement of tourism activities; basic
services for economy and rural population; village renewal and
development; and conservation and upgrading of rural heritage'.

## DROGHEDA PARTNERSHIP COMPANY

Workspace, Mayoralty Street, Drogheda, Co Louth  T: (041) 984 2088
F: (041) 984 3358  E: info@droghedapartnership.ie
W: www.droghedapartnership.ie  C: Mary-Ann McGlynn, Manager
**Categories:** Community & Rural Development; Information; Training

Through the Local Development Social Inclusion programme,
Drogheda Partnership supports enterprise in the Drogheda area,
helping to make jobs, create businesses and find jobs for the
unemployed.

## DUBLIN BUSINESS INNOVATION CENTRE

The Tower, TCD Enterprise Centre, Pearse Street, Dublin 2
T: (01) 671 3111  F: (01) 677 5655  E: info@dbic.ie  W: www.dbic.ie
C: John McInerney
**Categories:** Business Plans; Incubator; Marketing; Training

DBIC is a licensed member of an EU-supported network of 160 Business
Innovation Centres operating throughout Europe known as European
Business Network. It has helped over 330 businesses get up and
running and expand, with 85% still in business after five years.

## DUBLIN CITY ENTERPRISE BOARD

5th Floor, O'Connell Bridge House, D'Olier Street, Dublin 2
T: (01) 635 1144  F: (01) 635 1811  E: info@dceb.ie  W: www.dceb.ie
C: Greg Swift, CEO
**Categories:** Debt; Equity; Grants; Information; Mentoring; Training

Dublin City Enterprise Board supports enterprise development in Dublin city, thus strengthening the sustainability of local economies to provide employment opportunities within their own communities.

## DUBLIN CITY UNIVERSITY

Invent, Glasnevin, Dublin 9  T: (01) 700 5175 (Direct) F: (01) 836 0830
E: richard.stokes@invent.dcu.ie  W: www.invent. dcu.ie
C: Richard Stokes, CEO, Invent
**Categories:** Consulting; Incubator; R & D; Training

Invent is a state-of-the-art innovation and enterprise centre at DCU. Its mission is to transform knowledge into commercial success and to provide the critical link between the university and the marketplace.

## DUBLIN EMPLOYMENT PACT

Strand House, 1st Floor, 22 Great Strand Street, Dublin 1  T: (01) 878 8900  E: info@dublinpact.ie  C: Philip O'Connor, Co-ordinator
**Categories:** Community & Rural Development

Dublin Employment Pact is supported under the Local Development Social Inclusion Programme in achieving local development through the promotion of sustainable enterprise.

## DUBLIN INNER CITY PARTNERSHIP

Equity House, 16-17 Upper Ormond Quay, Dublin 7  T: (01) 872 1321
F: (01) 872 1330  E: office@dicp.ie  W: www.dicp.ie
C: Peter Nolan, Employment & Enterprise Co-ordinator
**Categories:** Community & Rural Development; Information; Training

Dublin Inner City Partnership is supported under the Local Development Social Inclusion Programme in achieving local development through the promotion of sustainable enterprise.

## DUBLIN INSTITUTE OF TECHNOLOGY

Directorate of Research & Enterprise, 143-149 Rathmines Road, Dublin 6
T: (01) 402 3370  E: research@dit.ie
W: www.dit.ie/researchandenterprise  C: Professor Ellen Hazelkorn
**Categories:** Consulting; Information; R & D; Training

DIT encourages and supports the development of new business ventures and has strategically clustered activity aligned to its interdisciplinary Research Institutes and Centres in environmental sustainability; creative arts and media; food and health sciences; new materials and technologies; information and communication technologies; and social, economic and business development.

## DÚN LAOIRE ENTERPRISE CENTRE

The Old Firestation, George's Place, Dún Laoire, Co Dublin
T: (01) 202 0056  F: (01) 230 1044  E: dlenterprise@clubi.ie
C: Harry Cullen, Manager
**Categories:** Incubator; Workspace

An incubation centre offering workspace.

## DÚN LAOIRE RATHDOWN COUNTY ENTERPRISE BOARD

Nutgrove Enterprise Centre, Nutgrove Way, Rathfarnham, Dublin 14
T: (01) 494 8400  F: (01) 494 8410  E: michael@dlrceb.ie
W: www.dlrceb.ie  C: Michael Johnson, CEO
**Categories:** Debt; Equity; Grants; Information; Mentoring; Training

The Enterprise Board supports the growth and development of micro enterprises in Dún Laoire Rathdown County, Dublin. It offers information packs on all aspects of setting up a small business.

## DUNDALK EMPLOYMENT PARTNERSHIP LTD

Partnership Court, Park Street, Dundalk  T: (042) 933 0288
F: (042) 933 0552  C: John Butler, Chief Executive
**Categories:** Community & Rural Development; Information; Training;
Women; Workspace

The Partnership operates wholly-owned subsidiary companies that directly create jobs for long-term unemployed people. It also provides services to individuals and groups planning to set up their own business, including subsidised workspace training and business advice.

## DUNDALK INSTITUTE OF TECHNOLOGY

Dublin Road, Dundalk, Co Louth  T: (042) 937 0200  F: (042) 933 3505
E: gerry.carroll@dkit.ie  W: www.dkit.ie
C: Gerry Carroll, Head of Development
**Categories:** Incubator; Training

Dundalk IT operates the Regional Development Centre, which provides services to industry, and offers the Novation Enterprise Programme.

## DUNGANNON ENTERPRISE CENTRE LTD

2 Coalisland Road, Dungannon, Co Tyrone BT71 6JT  T: (028) 8772 3489
F: (028) 8775 2200  E: info@dungannonenterprise.com
W: www.dungannonenterprise.com
C: Brian MacAuley, Chief Executive
**Categories:** Information; Training; Workspace

Dungannon Enterprise Centre is a member of Enterprise Northern Ireland. As the Local Enterprise Agency for South Tyrone, Dungannon Enterprise Centre's aims are: to help new businesses start up; to encourage existing businesses to expand; and to encourage the development of local economy through the fostering of the local enterprise culture.

## EAST BELFAST ENTERPRISE PARK LTD

308 Albertbridge Road, Belfast BT5 4GX  T: (028) 9045 5450
F: (028) 9073 2600  E: info@eastbelfast.org  W: www.eastbelfast.org
C: Kenny Rodgers, Business Development Manager
**Categories:** Information; Training; Workspace

East Belfast Enterprise Park is a member of Enterprise Northern Ireland. It is the Local Enterprise Agency for East Belfast and the starting point for anyone wishing to start a business or improve and grow their current business. Its mission is to 'lead enterprise and business development in the community'.

## ENTERPRISE ACCELERATION CENTRE

Limerick IT, Moylish Park, Limerick  T: (061) 208208 F: (061) 490148
E: eac@lit.ie  W: www.eac.ie
**Categories:** Incubator; Training

Limerick Institute of Technology's Enterprise Acceleration Centre (EAC) is a business incubation centre serving the Mid-West region of Limerick. Its mission is to deliver a unique business environment that stimulates innovation, research commercialisation and entrepreneurship. It also offers the LEAP Enterprise Platform Programme.

## ENTERPRISE EQUITY (IRL) LTD

Dublin Road, Dundalk, Co Louth  T: (042) 933 3167  F: (042) 933 4857
E: info@enterpriseequity.ie  W: www.eeirl.com.ie
C: Conor O'Connor, Chief Executive
**Categories:** Equity

Enterprise Equity provides venture capital of between €100,000 and €1 million to new and expanding businesses in the BMW regions, comprising Cavan, Donegal, Galway, Laois, Leitrim, Longford, Louth, Mayo, Monaghan, Offaly, Roscommon, Sligo and Westmeath. It was established by the International Fund for Ireland.

## ENTERPRISE EUROPE NETWORK

Enterprise Ireland, The Plaza, East Point Business Park, Dublin 3
T: (01) 727 2729   F: (01) 727 2069  E: jan.gerritsen@enterprise-ireland.com
W: www.enterprise-ireland.com
**Categories:** EU Information

The Enterprise Europe Network – in Cork, Dublin, Galway, Sligo and Waterford (see below for contact details) – provides local access to EU information for SMEs.

## ENTERPRISE EUROPE NETWORK CORK

Cork Chamber, Fitzgerald House, Summerhill North, Cork
T: (021) 450 9044   F: (021) 450 8568  E: cosullivan@corkchamber.ie
W: www.corkchamber.ie  C: Cathy O'Sullivan
**Categories:** EU Information

## ENTERPRISE EUROPE NETWORK DUBLIN

Dublin Chamber of Commerce, 7 Clare Street, Dublin
T: (01) 644 7200   F: (01) 676 6043   E: marion@dublinchamber.ie
W: www.dublinchamber.ie   C: Marion Jammet
**Categories:** EU Information

## ENTERPRISE EUROPE NETWORK GALWAY

Galway Chamber of Commerce & Industry, Commerce House,
Merchants Road, Galway   T: (091) 563536   F: (091) 561963
E: cbrady@galwaychamber.com   W: www.galwaychamber.com
C: Carol Brady
**Categories:** EU Information

## ENTERPRISE EUROPE NETWORK SLIGO

Chamber of Commerce & Industry, 16 Quay Street, Sligo
T: (071) 916 1274   F: (071) 916 0912   E: lorraine@sligochamber.ie
W: www.sligochamber.ie   C: Lorraine McDonnell
**Categories:** EU Information

## ENTERPRISE EUROPE NETWORK WATERFORD

Waterford Chamber of Commerce Ltd, 8 George's Street, Waterford
T: (051) 311138   F: (051) 876002
E: michelle.mchugh@waterfordchamber.ie
W: www.waterfordchamber.ie   C: Michelle McHugh
**Categories:** EU Information

## ENTERPRISE IRELAND

The Plaza, East Point Business Park, Dublin 3
T: (01) 727 2000 E: client.service@enterprise-ireland.com
W: www.enterprise-ireland.com
**Categories:** Competitions; Equity; Grants; Information; Mentoring;
Young Enterprise

Enterprise Ireland is the government organisation charged with assisting the development of Irish enterprise. Its mission is: 'to work in partnership with client companies to develop a sustainable competitive advantage, leading to a significant increase in profitable sales, exports and employment'. Its clients are mainly manufacturing and internationally-traded services companies employing more than 10 people. Enterprise Ireland's services are fully described on its website.

## ENTERPRISE LINK

The Plaza, East Point Business Park, Dublin 3  Helpline: 1850 35 33 33
T: (01) 808 2000 F: (01) 808 2802 W: www.enterprise-ireland.com
**Categories:** Information

Enterprise Link is an initiative of the Department of Enterprise, Trade & Employment, operated by Enterprise Ireland, to direct would-be entrepreneurs to the information or assistance they need. It provides a single source of information for all sources of support to start-up and small businesses in Ireland, just by dialling 1850 35 33 33.

## ENTERPRISE NORTHERN IRELAND

Aghanloo Industrial Estate, Aghanloo Road, Limavady BT49 0HE
T: (028) 7776 3555 F: (028) 7776 9049 E: pa@enterpriseni.com
W: www.enterpriseni.com

Enterprise Northern Ireland (ENI) is the organisation representing the network of Local Enterprise Agencies (LEAs) in Northern Ireland, which are independent, locally based not-for-profit companies set up to support small business development and to undertake economic development activity. ENI has 32 member agencies, with coverage across all local council areas in Northern Ireland. See individual entries for: Acorn Business Centre; Antrim Enterprise Agency Ltd; Ards Business Centre Ltd; Armagh Business Centre Ltd; Ballymena Business Development Centre Ltd; Banbridge District Enterprises Ltd; Carrickfergus Enterprise Agency Ltd; Castlereagh Enterprises Ltd

Causeway Enterprise Agency; Cookstown Enterprise Centre Ltd; Craigavon Industrial Development Organisation Ltd; Down Business Centre; Dungannon Enterprise Centre Ltd; East Belfast Enterprise Park Ltd; Fermanagh Enterprise Ltd; Glenwood Enterprises Ltd; Larne Enterprise Development Company Ltd; Lisburn Enterprise Organisation Ltd; Mallusk Enterprise Park; Moyle Enterprise Company Ltd; Newry & Mourne Enterprise Agency; North City Business Centre Ltd; North Down Development Organisation Ltd; North West Marketing; Omagh Enterprise Company Ltd; Ormeau Enterprises; ORTUS; Roe Valley Enterprises Ltd; Strabane Enterprise Agency; Townsend Enterprise Park; Work West Enterprise Agency; and Workspace (Draperstown) Ltd.

## ENTERPRISE PLATFORM PROGRAMMES

The Enterprise Platform Programmes are 12-month incubation programmes, targeted primarily at technology entrepreneurs, offered by the Institutes of Technology. Participants receive training, mentoring and incubation space. EPPs currently operate in: Athlone / GMIT – Midlands & West; Cork – Genesis; Dundalk – Novation; Dublin – M50, DIT HotHouse and Synergy; Limerick – LEAP; Sligo / Letterkenny – CÉIM; Waterford – South East Enterprise Platform Programme.

## ENVIRONMENTAL PROTECTION AGENCY

P.O. Box 3000, Johnstown Castle Estate, Co Wexford  T: (053) 916 0600
F: (053) 916 0699  E: info@epa.ie  W: www.epa.ie
**Categories:** Information; Regulator & Standards

The Environmental Protection Agency has responsibilities for a wide range of licensing, enforcement, monitoring and assessment activities associated with environmental protection. Its website provides information on how EPA performs its duties in these areas, as well as the rules and procedures it follows in administering the applicable environmental laws and regulations.

# EQUITYNETWORK

InterTradeIreland, The Old Gasworks Business Park, Kilmorey Street,
Newry, Co. Down BT34 2DE  T: 028 3083 4151  F: 028 3083 4155
E: equity@intertradeireland.com  W: www.intertradeireland.com
**Categories:** Business Angels; Cross-Border; Equity; Information

An initiative of InterTradeIreland, EquityNetwork provides free, value-added advisory services to businesses to assist in making them 'investor-ready', as well as signposting and advice for businesses seeking equity.

# ERNST & YOUNG

Ernst & Young Building, Harcourt Centre, Harcourt Street, Dublin 2
T: (01) 475 0555  F: (01) 475 0599  W: www.ey.com/IE/en/home
C: Entrepreneurial Services Department
**Categories:** Accountants; Consulting

Ernst & Young provides audit, accounting, taxation, payroll and consulting services for companies of all sizes. The firm also is a sponsor of the Entrepreneur of the Year Awards.

# EUROPA

E: europwebmaster@cec.eu.int  W: europa.eu.int
**Categories:** EU Information; Website

The European Union's website, Europa, features information on the objectives of the EU, details on its agencies and the latest news. The URL http://europa.eu.int/comm/enterprise/index_en.htm is specific to enterprise.

# EUROPE DIRECT.IE

**Categories:** EU Information

Europe Direct Ireland is delivered by the public libraries service on behalf of the European Commission Representation in Ireland and accessible at a number of locations.

# EUROPE DIRECT.IE BLANCHARDSTOWN

Blanchardstown, Library & Offices, Blanchardstown Centre, Fingal,
Dublin 15  T: (01) 890 5563  F: (01) 890 5786  E: blanchlib@fingalcoco.ie
W: www.fingalcoco.ie/livinginfingal/libraries/  C: Betty Boardman
**Categories:** EU Information

## EUROPE DIRECT.IE CARRAROE & BALLINASLOE

Carraroe Branch Library, An Scailp Chultúrtha, An Cheathrún Rua,
Co na Gaillimhe  T: (091) 595 733  F: (091) 565 039
E: carraroelibrary@eircom.net  W: www.galwaylibrary.ie  C: Peigí
Vaughan / Ballinasloe Library, Fairgreen, Ballinasloe, Co Galway
T: (090) 964 3464  F: (091) 565 039  E: ballinasloe@galwaylibrary.ie
C: Mary Dillon
**Categories:** EU Information

## EUROPE DIRECT.IE DUNDALK

Roden Place, Dundalk  T: (042) 935 3190  F: (042) 933 7635
E: libraryhelpdesk@louthcoco.ie
**Categories:** EU Information

## EUROPE DIRECT.IE KILLARNEY

Rock Road, Killarney  T: (064) 663 2655  F: (064) 663 6065
E: killarney@kerrycolib.ie  W: www.kerrylibrary.ie/killarneybranch.asp
C: Mary Murray
**Categories:** EU Information

## EUROPE DIRECT.IE LETTERKENNY

Central Library, Oliver Plunkett Road, Letterkenny, Co Donegal
T: (074) 912 4950  F: (074) 912 4950  E: library@donegallibrary.ie
W: www.donegallibrary.ie  C: Marianne Lynch
**Categories:** EU Information

## EUROPE DIRECT.IE THURLES

The Source, Cathedral Street, Thurles, Co Tipperary  T: (0504) 29720
F: (0504) 21344  E: eudirect@tipperarylibraries.ie
W: www.tipperarylibraries.ie  C: Ann Marie Brophy
**Categories:** EU Information

## EUROPE DIRECT.IE WATERFORD CITY

Lady Lane, Waterford  T: (051) 849 975
E: europedirect@waterfordcity.ie  W: www.waterfordcity.ie
C: Sinead O'Higgins
**Categories:** EU Information

# EXCELLENCE IRELAND QUALITY ASSOCIATION

9 Appian Way, Ranelagh, Dublin 6  T: (01) 660 4100  F: (01) 660 4280
E: info@eiqa.com  W: www.eiqa.com  C: Petrina Duggan
**Categories:** Information; Regulator & Standards

Excellence Ireland promotes continuous improvement and business excellence among Irish companies. It organises the Q-Mark and Hygiene Mark schemes, the National Quality Hygiene Awards and the Irish Business Excellence Model. The Foundation Mark is a management development programme accredited by Excellence Ireland for established small companies. The EIQA website offers useful online business resources.

# EXECUTIVE VENTURE PARTNERS

Arena House, Arena Road, Sandyford Industrial Estate, Dublin 18
T: (01) 213 0711  F: (01) 213 0515  E: info@evp.ie  W: www.evp.ie
C: Gerry Jones
**Categories:** Equity

EVP provides a comprehensive range of services that covers virtually every start-up aspect, from finance, through investor relations to sales and marketing, channel advice, Enterprise Ireland relations and risk reduction. It provides direct funding of up to €750,000.

# EXPERTISEIRELAND.COM

W: www.expertiseireland.com
**Categories:** Information; Website

Expertiseireland.com is the gateway to the island's knowledge base, bringing together innovators and those at the forefront of developing the knowledge economy, be they from a business or academic background. It provides a searchable database, with up-to-date details of academic expertise and business expertise, funding information, technology transfer and collaborative opportunities.

# FÁILTE IRELAND

88-95 Amiens Street, Dublin 1  T: (01) 884 7700
E: info@failteireland.ie  W: www.failteireland.ie

**Categories:** Information; Marketing; Tourism Development; Training

Fáilte Ireland provides an extensive range of training and support services and business solutions to tourism enterprises, designed to develop and sustain Ireland as a high-quality, competitive tourist destination.

# FÁS

Services to Business, 27–33 Upper Baggot Street, Dublin 4
T: (01) 607 0500  F: (01) 607 0608  E: info@fas.ie  W: www.fas.ie
C: John Dolan, Services to Industry

**Categories:** Training

Through a regional network of Employment Services offices and Training Centres, FÁS operates training and employment programmes, provides a recruitment service to job-seekers and employers, an advisory service for industry and supports community-based enterprises. Ireland's national standard for human resource management, 'Excellence Through People', is awarded by FÁS.

# FERMANAGH ENTERPRISE LTD

Enniskillen Business Centre, Lackaghboy Industrial Estate, Tempo
Road, Enniskillen BT74 4RL  T: (028) 6632 7348  F: (028) 6632 7878
E: info@fermanaghenterprise.com  W: www.fermanaghenterprise.com
C: John Treacy, Manager

**Categories:** Information; Training; Workspace

Fermanagh Enterprise is a member of Enterprise Northern Ireland. Its mission is 'to strengthen the economy of Fermanagh through encouraging, assisting and advising individuals and groups, in undertaking opportunities for enterprise development, and seeking, by support, an optimum output from a development enterprise culture, which reflects the delivery of that competent support in the creation and development of small businesses in the County'.

# FGS

Molyneux House, Bride Street, Dublin 8  T: (01) 418 2000
F: (01) 418 2044 E: fgs@fgs.ie  W: www.fgs.ie
**Categories:** Accountants; Consulting

An independent firm of business advisers and consultants, FGS is one of Ireland's top 10 accountancy practices. It provides a range of accountancy services, including audit, due diligence and corporate compliance, and an advisory service.

# FINGAL COUNTY ENTERPRISE BOARD

Mainscourt, 23 Main Street, Swords, Co Dublin  T: (01) 890 0800
F: (01) 813 9991  E: info@fingalceb.ie  W: www.fingalceb.ie
C: Oisin Geoghegan, CEO
**Categories:** Debt; Equity; Grants; Information; Mentoring; Training

Fingal CEB provides financial and other assistance to existing and potential small business promoters located in Fingal County (north County Dublin).

# FINGAL LEADER PARTNERSHIP

Unit 14, Beat Centre, Stephenstown Industrial Estate, Balbriggan, Fingal, Co. Dublin  T: (01) 802 0484  E: emulligan@fingalleaderpartnership.ie
W: fingal.leaderpartnership.ie  C: Emer Mulligan, CEO
**Categories:** Community & Rural Development

Fingal Leader Partnership is supported under the Local Development Social Inclusion Programme and LEADER in achieving local development through the promotion of sustainable enterprise.

# FINGLAS BUSINESS INITIATIVE

Rosehill House, Finglas Road, Dublin 11  T: (01) 836 1666  F: (01) 864 0211 E: info@fcp.ie  W: www.fcp.ie  C: David Orford
**Categories:** Business Plans; Grants; Information; Mentoring

The Finglas Business Initiative is operated by the Finglas / Cabra Partnership and offers mentoring, business information and advice, assistance with business planning and funding applications and loan finance to businesses in the Finglas area of Dublin.

## FIRST STEP

Jefferson House, Eglinton Road, Donnybrook, Dublin 4   T: (01) 260 0988
F: (01) 260 0989  E: info@first-step.ie  W: www.first-step.ie
**Categories:** Debt

First Step provides micro-finance (loans less than €25,000) to individuals
who cannot access funds through normal channels. First Step receives
funding from Enterprise Ireland through the EU Seed and Venture
Capital Fund and the Social Finance Foundation. It is also the
beneficiary of an SME Guarantee Facility created within the framework
of the Competitiveness and Innovation Framework Programme (CIP) of
the European Community.

## FIRST TRUST BANK

4 Queen Street, Belfast BT1 3DJ  T: (028) 9032 5599
W: www.firsttrustbank.co.uk
**Categories:** Debt

First Trust Bank is Allied Irish Bank's Northern Ireland business
banking service.

## FIRST TUESDAY

Zircol Ltd, DCU Ryan Academy, 3013 Lake Drive, CityWest Business
Campus, Dublin 24  T: 01 700 8508  F: 01 413 3543
W: www.firsttuesday.ie
**Categories:** Business Angels; Networking; Website

First Tuesday is a forum for entrepreneurs to meet investors, potential
customers and future partners.

## FLAX TRUST

Brookfield Business Centre, 333 Crumlin Road, Belfast BT14 7EA
T: (028) 9074 5241  F: (028) 9074 8025  E: info@flaxtrust.com
W: www.flaxtrust.com
**Categories:** Community & Rural Development; Incubator; Workspace

The Flax Trust is one of the largest and longest-established community
regeneration projects in the whole of Ireland and is committed to the
'reconciliation of a divided community through economic and social
development, bringing peace to both communities, one person and one
job at a time'.

## FOOD PRODUCT DEVELOPMENT CENTRE

Dublin Institute of Technology, Cathal Brugha Street, Dublin 1
T: (01) 814 6080  F: (01) 874 8572  E: fpdc@dit.ie  W: www.fpdc.dit.ie
C: Mary Dineen
**Categories:** Consulting; R & D; Training

The Food Product Development Centre at the Dublin Institute of Technology develops innovative food concepts through investigating value-added opportunities in Irish and European markets. Its confidential development work includes: idea generation; concept and prototype development; ingredient sourcing and testing; shelf-life studies; sensory assessment and market research; nutritional declaration; and labelling. The Centre also offers training workshops.

## FOOD SAFETY AUTHORITY OF IRELAND

Abbey Court, Lower Abbey Street, Dublin 1  T: (01) 817 1300
F: (01) 817 1301  E: info@fsai.ie  W: www.fsai.ie
**Categories:** Information; Regulator & Standards

The Food Safety Authority of Ireland's mission is to protect consumers' health by ensuring that food consumed, distributed, marketed or produced in Ireland meets the highest standards of food safety and hygiene. It offers information to industry on all aspects of food safety, including the safe handling and preparation of food, food safety and training, Hazard Analysis Critical Control Point (HACCP), labelling and food safety legislation. FSAI has also produced a fact sheet outlining the steps to be taken when starting a food business in Ireland. An Advice Line is available at 1890 33 66 77.

## FORFÁS

Wilton Park House, Wilton Place, Dublin 2  T: (01) 607 3000
F: (01) 607 3030  E:aideen.fitzgerald@forfas.ie  W: www.forfas.ie
C: Aideen Fitzgerald, Communications Manager
**Categories:** Policy

Forfás is the national policy and advisory board for enterprise, trade, science, technology and innovation and the body through which powers are delegated to Enterprise Ireland for promotion of indigenous industry and to IDA Ireland for promotion of inward investment. Science Foundation Ireland is a third agency of Forfás.

# FORUM CONNEMARA

Ellis Hall, Letterfrack, Connemara, Co. Galway  T: (095) 41116
F: (095) 41198 E: forum@indigo.ie  W: www.forumconnemara.ie
C: Johnny Coyne, CEO
**Categories:** Community & Rural Development

Forum Connemara is supported under the Local Development Social
Inclusion Programme and LEADER in achieving local development
through the promotion of sustainable enterprise.

# FOUNTAIN HEALTHCARE PARTNERS

Delta Partners, Guild House, 4th Floor, Guild Street, IFSC, Dublin 1
T: (01) 522 5100  F: (01) 636 6230  E: manus@fh-partners.com
W: www.fh-partners.com  C: Manus Rogan
**Categories:** Equity

A spin-out group from Elan Corporation's corporate venture capital
group, Fountain Healthcare partners is an Irish-based life science fund
that provides risk capital and expertise to assist entrepreneurs in
building the next generation of leading global life science companies.

# FR KELLY & CO

27 Clyde Road, Ballsbridge, Dublin 4  T: (01) 231 4848   F: (01) 614 4756
E: info@frkelly.com  W: www.frkelly.com
C: Patents: Philip Coyle, Trade Marks: Shane Smyth
**Categories:** Intellectual Property

FR Kelly & Co offers expertise and experience in all aspects of
intellectual property law, trade marks and brand name protection.

# FRANCHISEDIRECT

Suite 106, The Capel Building, Capel Street, Dublin 7  T: (01) 865 6370
W: www.franchisedirect.co.uk
**Categories:** Business Sales / Purchases; Franchises; Information; Website

FranchiseDirect is a leading international franchising resource, which
provides views, news and advice to entrepreneurs and franchisers.

## GAHAN & CO

14 South Lotts Road, Dublin 4  T: (01) 668 4411  F: (01) 668 4428
E: pgahan@gahan.ie  W: www.gahan.ie  C: Patrick Gahan
**Categories:** Accountants; Training

A firm of chartered accountants. In addition to the usual accountancy / auditing services, Gahan also provides workshops in effective financial management and strategic planning.

## GALWAY CITY PARTNERSHIP

3 The Plaza, Headford Road, Galway  T: (091) 773466  F: (091) 773468
E: info@gcp.ie  W: www.gcp.ie  C: Declan Brassil, Manager
**Categories:** Community & Rural Development; Information; Social Economy; Training

Galway City Partnership is supported under the Local Development Social Inclusion Programme in achieving local development through the promotion of sustainable enterprise.

## GALWAY COUNTY & CITY ENTERPRISE BOARD

Woodquay Court, Woodquay, Galway  T: (091) 565269  F: (091) 565384
E: enquiry@galwayenterprise.ie  W: www.galwayenterprise.ie
C: Charles Lynch, CEO
**Categories:** Debt; Equity; Grants; Information; Mentoring; Training; Website

Galway CEB provides a full range of supports for micro-enterprises in its region. Its website also offers online tools for entrepreneurs, as well as reference articles and other information.

## GALWAY RURAL DEVELOPMENT COMPANY

Mellowes Campus, Athenry, Co Galway  T: (091) 844335  F: (091) 845465
E: grdc@grd.ie  W: www.grd.ie  C: Delia Colahan, CEO
**Categories:** Community & Rural Development; Grants; Information; Training

Galway Rural Development is supported under LEADER and the Local Development Social Inclusion Programme in achieving local development through the promotion of sustainable enterprise.

## GALWAY TECHNOLOGY CENTRE

Mervue Business Park, Galway  T: (091) 770 007  F: (091) 755 635
E: gtc@iol.ie  W: www.gtc.ie
**Categories:** Workspace

The Galway Technology Centre provides flexible workspace for early-stage and developing enterprises.


## GALWAY–MAYO INSTITUTE OF TECHNOLOGY

Dublin Road, Galway  T: (091) 753161  F: (091) 751107
E: iibcgalway@gmit.ie; iibccastlebar@gmit.ie  W: www.gmit.ie
C: George McCourt (IiBC, Galway); Maria Staunton (IiBC, Castlebar)
**Categories:** Incubator; R & D; Training

GMIT operates Innovation in Business Centres (IiBCs) at its campuses in Galway and Castlebar, which offer incubation facilities and a supportive environment to potential entrepreneurs to assist them in taking their ideas from concept to full commercialisation. It also offers the Midlands & West Enterprise Programme in association with Athlone IT.


## GENESIS ENTERPRISE PROGRAMME

Rubicon Centre, CIT Campus, Bishopstown, Cork  T: (021) 492 8900
E: info@gep.ie  W: www.gep.ie  C: Denise Kennedy
**Categories:** Incubator; Mentoring; Training

The Genesis Enterprise Programme is a 12-month rapid incubation programme to support and accelerate graduate entrepreneurs in developing a business, which accelerates the learning process for participants through formal training, a mentor and the shared knowledge of other participants.

## GLENWOOD ENTERPRISES LTD

Glenwood Business Centre, Springbank Industrial Estate, Poleglass,
Belfast BT17 0QL T: (028) 9061 0311  F: (028) 9060 0929
E: office@glenwoodbc.com  W: www.glenwoodbc.com
C: Eamonn Foster, Chief Executive
**Categories:** Community & Rural Development; Information;
Social Economy; Training; Workspace

Glenwood Enterprises is a member of Enterprise Northern Ireland and
is 'committed to the promotion of job creation and economic
development in the Twinbrook, Poleglass and Lagmore areas through
practical support for small businesses'.

## GOV.IE

W: www.gov.ie
**Categories:** Information; Website

This website provides detailed information on the operation of the State,
with links to Government departments and local authorities. See also
BASIS.

## GOVERNMENT PUBLICATIONS

51 St Stephen's Green, Dublin 2 / Sales Office: Sun Alliance House,
Molesworth Street, Dublin 2    T: (01) 647 6000  F: (01) 661 0747
E: pubsales@opw.ie
**Categories:** Information; Publications

All Government publications are available from the sales office,
including Central Statistics Office reports.

## GREENHOUSE START-UP INCUBATOR

Waterloo Lodge, Coolbawn, Nenagh, Co Tipperary  T: (061) 748911
E: contactevert@gmail.com  W: www.greenhouselimerick.com
C: Evert Bopp
**Categories:** Incubator; Training

The Greenhouse is a start-up incubator that provides exciting and
innovative start-ups with the facilities, services, knowledge and
network needed to grow from an idea into a reality. The Greenhouse
also runs seminars, courses and conferences dealing with all aspect of
starting, funding, running and marketing a business.

## GROW SOUTH ANTRIM

Antrim Civic Centre, 50 Stiles Way, Antrim BT41 2UB  T: (028) 9448
1311  F: (028) 9448 1324  E: info@growsouthantrim.com
W: www.growsouthantrim.com  C: Emma Stubbs
**Categories:** Community & Rural Development

GROW South Antrim manages and delivers funding under the
Northern Ireland Rural Development Programme 2007-2013 across
rural South Antrim.

## GROWCORP INNOVATION CENTRE

3015 Lake Drive, CityWest Business Campus Park, Dublin 24  T: (01) 466
1000  F: (01) 466 1002  E: grow@growcorp.net  W: www.growcorp.net
**Categories:** Equity; Incubator

Growcorp is a leading integrated bioscience investment, advisory and
incubation organisation. It invests at an early stage in amounts up to
Euro €1.27 million and has led syndicates in excess of €20 million to take
businesses to product launch. The Growcorp team works with
entrepreneurs to get their business from start-up to commercial reality,
offering services from strategy optimisation, IP exploitation to fund-
raising and team building advice.

## GUARANTEED IRISH LTD

1 Fitzwilliam Place, Dublin 2  T: (01) 661 2607  F: (01) 661 2633
E: info@guaranteedirish.ie  W: www.guaranteedirish.ie
**Categories:** Marketing; Regulator & Standards

Guaranteed Irish Ltd aims to increase awareness of and demand for
Irish products and services, thereby maximising employment and
prosperity in Ireland. The Guaranteed Irish symbol has become the
definitive mark of excellence for Irish products and services.

## GUINNESS ENTERPRISE CENTRE

Taylor's Lane, Dublin 8  T: (01) 410 0600  F: (01) 410 0602
E: info@guinness-enterprisectr.com  W: www.guinness-
enterprisectr.com  C: Dolores Dempsey, Administration Manager
**Categories:** Incubator; Workspace

A 77-unit, 6,000 square metre enterprise / incubation centre managed by
Dublin Business Innovation Centre.

## GUINNESS WORKERS' EMPLOYMENT FUND LTD

St James's Gate, Dublin 8  T: (01) 453 6700  F: (01) 454 6520
C: Rowena Thornburgh; Andy Shirran (Part-time)
**Categories:** Debt

Funded by Guinness workers and pensioners, the Fund provides start-up businesses with financial assistance, and supports expansion of existing businesses, usually by way of a term loan, at interest rates below those charged by the commercial banks. Entrepreneurs must submit applications on the fund's official application form. GWEF also helped to fund the development of the Guinness Enterprise Centre.

## HALO BUSINESS ANGEL PARTNERSHIP

Guinness Enterprise Centre, Taylors Lane, Dublin 8  T: (01) 410 0818
F: (01) 671 3330  E: info@businessangels.ie  W: www.businessangels.ie
**Categories:** Business Angels; Equity

The HALO Business Angel Partnership matches private investors with pre-screened investment opportunities in start-up, early stage and developing businesses. It is managed by the Business & Innovation Centres.

## HEALTH & SAFETY AUTHORITY

The Metropolitan Building, James Joyce Street, Dublin 1  T: (01) 614 7000
F: (01) 614 7020  E: wcu@hsa.ie  W: www.hsa.ie
**Categories:** Information; Regulator & Standards

The HSA has overall responsibility for the administration and enforcement of health and safety at work in Ireland. The Safety, Health & Welfare at Work Act, 1989 covers all who work, all workplaces, visitors and passers-by and also places responsibilities on manufacturers and suppliers (including designers, installers and erectors).

## HEALTH & SAFETY EXECUTIVE FOR NORTHERN IRELAND

83 Ladas Drive, Belfast BT6 9FR  T: (028) 9024 3249  F: (028) 9023 5383
E: hseni@detini.gov.uk W: www.hseni.gov.uk
**Categories:** Information; Regulator & Standards

HSENI is the lead body responsible for the promotion and enforcement of health and safety at work standards in Northern Ireland. Its mission is to see that the risks to people's health and safety arising from work activities are effectively controlled, thereby contributing to the overall economic and social well-being of the community.

## HM REVENUE & CUSTOMS

Custom House, Belfast BT1 3ET  T: (028) 9056 2600  F: (028) 9056 2971
E: enquiries.ni@hmne.gsi.gov.uk  W: www.hmrc.gov.uk
VAT Registration Unit, PO Box 40, Carnbane Way, Damolly, Newry,
Co Down BT35 6PJ T: (028) 3026 1114  F: (028) 3026 4165
**Categories:** Regulator & Standards

For advice on VAT, contact your nearest VAT Business Advice Centre. HMRC's website provides a list of centres.

## IBEC

Confederation House, 84–86 Lower Baggot Street, Dublin 2  T: (01) 605 1500  F: (01) 638 1500  E: info@ibec.ie  W: www.ibec.ie
**Categories:** Information

IBEC (The Irish Business & Employers Confederation) represents and provides economic, commercial, employee relations and social affairs services to some 7,000 companies and organisations from all sectors of economic and commercial activity. It works to shape policies and influence decision-making in a way that develops and protects members' interests and contributes to the development and maintenance of an economy that promotes enterprise and productive employment.

# IDA IRELAND

Wilton Park House, Wilton Place, Dublin 2  T: (01) 603 4000
F: (01) 603 4040  E: idaireland@ida.ie  W: www.idaireland.com
**Categories:** Inwards Investment

IDA Ireland has national responsibility for securing new investment from overseas in manufacturing and international services sectors and for encouraging existing foreign enterprises in Ireland to expand their businesses. It markets Ireland as an attractive location through its offices abroad and reports to the Minister for Enterprise, Trade & Employment.

# IE DOMAIN REGISTRY LTD

Windsor House, 14 Windsor Terrace, Sandycove, Co Dublin
T: (01) 236 5400  F: (01) 230 0365  E: customerrelations@iedr.ie
W: www.domainregistry.ie
**Categories:** e-Business; Regulator & Standards

IEDR manages the .ie namespace in the interest of the Irish and global e-business communities. It is the Irish national Internet registry.

# INISHOWEN DEVELOPMENT PARTNERSHIP

St Mary's Road, Buncrana, Co Donegal  T: (074) 936 2218
F: (074) 936 2990  E: admin@inishowen.ie  W: www.inishowen.ie
**Categories:** Community & Rural Development

Inishowen Partnership Board is supported under LEADER and the Local Development Social Inclusion Programme in achieving local development through the promotion of sustainable enterprise.

# INNOVATION PARTNERS

Midlands Innovation & Research Centre, Athlone IT, Dublin Road,
Athlone, Co Westmeath T: (090) 647 6332  F: (090) 648 9457
E: danny@innovation-partners.com  W: www.innovation-partners.com
C: Danny Gleeson, Managing director
**Categories:** Consulting; R & D; Training

An innovation management consultancy, Innovation Partners offers consulting and training in innovation and technology transfer.

## INNOVATOR

174 Ivy Exchange, Granby Place, Parnell Square, Dublin 1  T: (01) 879
4010  F: (01) 879 4001  E: info@innovator.ie  W: www.innovator.ie
C: James Bourke, Sean McNulty
**Categories:** Consulting; R & D; Training

Innovator is a leading consultancy that provides integrated innovation,
R&D and  intellectual property management, training and mentoring
services to SMEs, entrepreneurs and large companies.

## INSTITUTE FOR MINORITY ENTREPRENEURSHIP

Dublin Institute of Technology, Room 4-033, Aungier Street, Dublin 2
T: (01) 402 3041  E: info@ime.ie  W: www.ime.ie  C: Etain Kidney
**Categories:** Community & Rural Development; Training

The Institute for Minority Entrepreneurship was established to offer the
different minority groups in Ireland equal opportunity through
entrepreneurship education and training. The Institute aims to act as a
hub in the gathering and dissemination of information relevant to
minority entrepreneurship in Ireland.

## INSTITUTE OF ART, DESIGN & TECHNOLOGY

Kill Avenue, Dún Laoire, Co Dublin  T: (01) 214 4600
E: development@iadt.ie  W: www.iadt.ie
C: Dr Marian O'Sullivan, Head of Development
**Categories:** Incubator; Training

The Institute of Art, Design & Technology operates the Media Cube
incubation centre and offers the Create enterprise programme.

## INSTITUTE OF CERTIFIED PUBLIC ACCOUNTANTS IN IRELAND

17 Harcourt Street, Dublin 2  T: (01) 425 1000  F: (01) 425 1001
E: nbornschein@cpaireland.ie  W: www.cpaireland.ie
C: Nicole Bornschein
**Categories:** Accountants

ICPAI is one of the accountancy bodies whose members are permitted
to audit company accounts. It has 1,000+ members throughout the
island of Ireland. If you're looking for an accountant, ICPAI can direct
you to one of its members.

## INSTITUTE OF DIRECTORS IN IRELAND

Heritage House, Dundrum Office Park, Dublin 14  T: (01) 296 4093
F: (01) 296 4127  E: skirwan@iodireland.ie  W: www.iodireland.ie
C: Maura Quinn, Chief Executive
**Categories:** Information; Networking; Training

IOD Ireland is an independent body affiliated to the Institute of Directors worldwide. It offers members access to a wide range of networking, database, and reciprocal service opportunities, provides a forum for the exchange of ideas and information, encourages members to improve their standards and performance as directors and principals, and represents the views of business leaders to government and other organisations.

## INSTITUTE OF MANAGEMENT CONSULTANTS & ADVISERS

19 Elgin Road, Dublin 2  T: (01) 634 9636  F: (01) 281 5330
E: info@imca.ie  W: www.imca.ie
C: Tom Moriarty, Development Executive
**Categories:** Consulting; Information

A management consultant is an independent and qualified person who provides a professional service identifying and investigating problems concerned with strategy, policy, markets, organisation, procedures, systems, practices and methods, and formulating recommendations for appropriate action. IMCA's website gives guidelines on how to choose and use consultants, as well as a listing of registered practices.

## INSTITUTE OF PUBLIC ADMINISTRATION

57-61 Lansdowne Road, Dublin 4  T: (01) 240 3600  F: (01) 668 9135
E: information@ipa.ie  W: www.ipa.ie
**Categories:** Information; Publications

Publisher of the *Administration Yearbook & Diary*, a reference database of 6,000+ entries about Ireland, a useful research resource for any business.

## INSTITUTE OF TECHNOLOGY BLANCHARDSTOWN

Blanchardstown Road North, Blanchardstown, Dublin 15
T: (01) 885 1000  F: (01) 885 1001  E: info@itb.ie  W: www.itb.ie
C: Tom Doyle, Head of Development
**Categories:** Consulting; Incubator; R & D; Training

IT Blanchardstown's Learning and Innovation Centre (LINC) provides
on-campus Research & Development, as well as incubation facilities and
business training development services. The Institute of Technology
Blanchardstown runs the M50@LINC Enterprise Programme.

## INSTITUTE OF TECHNOLOGY CARLOW

Kilkenny Road, Carlow  T: (059) 917 0400  F: (059) 917 0500
E: info@itcarlow.ie  W: www.itcarlow.ie
C: Jim McEntee, Head of External Services
**Categories:** Consulting; Incubator; R & D; Training

IT Carlow's Enterprise & Research Incubation Campus provides
services to local industry, including research, training and consultancy
in computing, applied sciences, civil, electronic and mechanical
engineering and business services, as well as offering an Enterprise
Platform Programme.

## INSTITUTE OF TECHNOLOGY SLIGO

Ballinode, Sligo  T: (071) 915 5222  F: (071) 916 0475
E: info@itsligo.ie  W: www.itsligo.ie
C: Padraig Ryan, Head of Learning Environment
**Categories:** Consulting; Incubator; R & D; Training

The Technology Transfer & Innovation Unit provides a single point of
contact for external linkages with IT Sligo and provides advice and
assistance on a range of activities, including sources of funding for
collaborative projects, open and distance learning consultancy and state-
of-the art communication and business facilities. It fosters innovation
through the IT Sligo Business Innovation Centre and the Céim
Enterprise Development Programme.

## INSTITUTE OF TECHNOLOGY TRALEE

Clash, Tralee, Co Kerry  T: (066) 714 5600 / 714 5611 (Development)
F: (066) 714 5636  E: brenda.clifford@ittralee.ie  W: www.ittralee.ie
C: Brenda Clifford, Development Department
**Categories:** Consulting; R & D; Training

The Tom Crean Business Centre at IT Tralee assists entrepreneurs in taking their ideas from proof of principle to full commercial success. The Centre also supports the Young Entrepreneur programme.

## INSTITUTES OF TECHNOLOGY

There are Institutes of Technology in Athlone; Blanchardstown, Dublin; Carlow; Cork; Dún Laoire; Dundalk; Galway / Mayo; Letterkenny; Limerick; Sligo; Tallaght, Dublin; Tipperary; Tralee; and Waterford, which provide a range of services to industry. Also included here is the National College of Ireland.

## INTERTRADEIRELAND

The Old Gasworks Business Park, Kilmorey Street, Newry,
Co. Down BT34 2DE  T: (028) 3083 4100  F: (028) 3083 4155
E: info@intertradeireland.com  W: www.intertradeireland.com
**Categories:** Competitions; Cross-Border; Grants; Information; Policy

InterTradeIreland's remit is to accelerate trade and business development across the whole island of Ireland. It runs a number of programmes, including EquityNetwork, Acumen, Fusion and the annual Seedcorn Business Plan competition.

## INVEST NORTHERN IRELAND

Bedford Square, Bedford Street, Belfast, BT2 7ES  T: (028) 9069 8000
E: info@investni.com  W: www.investni.com
**Categories:** Grants; Information; Inwards Investment

InvestNI is Northern Ireland's regional economic development agency. Its role is to grow the economy by helping new and existing businesses to compete internationally, and by attracting new investment to Northern Ireland. It offers the Northern Ireland business community a single organisation providing high-quality services, programmes, support and expert advice, principally supporting businesses in the manufacturing and tradable services sectors.

# INVEST-TECH

27 Ardmeen Park, Blackrock, Co Dublin  T: (01) 283 4083
F: (01) 278 2391  E: info@planware.org  W: www.planware.org
C: Brian Flanagan
**Categories:** Business Plans; Consulting; Information

Invest-Tech provides advice and assistance to start-ups and SMEs in business planning, strategy development and financial plans. It also offers freeware, shareware and software for writing a business plan, making financial forecasts and strategic planning.

# IRD DUHALLOW LTD

James O'Keeffe Institute, Newmarket, Co Cork  T: (029) 60633  F: (029) 60694  E: duhallow@eircom.net  C: Maura Walsh, Manager
**Categories:** Community & Rural Development

IRD Duhallow is a community-based rural development company, supported under LEADER and the Local Development Social Inclusion Programme in achieving local development through the promotion of sustainable enterprise.

# IRD KILTIMAGH

Enterprise House, Aiden Street, Kiltimagh, Co Mayo  T: (094) 938 1494
F: (094) 938 1884  E: manager@ird-kiltimagh.ie; ird@iol.ie
W: www.ird-kiltimagh.ie  C: Joe Kelly, Chief Executive
**Categories:** Community & Rural Development

IRD Kiltimagh's mission is the development of the economic potential of Kiltimagh and its hinterland to the fullest and in a way which will benefit the whole community'. It operates two Enterprise Centres, and has undertaken the successful implementation of a re-development programme for the Kiltimagh area in conjunction with the State and private sectors.

## IRISH BUSINESS SALES & CORPORATE FINANCE COMPANY

Unit 3, Riverview House, Barrett Street, Ballina, Co Mayo T: (096) 78804
F: (096) 76983  E: info@irishbusinesssales.com
W: www.irishbusinesssales.com  C: Eamonn Gaffney, Gerry Walsh
**Categories:** Business Sales / Purchases

IBSCI is a facilitator in: the buying and selling of businesses; effecting management buy-outs / buy-ins; sourcing partners / investors; and raising project finance. Its website provides a range of businesses for sale and acquisitions sought, as well as investors seeking businesses / projects and businesses seeking investment.

## IRISH CO-OPERATIVE SOCIETY LTD

Plunkett House, 84 Merrion Square, Dublin 2  T: (01) 676 4783
F: (01) 662 4502  E: info@icos.ie  W: www.icos.ie
**Categories:** Co-operatives; Information

As the co-ordinating organisation for co-operatives in Ireland, ICOS provides a range of services to its member co-operatives and represents them in national and international organisations. It can also advise on, and provide Model Rules for, the setting-up of a co-operative.

## IRISH COUNTRYWOMEN'S ASSOCIATION

An Grianán, Termonfeckin, Co Louth  T: (041) 982 2119
E: admin@an-grianan.ie  W: www.ica.ie
**Categories:** Information; Networking; Training; Women

The ICA is the largest women's organisation in Ireland, with members across the country, in villages, towns and cities. Members are involved in a wide range of activities within the ICA and in the community, including the residential adult education college at An Grianán.

## IRISH DIRECT MARKETING ASSOCIATION

8 Upper Fitzwilliam Street, Dublin 2  T: (01) 661 0470  F: (01) 830 8914
E: info@idma.ie  W: www.idma.ie
**Categories:** Information; Marketing; Training

The IDMA is the trade association for companies that practise in or supply the direct marketing industry in Ireland. IDMA offers training in direct marketing techniques.

## IRISH EXPORTERS ASSOCIATION

28 Merrion Square, Dublin 2  T: (01) 661 2182  F: (01) 661 2315
E: iea@irishexporters.ie  W: www.irishexporters.ie
C: John Whelan, Chief Executive
**Categories:** Information; Networking; Training

The Irish Exporters Association represents and promotes exporters' interests. The Association has regional branches in Cork, Dublin, Dundalk, Galway and Limerick. It offers a Diploma in International Trade and Marketing, as well as a series of short courses on aspects of international trade practice.

## IRISH FILM BOARD

Queensgate, 23 Dock Road, Galway  T: (091) 561398  F: (091) 561405
E: info@filmboard.ie  W: www.filmboard.ie
**Categories:** Debt; Equity

The Irish Film Board provides loans and equity investment to independent Irish film-makers to assist in the development and production of Irish films.

## IRISH FRANCHISE ASSOCIATION

Kandoy House, 2 Fairview Strand, Dublin 3  T: (01) 813 4555
F: (01) 813 4575  E: info@irishfranchiseassociation.com
W: www.irishfranchiseassociation.com  C: David Killeen, Chairman
**Categories:** Franchises; Information

The Irish Franchise Association promotes the development of franchising in Ireland through exhibitions, seminars, newsletters, awards and networking. Its website provides information about the franchise sector which will be of use to potential franchisees wishing to start their own franchised business, and potential franchisors looking to expand their existing business through business format franchising.

## IRISH INSTITUTE FOR TRAINING & DEVELOPMENT

4 Sycamore House, Millennium Business Park, Naas, Co Kildare
T: (045) 881166  F: (045) 881192  E: info@iitd.com  W: www.iitd.ie
C: Sinead Heneghan, CEO
**Categories:** Information; Networking; Training

IITD is the professional body for human resource development professionals in Ireland. It conducts courses nationwide in training & development, leading to Certificate or Diploma level qualifications, and supports continuing professional development through a programme of events around the country. IITD keeps members updated on national training and development issues.

## IRISH INTERNET ASSOCIATION

The Digital Hub, 101 James Street, Dublin 8  E: info@iia.ie
W: www.iia.ie  C: Joan Mulvihill (CEO), Roseanne Smith (Membership),
Irene Dehaene (Events)
**Categories:** e-Business; Information; Networking; Website

The IIA is the professional body for those conducting business via the Internet in Ireland. IIA provides information to and runs seminars for members on e-business, education & training, security, employer / employee rights, raising capital, marketing, design & development and languages / platforms. The IIA website offers 'iia internet resources', with catalogued links and articles within each topic.

## IRISH LEADER NETWORK

James O'Keeffe Institute, Newmarket, Co. Cork  T: (029) 60633
E: info@irishleadernetwork.org  W: www.irishleadernetwork.org

The Irish LEADER Network is a network of 36 Local Action Groups. It operates within a legal co-operative framework, underpinned by a co-operative philosophy and mission. See individual entries for Avondhu / Blackwater Partnership; Ballyhoura Development Co. Ltd; Breffni Integrated Company; Carlow County Development Partnership; Cill Dara Ar Aghaidh Teo; Clare Local Development Company; Comhar na Oileáin Teo; County Kilkenny LEADER Partnership; County Wicklow Partnership; Donegal Local Development Co. Ltd; Fingal LEADER Partnership Co. Ltd; Forum Connemara; Galway Rural Development Co. Ltd; Inishowen Development Partnership; IRD Duhallow; Laois Partnership Co. Ltd; Leitrim Integrated Development Co. Ltd; Longford

Community Resources; Louth LEADER Partnership; Mayo North & East LEADER; Meath Partnership; Meitheal Forbatha na Gaeltachta Teo; Monaghan Integrated Development Co. Ltd; North & East Kerry Development; North Tipperary LEADER Partnership; Offaly Integrated Local Development Co.; Roscommon Integrated Development Company; Sligo LEADER Partnership Co. Ltd; South & East Cork Area Development; South Kerry Development Partnership; South Tipperary Development Company Ltd; South West Mayo Development; Waterford LEADER Partnership; Westmeath Community Development; West Cork Development Partnership Ltd; West Limerick Resources Ltd; Wexford Local Development.

## IRISH LEAGUE OF CREDIT UNIONS

33-41 Lower Mount Street, Dublin 2  T: (01) 614 6700  F: (01) 614 6701
E: info@creditunion.ie  W: www.creditunion.ie
**Categories:** Co-operatives; Debt; Information

Members of credit unions or businesses structured as co-operatives may qualify for a credit union loan. Each application is treated in the utmost confidence and will be considered on its own merits. In deciding whether to grant the loan, the member's record of saving and repayments, as well as ability to repay, and need will be taken into account. ILCU's website offers a database of credit unions in Ireland.

## IRISH MANAGEMENT INSTITUTE

Sandyford Road, Dublin 16  T: (01) 207 8400  F: (01) 295 5147
E: reception@imi.ie  W: www.imi.ie
**Categories:** Information; Networking; Training

Ireland's centre for management development, the IMI is a member organisation providing a forum for practising managers to exchange leading-edge experience, and facilitating access to Irish and international management experts. It offers full- and part-time courses, on-line support services and research resources.

## IRISH ORGANIC FARMERS & GROWERS ASSOCIATION

Main Street, Newtownforbes, Co Longford  T: (043) 334 2495
F: (043) 334 2496  E: info@iofga.org  W: www.iofga.org
C: Grace Maher, Development officer
**Categories:** Information

IOFGA is Ireland's leading organic certification body, with 25 years' experience of certifying, networking and training.

## IRISH SMALL & MEDIUM ENTERPRISES ASSOCIATION

17 Kildare Street, Dublin 2  T: (01) 662 2755  F: (01) 661 2157
E: info@isme.ie  W: www.isme.ie  C: Mark Fielding, Chief Executive
**Categories:** Information; Networking; Publications; Training

ISME's membership is composed exclusively of entrepreneurs who own and manage competitive businesses. It offers a range of services to members, including publications on wages and conditions, employers' obligations, Government-sponsored grant schemes and a member-to-member sourcing directory.

## IRISH SOFTWARE ASSOCIATION

Confederation House, 84-86 Lower Baggot Street, Dublin 2
T: (01) 605 1582  F: (01) 638 1582  E: isa@ibec.ie  W: www.software.ie
C: Kathryn Raleigh, Director
**Categories:** Information; Networking

The Irish Software Association represents Irish and multi-national software and computing services companies.

## IRISH VENTURE CAPITAL ASSOCIATION

3 Rectory Slopes, Bray, Co Wicklow  T: (01) 276 4647  F: (01) 274 5915
E: secretary@ivca.ie  W: www.ivca.ie  C: Ciara Burrowes, Administrator
**Categories:** Equity

The IVCA represents the venture capital industry in Ireland. Its website has a list of members and associates.

# IRISH WIND ENERGY ASSOCIATION

Sycamore House, Millennium Business Park, Naas, Co Kildare
T: (045) 899341  F: (045) 854958  E: office@iwea.com  W: www.iwea.com
C: Michael Walsh, CEO
**Categories:** Information; Networking

The IWEA promotes the use of wind energy in Ireland. Its members are business people, environmentalists, academics and farmers who recognise that wind energy will soon become one of Ireland's most significant sources of energy.

# ITT DUBLIN

Tallaght, Dublin 24  T: (01) 404 2000  F: (01) 404 2700
E: eamon.tuffy@it-tallaght.ie  W: www.it-tallaght.ie
C: Eamon Tuffy, Head of Development and External Services
**Categories:** Consulting; Incubator; R & D; Training

The Development and External Services Department provides advanced business and technical training and R & D consultancy. The Synergy Centre offers the Synergy EPP and other training programmes, as well as incubator facilities.

# JUNIOR ACHIEVEMENT IRELAND

8 Longford Place, Monkstown, Co Dublin  T: (01) 236 6644  F: (01) 280 3758  E: info@juniorachievement.ie  W: www.juniorachievement.ie
C: Della Clancy, Executive Director
**Categories:** Young Enterprise

Creating a culture of enterprise in the schools system, from Senior Infants to Leaving Certificate, Junior Achievement programmes use hands-on activities to help young people understand the economics of life.

# KERNEL CAPITAL PARTNERS

Rubicon Centre, Rossa Avenue, Bishopstown, Cork  T: (021) 492 8974
F: (021) 492 8977  E: nolden@kernelcapital.ie  W: www.kernelcapital.ie
C: Niall Olden
**Categories:** Equity

Kernel is one of Ireland's  most active venture capital funds. It has a portfolio of investee companies across, technology, life science and general industry and targets opportunities in the €100k to €5m range.

## KERRY COUNTY ENTERPRISE BOARD

County Buildings, Tralee, Co Kerry  T: (066) 718 3522  F: (066) 712 6712
E: kerryceb@kerrycoco.ie  W: www.kerryenterprise.ie
C: Tomas Hayes, CEO

**Categories:** Debt; Equity; Grants; Information; Mentoring; Training

Kerry County Enterprise Board provides a wide range of supports for local SMEs and intending entrepreneurs.

## KILDARE COUNTY ENTERPRISE BOARD

The Woods, Clane, Co Kildare  T: (045) 861707  F: (045) 861712
E: info@kildareceb.ie  W: www.kildareceb.ie  C: Donal Dalton, CEO

**Categories:** Debt; Equity; Grants; Information; Mentoring; Training; Women

Kildare CEB offers a wide range of supports to SMEs and intending entrepreneurs. Business Advice clinics are held on an ongoing basis, aimed at anyone who wishes to talk on a one-to-one basis with a staff member from the CEB. It operates a 'Women in Business' programme to foster and encourage entrepreneurship, self-employment and enterprise.

## KILKENNY COUNTY ENTERPRISE BOARD

42 Parliament Street, Kilkenny  T: (056) 775 2662  F: (056) 775 1649
E: enquiries@kceb.ie  W: www.kceb.ie  C: Sean McKeown, CEO

**Categories:** Debt; Equity; Grants; Information; Mentoring; Training

Kilkenny County Enterprise Board offers a wide range of supports, including advice, training, mentoring and financial assistance, to those wishing to start or expand their business.

## KPMG

1 Stokes Place, St Stephen's Green, Dublin 2  T: (01) 410 1000
F: (01) 412 1122  E: webmaster@kpmg.ie  W: www.kpmg.ie

**Categories:** Accountants; Consulting

KPMG is a major firm of chartered accountants and business advisers, providing services to clients in all sectors of Irish business. It is the Irish national practice of the accountancy organisation, KPMG International.

## LAGAN RURAL PARTNERSHIP

Economic Development Unit, Lisburn City Council, Island Civic Centre,
The Island, Lisburn, BT27 4RL  T: (028) 9250 9419
E: info@laganruralpartnership.com  W: www.laganruralpartnership.com
C: Padraic Murphy, Rural Development Manager
**Categories:** Community & Rural Development

Lagan Rural Partnership is the delivery agent for Axis 3 of the Northern
Ireland Rural Development Programme 2007-2013 – Rural Life. The
Partnership will deliver funding for projects in eligible rural areas within
Lisburn City, Castlereagh Borough and Belfast City Council areas.

## LAOIS COUNTY ENTERPRISE BOARD

Portlaoise Enterprise Centre, Clonminam Business Park, Portlaoise, Co
Laois  T: (057) 866 1800  F: (057) 866 6989  E: admin@laoisenterprise.com
W: www.laoisenterprise.com  C: Maria Callinan, CEO
**Categories:** Debt; Equity; Grants; Information; Mentoring; Training

The Laois County Enterprise Board empowers local enterprise through
advice, training, mentoring and financial assistance for those wishing to
start or expand their business.

## LAOIS PARTNERSHIP COMPANY

Pepper's Court, Portlaoise, Co Laois  T: (057) 866 1900
E: agoodwinll@eircom.net  C: Anne Goodwin, CEO
**Categories:** Community & Rural Development

Laois Partnership is supported under LEADER and the Local
Development Social Inclusion Programme in achieving local
development through the promotion of sustainable enterprise.

## LARNE ENTERPRISE DEVELOPMENT COMPANY LTD

LEDCOM Industrial Estate, Bank Road, Larne, Co Antrim BT40 3AW
T: (028) 2827 0742  F: (028) 2827 5653  E: info@ledcom.org
W: www.ledcom.org  C: David Gillespie
**Categories:** Information; Social Economy; Training; Workspace

LEDCOM is a member of Enterprise Northern Ireland and one of
Northern Ireland's longest established enterprise agencies. It provides
an effective local focus for business support, acting as a catalyst for
economic development.

# LAW SOCIETY OF IRELAND

Blackhall Place, Dublin 7  T: (01) 672 4800  F: (01) 672 4801
E: general@lawsociety.ie  W: www.lawsociety.ie
C: Ken Murphy, Director General
**Categories:** Legal

The Law Society exercises statutory functions under the Solicitors Acts 1954-1994 in relation to the education, admission, enrolment, discipline and regulation of over 6,000 solicitors in Ireland. If you're looking for a lawyer, the Law Society can direct you to one of its members.

# LAW SOCIETY OF NORTHERN IRELAND

96 Victoria Street, Belfast BT1 3GN  T: (028) 9023 1614  F: (028) 9023 2606
E: info@lawsoc-ni.org  W: www.lawsoc-ni.org
**Categories:** Legal

The Law Society regulates the solicitors' profession in Northern Ireland with the aim of protecting the public. If you're looking for a lawyer, it can direct you to one of its members.

# LEADER

See Irish Leader Network.

# LEAP ENTERPRISE PLATFORM PROGRAMME

Enterprise Acceleration Centre, Limerick Institute of Technology, Moylish Park, Limerick  T: (061) 490152  E: leap@lit.ie  W: www.leap.ie
C: Graham Royce, Programme Manager
**Categories:** Incubator; Mentoring; Training

The Enterprise Acceleration Centre at LIT offers the LEAP EPP, a one-year full-time training and enterprise support programme aimed at the needs of entrepreneurs in a business start-up situation.

# LEGAL-ISLAND

Steeple Road, Antrim, BT41 1DN  T: (028) 9446 3888  F: (028) 9446 3516
E: legal@legal-island.com  W: www.legal-island.com
**Categories:** Cross-Border; Information; Legal

The leading source for legal information and advice relevant to both Northern Ireland and the Republic of Ireland.

## LEITRIM INTEGRATED DEVELOPMENT COMPANY LTD

Church Street, Drumshambo, Co Leitrim  T: (071) 964 1770  F: (071) 964
1741  E: info@ldco.ie  W: www.ldco.ie  C: Tom Lavin, CEO
**Categories:** Community & Rural Development

Leitrim Integrated Development Company is supported under
LEADER and the Local Development Social Inclusion Programme in
achieving local development through the promotion of sustainable
enterprise.

## LEITRIM COUNTY ENTERPRISE BOARD

Carrick-on-Shannon Business Park, Dublin Road, Carrick-on-Shannon,
Co Leitrim  T: (071) 962 0450  F: (071) 962 1491
E: info@leitrimenterprise.ie  W: www.leitrimenterprise.ie
C: Joe Lowe, CEO
**Categories:** Debt; Equity; Grants; Information; Mentoring; Training

Leitrim County Enterprise Board seeks to stimulate and support the
indigenous business development potential in Co. Leitrim with the
creation of new, sustainable employment opportunities.

## LETTERKENNY INSTITUTE OF TECHNOLOGY

Port Road, Letterkenny, Co Donegal  T: (074) 918 6000  F: (074) 918 6005
E: john.bonnar@lyit.ie  W: www.lyit.ie
C: John Andy Bonnar, Head of Development
**Categories:** Consulting; Incubator; R & D; Training; Workspace

Through its Development Office, Letterkenny IT provides training
programmes (including the Céim Enterprise Development Programme),
consultancy and research expertise to meet the education and
development needs of the industrial and commercial sector and wider
community, while the Business Development Centre provides campus-
based incubation facilities to start-up companies.

# LIFFEY TRUST

117–126 Upper Sheriff Street, Dublin 1  T: (01) 836 4645  F: (01) 855 6798
E: liffey-trust@clubi.ie  W: www.liffey-trust.com
C: Michelle McDermott

**Categories:** Business Plans; Consulting; Incubator; Marketing; Training

Financed entirely by its own efforts and without Government assistance, the Liffey Trust helps to prepare business plans, feasibility studies and grant applications, free of charge; advises on raising finance; provides guidance on how to set up accountancy and control systems; provides free management and marketing consultancy; takes care of bureaucratic procedures; and rents incubator units at reduced rents until enterprises are established.

# LIMERICK CITY ENTERPRISE BOARD

The Granary, Michael Street, Limerick  T: (061) 312611  F: (061) 311889
E: info@limceb.ie  W: www.limceb.ie  C: Eamon Ryan, CEO

**Categories:** Debt; Equity; Grants; Information; Mentoring; Training

Limerick City CEB's mission is to facilitate the creation of sustainable jobs through the development of an Enterprise Culture and the provision of support to enterprise in Limerick City. It offers financial assistance and advice, business guidance and training support.

# LIMERICK COUNTY ENTERPRISE BOARD

Lissanalta House, Dooradoyle, Co. Limerick T: (061) 496 520  F: (061) 582 954 E: info@lcoeb.iol.ie  W: www.lcoeb.ie  C: Ned Toomey, CEO

**Categories:** Debt; Equity; Grants; Information; Mentoring; Training

Limerick County Enterprise Board assists entrepreneurs in developing a business from the initial idea to start-up and at all stages of its development.

# LIMERICK ENTERPRISE DEVELOPMENT PARTNERSHIP

Roxboro Road, Limerick  T: (061) 469060  F: (061) 313786
E: lmcelligott@ledp.ie W: www.ledp.ie  C: Liam McElligott, CEO

**Categories:** Workspace

LEDP operates an Enterprise Centre on the site of the former Krups factory and works closely with other regeneration agencies in Limerick.

## LIMERICK INSTITUTE OF TECHNOLOGY

Moylish Park, Limerick  T: (061) 208208  F: (061) 208209
E: information@lit.ie  W: www.lit.ie  C: Colin McLean, Head of External
Services / Dr Fergal Barry, Head of Development
**Categories:** Consulting; Incubator; R & D; Training

Limerick Institute of Technology is a centre for research and development in the Mid-West region. Its Enterprise Acceleration Centre provides the LEAP Enterprise Platform Programme and other programmes and supports the development of entrepreneurial skills among students in LIT.

## LINC CENTRE

IT Blanchardstown, Blanchardstown Road North, Dublin 15
T: (01) 886 1186  E: assumpta.harvey@itb.ie  W: www.itblinc.ie
C: Assumpta Harvey
**Categories:** Incubator; Training

The LINC Centre at IT Blanchardstown links academia and industry through: support for start-up businesses; office space, business support, access to college resources and training; applied research / collaborative research between college and industry; and industry training programmes to improve the competitiveness of SMEs in the region. It also offers the M50 Enterprise Platform Programme.

## LISBURN ENTERPRISE ORGANISATION LTD

Enterprise Crescent, Ballinderry Road, Lisburn, Co Antrim BT28 2BP
T: (028) 9266 1160  F: (028) 9260 3084  E: centre@lisburn-enterprise.co.uk
W: www.lisburn-enterprise.co.uk
**Categories:** Consulting; Information; Training; Workspace

Lisburn Enterprise Organisation is a member of Enterprise Northern Ireland. It is a business information and advice service, offering assistance to both new and established businesses within Co. Antrim.

# LOMBARD

Ulster Bank Group Centre, Georges Quay, Dublin 2
T: (01) 608 5499 / (1850) 215 000  W: www.lombard.ie
**Categories:** Debt

Part of the RBS Group, Lombard provides asset finance, through hire purchase, contract hire and leasing.

# LONGFORD COMMUNITY RESOURCES LTD

Longford Community Enterprise Centre, Templemichael, Ballinalee
Road, Longford  T: (043) 334 5555  F: (043) 334 4093
E: enquiries@lcrl.ie  W: www.lcrl.ie  C: Adrian Greene, Manager
**Categories:** Community & Rural Development

Longford Community Resources is supported under LEADER and the Local Development Social Inclusion Programme in achieving local development through the promotion of sustainable enterprise.

# LONGFORD COUNTY ENTERPRISE BOARD

Longford Community Enterprise Centre, Templemichael, Ballinalee
Road, Longford  T: (043) 334 2757  F: (043) 334 0968
E: info@longfordceb.ie  W: www.longfordceb.ie  C: Michael Nevin, CEO
**Categories:** Debt; Equity; Grants; Information; Mentoring; Training

Longford CEB provides a full range of financial and other supports for micro-enterprises in its area.

# LOUTH COUNTY ENTERPRISE BOARD

Enterprise House, Quayside Business Park, Mill Street, Dundalk,
Co Louth  T: (042) 932 7099  F: (042) 932 7101  E: info@lceb.ie
W: www.lceb.ie  C: Ronan Dennedy, CEO
**Categories:** Cross-Border; Debt; Equity; Grants; Information;
Mentoring; Training; Women

Louth CEB provides business support and services to micro-enterprises in the county, including business information, training and mentoring, management development / international product transfer programmes and financial assistance.

## LOUTH CRAFTMARK

Highlanes Gallery, St Laurence Street, Drogheda, Co Louth  T: (041) 980
3283  E: shop@louthcraftmark.com  W: www.louthcraftmark.com
C: Sarah Daly, Crafts Development Officer
**Categories:** Information; Training; Website

Louth Craftmark showcases the work of local artists and craftspeople. It
has a strategic focus to tackle economic hardship, entrepreneurship
skills deficits and social barriers faced by craftspeople living and
working in Co. Louth.

## LOUTH LEADER PARTNERSHIP

Market Street, Ardee, Co Louth  T: (041) 685 7375  F: (041) 685 6787
E: info@louthleader.com  W: www.louthleader.com  C: John Butler
**Categories:** Community & Rural Development

Louth LEADER Partnership is supported under LEADER and the Local
Development Social Inclusion Programme in achieving local
development through the promotion of sustainable enterprise.

## M50 ENTERPRISE PLATFORM PROGRAMME

LINC Centre, Institute of Technology Blanchardstown, Blanchardstown
Road North, Blanchardstown, Dublin 15 T: (01) 885 1000
F: (01) 885 1001 E: info@itb.ie  W: www.itb.ie
C: Claire Quigley, Programme Manager
**Categories:** Incubator; Mentoring; Training

IT Blanchardstown's LINC Centre runs the M50 Enterprise Platform
Programme, which aims to provide the participants with the skills to
develop a business idea to launch-stage or, in the case of businesses
already trading, to strengthen their market and trading position.
Participants must have an innovative business idea and a third level
qualification in any discipline.

# MAC

Suparule House, Lonsdale Road, Plassey Technology Park, Limerick
T: (061) 334699  F: (061) 338500  E: info@mac.ie  W: www.mac.ie
C: Dr John J. O'Flaherty, MD
**Categories:** Consulting; R & D

MAC, the National Microelectronics Application Centre, is Ireland's primary electronics / software concept-to-product development company. It develops and web-enables products / services for entrepreneurs and industry, and provides complete end-to-end solutions that integrate embedded electronics, wireless communications and intelligent transactional web services.

# MACLACHLAN & DONALDSON

47 Merrion Square, Dublin 2  T: (01) 676 3465  F: (01) 661 2083
E: mail@maclachlan.ie  W: www.maclachlan.ie
**Categories:** Intellectual Property

MacLachlan & Donaldson are European Patent and Community Trade Mark attorneys.

# MALLUSK ENTERPRISE PARK

Mallusk Drive, Newtownabbey BT36 4GN  T: (028) 9083 8860
F: (028) 9084 1525  E: info@mallusk.org  W: www.mallusk.org
C: Melanie Humphrey, Chief Executive
**Categories:** Consulting; Information; Training; Workspace

Mallusk Enterprise Park provides help and support to over 100 new businesses each year and has won several awards for its work. It is a member of Enterprise Northern Ireland.

# MAMUT LTD

1 Regus House, Harcourt Centre, Harcourt Road, Dublin 2  T: (1800)
944688  E: info@mamut.ie  W: www.mamut.com/ie/
**Categories:** Accountants

Mamut is a leading European provider of complete, integrated software solutions and internet services for SMEs, including accounting software.

## MARINE INSTITUTE

80 Harcourt Street, Dublin 2  T: (01) 476 6500  F: (01) 478 4988
W: www.marine.ie
**Categories:** Information; R & D

The Marine Institute is the national agency responsible for undertaking, co-ordinating, promoting and assisting in marine research and development, and providing such services related to marine research and development that, in the opinion of the Institute, will promote economic development, create employment and protect the environment.

## MARKETING CENTRE FOR SMALL BUSINESS

University of Limerick, Limerick  T: (061) 202 986  F: (061) 202 588
E: mcsb.info@ul.ie  W: www.mcsb.ul.ie
C: Marguerite O'Rourke, Manager
**Categories:** Consulting; Marketing

The Marketing Centre for Small Business (MCSB) is a marketing and market research consultancy, which offers marketing assistance to start-up companies operating in the Shannon Region. The MCSB is a campus company of the University of Limerick, operated with the assistance of the Department of Management & Marketing.

## MARKETING INSTITUTE OF IRELAND

Marketing House, South County Business Park, Leopardstown, Dublin 18  T: (01) 295 2355  F: (01) 295 2453  E: info@mii.ie  W: www.mii.ie
C: Tom Trainor, Chief Executive
**Categories:** Information; Marketing; Training

The Marketing Institute is the professional representative body for marketing people in Ireland. Its aim is to set, promote and develop high standards of marketing practice in Irish business.

## MAYO COUNTY ENTERPRISE BOARD

Top Floor, The Cedar Building, Moneen, Castlebar, Co Mayo
T: (094) 902 2887 E: info@mayoceb.com  W: www.mayoceb.com
C: Frank Fullard, CEO
**Categories:** Debt; Equity; Grants; Information; Mentoring; Training

The Mayo County Enterprise Board offers a range of financial supports, business advice, counselling and management development training to SMEs based in County Mayo.

## MAYO NORTH EAST LEADER PARTNERSHIP COMPANY TEO

Lower Main Street, Foxford, Co. Mayo  T: (094) 925 6745
E: monicaomalley@mnelp.com  W: www.mnelp.com
C: Monica O'Malley, CEO
**Categories:** Community & Rural Development

Mayo North East Leader is supported under the Local Development Social Inclusion Programme and LEADER in achieving local development through the promotion of sustainable enterprise. It also has offices in Kiltimagh and Ballina.

## MAZARS

Block 3, Harcourt Centre, Harcourt Road, Dublin 2  T: (01) 449 4400
F: (01) 475 0030  W: www.mazars.ie  C: Joe Carr, Managing Partner
**Categories:** Accountants; Consulting

Mazars is a leading firm of chartered accountants and business advisors, providing services in accounting audit, tax, consulting and corporate finance, providing services to companies in all sectors of Irish business, with a specific market focus and team dedicated to the SME sector.

## MEATH PARTNERSHIP

Tom Blake House, Bective Street, Kells, Co Meath  T: (046) 928 0790
F: (046) 924 9338  E: info@meathpartnership.ie
W: www.meathpartnership.ie  C: Michael Ludlow, CEO
**Categories:** Community & Rural Development

Meath Partnership is supported under the Local Development Social Inclusion Programme and LEADER in achieving local development through the promotion of sustainable enterprise.

## MEATH COUNTY ENTERPRISE BOARD

Navan Enterprise Centre, Trim Road, Navan, Co Meath  T: (046) 907
8400  F: (046) 902 7356  E: mhceb@meath.com  W: www.meath.com
C: Hugh Reilly, CEO

**Categories:** Debt; Equity; Grants; Information; Mentoring; Training

Meath CEB assists enterprise development in the county through the
creation of an enterprise culture, the provision of advice and support
and the granting of financial aid.

## MEITHEAL FORBARTHA NA GAELTACHTA TEO

An Mhainistir, An Daingean, Co Chiarraí  T: (066) 915 2280  F: (066) 915
1790  E: eolas@mfg.ie  W: www.mfg.ie  C: Antaine M Ó Sé

**Categories:** Community & Rural Development

Meitheal Forbatha na Gaeltachta is supported under LEADER and the
Local Development Social Inclusion Programme in achieving local
development through the promotion of sustainable enterprise. Sub-
groups of MFG include: Páirtíocht Gaeltacht Thír Chonaill, Dhún na
nGall; Comhlucht Forbatha Acla, Co Mhuigheo; Comhar Dhuibhne, Co
Chiarraí and Meitheal Mhuscraí, Co Chorcaí.

## MEITHEAL MHAIGH EO

Lower Main Street, Foxford, Co Mayo  T: (094) 56745  F: (094) 56749
E: meithealm@eircom.net  C: Justin Sammon, Manager

**Categories:** Community & Rural Development; Information; Training

An Area Partnership, currently delivering the Local Development
Social Inclusion Programme as part of the Government's National
Development Plan.

## MIDLANDS & WEST ENTERPRISE PROGRAMME

Midlands Innovation & Research Centre, Athlone Institute of
Technology, Dublin Road, Athlone, Co Westmeath / Innovation in
Business Centre, GMIT, Galway  T: (090) 647 1882  F: (090) 644 2570
E: mlonergan@ait.ie  W: www.mirc.ie
C: Michael Lonergan, Centre Manager

**Categories:** Incubator; Training

The Midlands & West Enterprise Programme is a 12-month incubation
programme run jointly by Athlone IT and GMIT.

## MOMENTUM

NISoft House, Ravenhill Business Park, Ravenhill Road, Belfast BT6
8AW  T: (028) 9045 0101  F: (028) 9045 2123  E: info@momentumni.org
W: www.momentumni.org
**Categories:** Information; Networking

Momentum represents Northern Ireland companies with a common interest in the growth and development of the software industry. Membership includes software developers, in-house computing departments, hardware suppliers, computer services companies, universities and colleges, and consultants.

## MONAGHAN COUNTY ENTERPRISE BOARD

Unit 9, M:TEK Building, Knockaconny, Monaghan T: (047) 71818
F: (047) 84786  E: info@mceb.ie  W: www.mceb.ie  C: John McEntegart
**Categories:** Debt; Equity; Grants; Information; Mentoring; Training

The role of the Monaghan County Enterprise Board is to develop indigenous potential and stimulate economic activity at local level, primarily through the provision of financial and technical assistance, as well as ongoing non-financial enterprise supports.

## MONAGHAN INTEGRATED DEVELOPMENT COMPANY

Monaghan Road, Castleblaney, Co Monaghan  T: (042) 974 9500
F: (042) 974 9504  E: info@monaghanpartnership.ie  W: www.planet.ie
C: Gabriel O'Connell
**Categories:** Community & Rural Development

Monaghan Integrated Development is supported under LEADER and the Local Development Social Inclusion Programme in achieving local development through the promotion of sustainable enterprise.

## MOUNTMELLICK DEVELOPMENT ASSOCIATION

Irishtown, Mountmellick, Co Laois  T: (057) 862 4525  F: (057) 864 4343
E: info@moutmellickdevelopment.com
W: www.mountmellickdevelopment.com  C: Mary Dolan, Manager
**Categories:** Community & Rural Development

Mountmellick Development Association works to improve the social, cultural and economic development of the town of Mountmellick and its surrounding area.

# MOVETOIRELAND.COM

E: info@irishireland.com  W: www.movetoireland.com
**Categories:** Information; Inwards Investment; Website

MoveToIreland.com provides useful information (from an American now resident in Ireland) on preparing, making and surviving the move. Part of the site is free; part available only on subscription (US$45 pa).

# MOYLE ENTERPRISE COMPANY LTD

61 Leyland Road, Ballycastle, Co Antrim BT54 6EZ T: (028) 2076 3737
F: (028) 2076 9690  E: info@moyle-enterprise.com
W: www.moyle-enterprise.com  C: Marc McGerty, Manager
**Categories:** Information; Training; Workspace

Moyle Enterprise is a member of Enterprise Northern Ireland. It is the Local Enterprise Agency for Moyle, working in close partnership with Moyle District Council to deliver a co-ordinated approach to local economic development, providing support, help and guidance for entrepreneurs thinking about starting a business right through to businesses looking to become global.

# NATIONAL ASSOCIATION OF BUILDING CO-OPERATIVES LTD

33 Lower Baggot Street, Dublin 2  T: (01) 661 2877  F: (01) 661 4462
E: admin@nabco.ie  : www.nabco.ie
**Categories:** Co-operatives; Information

One of the organisations that provides Model Rules for the formation of worker and community co-operatives.

# NATIONAL COLLEGE OF IRELAND

Mayor Street, IFSC, Dublin 1  T: (01) 449 8500  F: (01) 497 2200
E: info@ncirl.ie  W: www.ncirl.ie  C: Bertie Kelly
**Categories:** Incubator; Information; Training

Through its new campus in the IFSC, its network of 40 off-campus centres, on-site educational hubs within industry, and online programme, NCI provides leading edge programmes in Business, Management, Financial Services, Informatics, Humanities, and related fields. It also operates a Business Incubation Centre at its IFSC site.

## NATIONAL GUILD OF MASTER CRAFTSMEN

3 Greenmount Lane, Harolds Cross, Dublin 12  T: (01) 473 2543
F: (01) 473 2018  E: info@nationalguild.ie  W: www.nationalguild.ie
**Categories:** Information; Regulator & Standards

An organisation dedicated to achieving the highest standards of quality and workmanship in all trades and disciplines. It operates a referral system for members.

## NATIONAL IRISH BANK LTD

National House, Airton Road, Dublin 24  T: (01) 638 5000
F: (01) 638 5198  W: www.nib.ie  C: Brian Leydon
**Categories:** Debt

NIB offers a range of banking facilities to assist in the creation and development of small and medium-sized businesses. Access is through any of NIB's branches or the specialist regional offices.

## NATIONAL SOFTWARE CENTRE

NSC Campus, Mahon, Cork  T: (021) 230 7000  F: (021) 230 7020
E: info@nsc-campus.com  W: www.nsc-campus.com
C: Sue O'Brien, Facilities Manager
**Categories:** Workspace

The Centre has been funded on a public-private partnership basis, and is managed by Cork Business Innovation Centre as a software development hub in the southern region.

## NATIONAL STANDARDS AUTHORITY OF IRELAND

1 Swift Square, Northwood, Santry, Dublin 9  T: (01) 807 3800
F: (01) 807 3838  E: info@nsai.ie  W: www.nsai.ie
**Categories:** Information; Regulator & Standards

NSAI formulates, publishes and sells Irish Standards, part of the harmonised European and worldwide system of standards in which NSAI is a designated 'National Standards Body. It also assists industry to understand and meet the technical, quality and safety requirements of harmonised European and international standards in the domestic and overseas markets and provides a comprehensive quality auditing and product certification service for industry and commerce in accordance with current European and international practice.

# NATIONAL TECHNOLOGY PARK

Limerick  T: (061) 336555  F: (061) 338065
E: corcoranj@shannondevelopment.ie  W: www.shannon-dev.ie
C: Joan Corcoran, Marketing Executive
**Categories:** Workspace

The National Technology Park is home to over 90 high-technology and knowledge-based companies, employing close to 5,000 skilled people and consists of 30+ buildings with a total floor area of circa 1.5 million sq.ft. It includes Shannon Development's InnovationWorks, part of Shannon Development's Knowledge Network.

# NATIONAL UNIVERSITY OF IRELAND GALWAY

University Road, Galway  T: (091) 524411  F: (091) 525700
E: joe.watson@mis.nuigalway.ie  W: www.nuigalway.ie
C: Dr Joe Watson, Industrial Liaison Officer
**Categories:** Community & Rural Development; Incubator; R & D;
Training

NUIG offers part-time Programmes in Rural Development, aimed at community leaders and development agents. It also provides an incubator and R & D services to industry.

# NCB VENTURES

3 George's Dock, IFSC, Dublin 1  T: (01) 611 5611  F: (01) 611 5766
E: will.prendergast@ncb.ie  W: www.ncb-ventures.com
C: Will Prendergast
**Categories:** Equity

NCB Ventures invests equity capital in fast-growing, private unquoted companies on a long-term basis. The €75 million Ulster Bank Diageo Venture Fund (managed by NCB Ventures) is actively seeking new opportunities in an investment range of €1 million to €5 million from sectors including ICT, support services, consumer products and services, leisure and fitness, cleantech, waste services, medtech and engineering. NCB Ventures invests across all development stages from early stage and expansion through to management buy-out.

# NETWORK IRELAND

P.O. Box 306, Naas, Co Kildare  T: (01) 499 1086
E: jacquieh@eircom.net  W: www.networkireland.ie
C: Jacquie Hennessey, National President
**Categories:** Information; Networking; Training; Women

Network is a national organisation for women in business, management, the professions and the arts. It facilitates women in the promotion and development of their careers through regular meetings and educational seminars.

# NEWRY & MOURNE ENTERPRISE AGENCY

Enterprise House, WIN Business Park, Canal Quay, Newry, Co Down
BT35 6PH  T: (028) 3026 7011  F: (028) 3026 1316  E: info@nmea.net
W: www.nmea.net  C: Conor Patterson, Chief Executive
**Categories:** Cross-Border; Debt; Information; Training; Workspace

Newry & Mourne Enterprise Agency is a member of Enterprise Northern Ireland. It offers a range of services to support start-up and existing businesses.

# NIBUSINESSINFO.CO.UK

W: www.nibusinessinfo.co.uk
**Categories:** Information; Website

An online business advice service provided by Invest Northern Ireland.

# NORIBIC

Northland Building, NWIFHE, Strand Road, Derry BT48 7AY
T: (028) 7126 4242  F: (028) 7126 9025  E: noribic@nwifhe.ac.uk
W: www.noribic.com  C: Dr Bernard R Toal, Chief Executive
**Categories:** Business Plans; Grants; Incubator; Information; Marketing; Training

NORIBIC, the Business Innovation Centre in Derry, provides support services for those seeking to start their own businesses or to develop existing businesses into sustainable, well-managed innovative businesses. It offers: business planning; acquisition of business start and development capital; market planning and development; development of innovative management techniques; creativity and innovation audits; 'Start Your Own Business' courses; and finance.

## NORTH & EAST KERRY DEVELOPMENT

Clash, Tralee, Co Kerry  T: (066) 718 0190  E: info@nekd.ie
W: www.nekd.ie  C: Eamonn O'Reilly, CEO
**Categories:** Community & Rural Development

North & East Kerry Development is supported under LEADER and the Local Development Social Inclusion Programme in achieving local development through the promotion of sustainable enterprise.

## NORTH CITY BUSINESS CENTRE LTD

2 Duncairn Gardens, Belfast BT15 2GG  T: (028) 9074 7470
F: (028) 9074 6565  E: mailbox@north-city.co.uk
W: www.north-city.co.uk  C: Michael McCorry, Manager
**Categories:** Information; Training; Workspace

North City Business Centre is a member of Enterprise Northern Ireland. It encourages the development of small and medium-sized businesses in the community, thereby creating employment and providing a focus for the social and economic regeneration of the district.

## NORTH DOWN DEVELOPMENT ORGANISATION LTD

Enterprise House, 2-4 Balloo Avenue, Balloo Industrial Estate, Bangor, Co Down BT19 7QT  T: (028) 9127 1525  F: (028) 9127 0080
E: mail@nddo.co.uk  W: www.nddo.co.uk  C: Lynne Vance, CEO
**Categories:** Information; Training; Workspace

North Down Development Organisation is a member of Enterprise Northern Ireland. Its objectives are the development of enterprise in North Down and assistance in the creation of jobs within the Borough.

## NORTH EAST RURAL DEVELOPMENT PROGRAMME

Ecos Centre, Kernohan's Lane, Ballymena, BT43 7QA  T: (028) 2563 8263
F: (028) 2563 8263  E: northeastrdp@ballymena.gov.uk
W: www.northeastrdp.com  C: Andrew McAlister, Strategy Manager
**Categories:** Community & Rural Development

The Northern Ireland Rural Development Programme 2007-2013 is delivered in the North East region using a 'LEADER' approach by a Joint Committee representing all five Councils and implemented by a Local Action Group. Ballymena Borough Council acts as the administrative Council with responsibility for finance and administration.

## NORTH TIPPERARY LEADER PARTNERSHIP

c/o Roscrea 2000 Ltd, Community Resource Centre, New Line, Roscrea,
Co. Tipperary  T: (0505) 23379  E: info@ntlp.ie  C: Michael Murray, CEO
**Categories:** Community & Rural Development

North Tipperary LEADER Partnership is supported under LEADER
and the Local Development Social Inclusion Programme in achieving
local development through the promotion of sustainable enterprise.

## NORTH WEST MARKETING

Skeoge Industrial Estate, Beraghmore Road, Londonderry BT48 8SE
T: (028) 7135 2693  F: (028) 7135 6293  E: info@north-westmarketing.com
W: www.north-westmarketing.com  C: John McGowan, Chief Executive
**Categories:** Consulting; Information; Marketing; Social Economy;
Training

A member of Enterprise Northern Ireland, North West Marketing
provides supports for entrepreneurs looking to set up a business.
Having opened an office in China in 2006, it provides a sourcing service
to companies looking to export or import from these markets.

## NORTHERN BANK LTD

Donegall Square West, Belfast BT1 6JS  T: (028) 9024 5277
F: (028) 9023 1349  W: www.nbonline.co.uk
**Categories:** Debt

As well as traditional banking services, Northern Bank offers specialist
services in foreign exchange, leasing and hire purchase, debtor finance,
corporate banking and agriculture.

## NORTHERN IRELAND CENTRE FOR ENTREPRENEURSHIP

University of Ulster, Shore Road, Newtownabbey, BT37 0QB
T: (028) 9036 6011  F: (028) 9036 6015  E: nicent@ulster.ac.uk
W: www.ulster.ac.uk/nicent/
**Categories:** Information; Training

NICENT is led by the University of Ulster, in partnership with Queen's
University Belfast. Its primary aim is to promote and support
entrepreneurship in science and technology subjects. It also aims to
embed a culture of entrepreneurship within the university community.

## NORTHERN IRELAND CHAMBER OF COMMERCE & INDUSTRY

22 Great Victoria Street, Belfast BT2 7BJ  T: (028) 9024 4113  F: (028) 9024
7024  E: mail@northernirelandchamber.com  W: www.nicci.co.uk
**Categories:** Information; Networking

NICCI represents 4,000 member businesses across Northern Ireland. It
provides members with a broad range of services and events.

## NORTHERN IRELAND FOOD & DRINK ASSOCIATION

Belfast Mills, 71-75 Percy Street, Belfast BT13 2HW  T: (028) 9024 1010
F: (028) 9024 0500  E: info@nifda.co.uk  W: www.nifda.co.uk
C: Michael Bell, Executive Director
**Categories:** Information; Marketing; Networking; Training

NIFDA is a voluntary organisation committed to helping Northern
Ireland food and beverage companies compete successfully and to
represent and promote their interests. It was established to provide
services to enhance, promote, inform, educate and develop member
businesses.

## NORTHERN IRELAND SCIENCE PARK

The Innovation Centre, Queen's Road, Queen's Island, Belfast, BT3 9DT
T: (028) 9073 7800  F: (028) 9073 7801  E: info@nisp.co.uk
W: www.nisp.co.uk  C: Norman Apsley, CEO
**Categories:** R & D; Workspace

NISP is headquartered at the main Science Park site at Queen's Island,
Belfast but aims to create a network of science park facilities throughout
Northern Ireland, with a thriving community of tenant businesses
seeking to exploit the university research base with industrial
applications and enabling tenant companies to focus on knowledge-
based entrepreneurialism.

## NORTHERN IRELAND STATISTICS & RESEARCH AGENCY

McAuley House, 2-14 Castle Street, Belfast BT1 1SA  T: (028) 9034 8100
E: info.nisra@dfpni.gov.uk  W: www.nisra.gov.uk
**Categories:** Information

NISRA is an Executive Agency within the Department of Finance and Personnel. It provides statistics, social research and registration services, and is responsible for the census of population.

## NORTHERN IRELAND TOURIST BOARD

59 North Street, Belfast BT1 1NB  T: (028) 9023 1221  F: (028) 9024 0960
E: info@nitb.com  W: www.discovernorthernireland.com
**Categories:** Grants; Information; Marketing; Tourism Development

NITB provides funding for marketing tourism projects in Northern Ireland.

## NORTHSIDE PARTNERSHIP

Coolock Development Centre, Bunratty Drive, Coolock, Dublin 17
T: (01) 848 5630  F: (01) 848 5661  E: cepta.dowling@northsidepartnership.ie
W: www.northsidepartnership.ie  C: Cepta Dowling
**Categories:** Community & Rural Development; Information; Training;
Workspace

The Northside Partnership provides an enterprise support service to unemployed local people. It is supported under the Local Development Social Inclusion Programme in achieving local development through the promotion of sustainable enterprise.

## NOVATION ENTERPRISE PROGRAMME

Regional Development Centre, Dundalk Institute of Technology, Dublin Road, Dundalk, Co Louth  T: (042) 933 1611 / 937 0413  F: (042) 933 1163
E: garrett.duffy@dkit.ie  W: www.rdc.ie  C: Garrett Duffy
**Categories:** Incubator; Training

The Novation programme is designed to assist entrepreneurs and existing small companies with technology-based product or service ideas. Entrepreneurs selected to participate in the programme are offered support services to help them through the early stages of business development.

# NOVAUCD

Belfield Innovation Park, University College Dublin, Belfield, Dublin 4
T: (01) 716 3700  F: (01) 716 3709  E: nova@ucd.ie  W: www.novaucd.ie
C: Dr Pat Frain, Director
**Categories:** Incubator; Intellectual Property; R&D

NovaUCD is an innovation and technology transfer centre on the UCD campus, providing support for entrepreneurs and campus companies. NovaUCD is also responsible for the management of intellectual property arising from UCD research programmes.

# NOVUS MODUS

Level 1, Block D, ESB Head Office, 27 Lower Fitzwilliam Street, Dublin 2
T: (01) 702 7905  F: (01) 669 2438 W: www.novusmodus.com
**Categories:** Equity

Novus Modus is a €200m fund, whose sole investor is the ESB, and whose mission is to provide capital, support and knowledge to companies, projects and management teams in the clean energy and energy efficiency sectors.

# OAK TREE PRESS

19 Rutland Street, Cork  T: (021) 431 3855  F: (021) 431 3496
E: brian.okane@oaktreepress.com  W: www.oaktreepress.com
C: Brian O'Kane, Managing Director
**Categories:** Information; Publications; Training; Website

Ireland's leading business book publisher, focussed on titles relevant to Irish SMEs, many of them standards in their field. Oak Tree Press is now an international developer and publisher of enterprise training and support materials. It also offers training for entrepreneurs – see website.

# OFFALY COUNTY ENTERPRISE BOARD

Enterprise House, Cormac Street, Tullamore, Co Offaly  T: (057) 935 2971  F: (057) 935 2972  E: info@offalyceb.ie  W: www.offalyceb.ie
C: Seán Ryan, CEO
**Categories:** Debt; Equity; Grants; Information; Mentoring; Training

The Offaly County Enterprise Board develops and supports local entrepreneurship and enterprise within an integrated county action plan so as to build a local economy of real strength and permanence.

## OFFALY INTEGRATED LOCAL DEVELOPMENT COMPANY

Millennium House, Main Street, Tullamore, Co Offaly  T: (057) 935 2467
/ 932 2850  F: (057) 935 2574  E: info@offalyldc.ie  W: www.offalyldc.ie
C: Carmel Ormond
**Categories:** Community & Rural Development

Offaly Integrated Local Development is supported under LEADER and the Local Development Social Inclusion Programme in achieving local development through the promotion of sustainable enterprise.

## OMAGH ENTERPRISE COMPANY LTD

Omagh Business Complex, Gortrush Industrial Estate, Great Northern Road, Omagh, Co Tyrone BT78 5LU  T: (028) 8224 9494  F: (028) 8224 9451  E: info@oecl.co.uk W: www.oecl.co.uk  C: Nicholas O'Shiel, CEO
**Categories:** Information; Training; Workspace

Omagh Enterprise Company is a member of Enterprise Northern Ireland. It offers a range of services to support start-ups and existing businesses.

## OPTIMUM RESULTS LTD

The Business Centre, Blackthorn Business Park, Dundalk, Co. Louth
T: (042) 933 3033  F: (042) 933 3233  E: info@optimumresults.ie
W: www.optimumresults.ie  C: Aidan Harte, Managing director
**Categories:** Consulting; Training

Optimum Results provides consulting and training for SMEs.

## ORGANIC COLLEGE

Dromcollogher, Co Limerick  T: (063) 83604  F: (063) 83903
E: oifig@eircom.net  W: www.organiccollege.com
**Categories:** Training

The Organic College offers courses in organic horticulture and practical sustainability.

## ORMEAU ENTERPRISES

8 Cromac Avenue, Belfast BT7 2AJ  T: (028) 9033 9906  F: (028) 9033 9937
E: info@ormeaubusinesspark.com  W: www.ormeaubusinesspark.com
C: Patricia McNeill, Business Development Manager
**Categories:** Information; Training; Workspace

Ormeau Enterprises is a member of Enterprise Northern Ireland. Its aims are to: promote enterprise awareness; assist in the development of new business start-ups and the further expansion of existing businesses; encourage entrepreneurs to fulfil their potential; and respond to local needs by supporting economic development in the area.

## ORTUS

Twin Spires Centre, Curran House, 155 Northumberland Street, Belfast
BT13 2JF  T: (028) 9031 1002  F: (028) 9031 1005  E: hq@ortus.org
W: www.ortus.org
**Categories:** Consulting; Information; Training; Workspace

ORTUS is a member of Enterprise Northern Ireland. Since its inception as a commercial social enterprise in 1988, it has been delivering quality business training and development programmes and providing high quality commercial units for rent.

## OSK ACCOUNTANTS & BUSINESS CONSULTANTS

East Point Plaza, East Point, Dublin 3  T: (01) 439 4200  F: (01) 439 4299
E: advice@osk.ie  W: www.osk.ie
**Categories:** Accountants; Consulting

OSK Small Business Support is the leading supplier of audit and taxation services in the SME market and provides a full-service package that assists and supports clients in all aspects of their business from start-up to development and expansion. OSK also provides advice on all areas of starting your own business including company set-up, business plans, raising finance, audit, and taxation services.

# PALO ALTO SOFTWARE UK

19 Catherine Place, Victoria, London SW1E 6DX  E: info@paloalto.co.uk
W: www.paloalto.co.uk
**Categories:** Business Plans

Palo Alto Software Ltd is the developer of the UK and Irish editions of
Business Plan Pro and Business Plan Premier, the award-winning
business planning software. See also bplans.ie.

# PARTAS

Bolbrook Enterprise Centre, Avonmore Road, Tallaght, Dublin 24
T: (01) 414 5700  F: (01) 414 5799  E: ltwamley@partas.ie
W: www.partas.ie  C: Linda Twamley, Enterprise Officer
**Categories:** Community & Rural Development; Social Economy;
Training; Workspace

Partas' aim is to build an inclusive and thriving community by being a
leading source of excellence in development of local enterprise and of
social economy.

# PATENTS OFFICE

Government Buildings, Hebron Road, Kilkenny  T: (056) 772 0111
F: (056) 772 0100  E: patlib@entemp.irlgov.ie
W: www.patentsoffice.ie  C: Yvonne Cassidy
**Categories:** Information; Intellectual Property

The principal statutory functions of the Office are: the granting of
patents; the registration of industrial designs and trade marks;
providing information in relation to patents, designs and trade marks;
and certain limited functions under the Copyright Act in relation to
copyright disputes.

# PAUL PARTNERSHIP LIMERICK

Unit 25a, The Tait Centre, Dominic Street, Limerick  T: (061) 419388
F: (061) 418098  E: info@paulpartnership.ie W: www.paulpartnership.ie
C: Anne Kavanagh, Manager
**Categories:** Community & Rural Development; Information; Training

Paul Partnership is supported under the Local Development Social
Inclusion Programme in achieving local development through the
promotion of sustainable enterprise.

## PDC

128-130 East Wall Road, Dublin 3  T: (01) 240 1300  F: (01) 240 1310
E: info@pdc.ie  W: www.pdc.ie  C: Bernadette O'Reilly
**Categories:** Equity; Incubator; Information; Training

PDC, the Project Development Centre, is an initiative of the Dublin Institute of Technology, and provides enterprise development programmes (including HotHouse), incubation space and facilities, business counselling, funding and access to R&D expertise as a package that allows entrepreneurs to start up and grow global businesses.

## PERMANENT TSB

56-59 St Stephen's Green, Dublin 2  T: (01) 669 5000
E: info@permanenttsb.ie  W: www.permanenttsb.ie
**Categories:** Debt

Though geared primarily towards the personal banking market, Permanent TSB offers current account facilities, overdrafts and loans to business customers.

## PKF O'CONNOR, LEDDY & HOLMES

Century House, Harold's Cross Road, Dublin 6W  T: (01) 496 1444
F: (01) 496 1637  E: info@pkf.ie  W: www.pkf.ie
**Categories:** Accountants

PKF O'Connor, Leddy & Holmes is a firm of chartered accountants and business consultants, which offers accountancy, taxation, business planning and funding application services to Irish companies.

## PLATO

58 Fitzwilliam Square North, Dublin 2  T: (01) 676 3973  F: (01) 676 3985
E: marion.walshe@plato.ie  W: www.plato.ie
C: Marion Walshe, Regional Manager
**Categories:** Cross-Border; Networking; Training

PLATO Ireland is a confidential business support forum and a business and management development network for owner / managers of SMEs.

# POBAL

Holbrook House, Holles Street, Dublin 2  T: (01) 240 0700  F: (01) 661
0411  E: enquiries@pobal.ie  W: www.pobal.ie
**Categories:** Enterprise Support

Pobal delivers its programmes, which support integrated local economic and social development, through Area Partnership Companies in the most disadvantaged areas of Ireland and Community Groups in non-disadvantaged areas. It administers the Local Development Social Inclusion Programme, through these Partnerships and Community Groups, on behalf of the Department of Community, Rural & Gaeltacht Affairs.

# POWERSCOURT CAPITAL PARTNERS

46 Upper Mount Street, Dublin 2  T: (01) 247 4050
W: www.powerscourt-capital.com
**Categories:** Equity

Powerscourt Capital Partners invests in high potential early-stage companies across a range of sectors, leveraging its industry experience, contacts and strategic partnerships.

# PREMIER BUSINESS CENTRES

3013 Lake Drive, CityWest, Dublin 24  T: (01) 469 3100 F: (01) 469 3115
E: info@premierbusinesscentres.com
W: www.premierbusinesscentres.com
**Categories:** Workspace

Premier Business Centres provide both serviced and unserviced office accommodation, offering traditional Georgian buildings in the heart of Dublin city centre and modern purpose-built facilities in suburban Dublin and Belfast city centre. It also offers a virtual office service, 'Premier Connection', which provides companies with a mailing address, dedicated phone number and line answering the company name.

# PRICEWATERHOUSECOOPERS

One Spencer Dock, North Wall Quay, Dublin 1  T: (01) 792 6000
F: (01) 792 6200  E: info@ie.pwc.com  W: www.pwc.ie
**Categories:** Accountants; Consulting

PricewaterhouseCoopers works with start-up entrepreneurs to develop business plans, prepare financial projections, raise finance, identify opportunities to avail of grant aid, and establish businesses in as tax-efficient a manner as possible.

# PRINCE'S TRUST NORTHERN IRELAND

Block 5, Jennymount Court, North Derby Street, Belfast BT15 3HN
T: (028) 9074 5454  E: webinfoni@princes-trust.org.uk
W: www.princes-trust.org.uk
**Categories:** Debt; Grants; Mentoring; Training; Young Enterprise

The Prince's Trust Northern Ireland is the largest cross-community charity investing in young people. It offers low interest loans, test marketing grants, bursaries and mentor support and incubation workspace. Applicants should be aged 18–30, unemployed, under-employed or of limited means; unable to raise all the necessary finance from banks, families or other sources; have completed an appropriate business training course, and have a viable business plan.

# PROFILES IRELAND

Harbour Business Centre, New Road, Kilcock, Co. Kildare
T: (01) 628 7037  F: (01) 628 7019  E: info@profilesireland.com
W: www.profilesireland.com / www.profilesinternational.com
C: Deiric McCann
**Categories:** Consulting

Profiles Ireland offers a number of online assessment tools for employers that help them to make better hiring, training, managing, and promoting decisions. The Profile answers four critical questions about a candidate for employment: Can the person do the job? Will the person do the job? Does the person have the personality to enjoy the job? Does the individual fit the job?

## PUBLIC RELATIONS CONSULTANTS ASSOCIATION

78 Merrion Square, Dublin 2 T: (01) 661 8004 F: (01) 676 4562
E: info@prca.ie W: www.prca.ie
**Categories:** Information

The Public Relations Consultant Association Ireland represents most of the PR consultancy businesses in Ireland. It can help with selection of a consultancy. The PRCA is for consultancies, while the PRII is for individual PR practitioners.

## PUBLIC RELATIONS INSTITUTE OF IRELAND

78 Merrion Square, Dublin 2 T: (01) 661 8004 F: (01) 676 4562
E: info@prii.ie W: www.prii.ie
**Categories:** Information

The Public Relations Institute of Ireland is the professional body for public relations practitioners (individuals) in Ireland. Note that the PRII is for individual PR practitioners, while the PRCA is for consultancies.

## QUBIS LTD

Northern Ireland Technology Centre, The Queen's University of Belfast, Cloreen Park, Malone Road, Belfast BT9 5HN T: (028) 9068 2321
F: (028) 9027 3015 E: info@qubis.co.uk W: www.qubis.co.uk
C: Panos Lioulias, Chief Executive
**Categories:** Equity; R & D

Qubis Ltd was established in 1984 by The Queen's University of Belfast to commercialise the University's research and development activities through the formation of 'spin-out' businesses. Qubis is an investment vehicle and holding company, which takes an equity holding in a new spin-out venture in return for an investment of cash and / or intellectual property. Qubis Ltd 'pulls through' appropriate R & D from the laboratory into the commercial market place.

## QUEEN'S UNIVERSITY BELFAST

Research & Regional Services, Lanyon North, Queen's University,
Belfast BT7 1NN  T: (028) 9027 2568  F: (028) 9027 2570  E: rrs@qub.ac.uk
W: www.qub.ac.uk/rrs/  C: Trevor Newsom, Director
**Categories:** Consulting; Incubator; R & D

Queen's University has a long-established reputation for research. The
Research & Regional Services department handles all consultancy
enquiries from business. The Northern Ireland Technology Centre, built
on the QUB campus, operates as a self-financing practical experience
centre dedicated to technology transfer. Qubis Ltd manages the
university's equity investments in campus companies.

## RABOBANK IRELAND PLC

George's Dock House, IFSC, Dublin 1  T: (01) 607 6100  F: (01) 670 1724
E: fm.ie.dublin.information@rabobank.com  W: www.rabobank.ie
**Categories:** Debt

Part of Rabobank International, Rabobank Ireland offers corporate
banking, structured finance investment banking and financial services
outsourcing.

## RATHMINES PEMBROKE COMMUNITY PARTNERSHIP

Rathmines Information Centre, 11 Wynnefield Road, Rathmines,
Dublin 6  T: (01) 496 5558  E: tara@rpcp.ie  C: Tara Smith, Manager
**Categories:** Community & Rural Development

Rathmines Pembroke Community Partnership is supported under the
Local Development Social Inclusion Programme in achieving local
development through the promotion of sustainable enterprise.

## REGISTRY OF BUSINESS NAMES

Companies Registration Office, Parnell House, 14 Parnell Square,
Dublin 1  T: (01) 804 5200  F: (01) 804 5222  E: info@cro.ie  W: www.cro.ie
**Categories:** Information; Regulator & Standards

By law, entrepreneurs are obliged to register their business with the
Registry of Business Names, or the relevant body in the case of co-
operatives, if it carries on a business under a name other than its own.
The CRO's website explains the procedures involved.

## REGISTRY OF FRIENDLY SOCIETIES

Parnell House, 14 Parnell Square, Dublin 1  T: (01) 804 5499
F: (01) 804 5498
**Categories:** Co-operatives; Information; Regulator & Standards

A co-operative society can be formed by any group of seven or more people over the age of 18, and can be registered with the Registry of Friendly Societies. The advantage of registration is limited liability. The Co-operative Development Society Ltd, Irish Co-operative Society Ltd, and National Association of Building Co-operatives Ltd have Model Rules for co-operatives that have been approved by the Registry of Friendly Societies for use by those wishing to form a co-operative.

## REVENUE COMMISSIONERS

W: www.revenue.ie
**Categories:** Information; Publications; Regulator & Standards; Website

Revenue's mission is to serve the community by fairly and efficiently collecting taxes and duties and implementing import and export controls. You can now submit returns online to the Revenue Commissioners using the Revenue Online Service (ROS) – see the Revenue website.

## ROE VALLEY ENTERPRISES LTD

Aghanloo Industrial Estate, Aghanloo Road, Limavady, Co Londonderry BT49 0HE  T: (028) 7776 2323  F: (028) 7776 5707
E: info@roevalleyenterprises.co.uk  W: www.roevalleyenterprises.com
C: Martin Devlin, Chief Executive
**Categories:** Information; Training; Workspace

Roe Valley Enterprises is a member of Enterprise Northern Ireland. Its aim is to develop enterprise within the Limavady Borough Council area by encouraging new business start-up and growth within the SME sector.

## ROSCOMMON COUNTY ENTERPRISE BOARD LTD

Library Buildings, Abbey Street, Roscommon  T: (090) 662 6263
F: (090) 662 5474  E: ceb@roscommon.ie  W: www.roscommon.ie
C: Peter Wrafter, Acting CEO
**Categories:** Debt; Equity; Grants; Information; Mentoring; Training

Roscommon County Enterprise Board is committed to the economic development of the county and, since its establishment, has provided an integrated service where business ideas have been translated into commercial reality with its assistance and guidance. As well as financial support, the CEB provides training, mentoring and other supports.

## ROSCOMMON INTEGRATED DEVELOPMENT COMPANY

The Enterprise Centre, Arigna, Carrick-on-Shannon, Co Roscommon
T: (071) 964 6186  E: mearley@iol.ie  C: Martina Earley, CEO
**Categories:** Community & Rural Development

Roscommon Integrated Development is supported under LEADER and the Local Development Social Inclusion Programme in achieving local development through the promotion of sustainable enterprise.

## RURAL COMMUNITY NETWORK

38A Oldtown Street, Cookstown, Co Tyrone BT80 8EF  T: (028) 8676
6670  F: (028) 8676 6006  E: rcn@ruralcommunitynetwork.org
W: www.ruralcommunitynetwork.org
**Categories:** Community & Rural Development; Information;
Networking

RCN is a voluntary organisation with over 500 members that identifies and provides a voice on issues of concern to rural communities in relation to poverty, disadvantage and community development.

## RURAL DEVELOPMENT COUNCIL

17 Loy Street, Cookstown, Co Tyrone BT80 8PZ  T: (028) 8676 6980
F: (028) 8676 6922  E: info@rdc.org.uk  W: www.rdc.org.uk
C: Martin McDonald, Chief Executive
**Categories:** Community & Rural Development

The Rural Development Council promotes positive and sustainable change in developing and regenerating rural areas.

## SAGE IRELAND

3096 Lake Drive, CityWest Business Park, Dublin 24 T: (01) 642 0800
F: (01) 642 0895  E: sales@sage.ie  W: www.sage.ie
**Categories:** Accountants

A leading supplier of accounting, payroll, CRM and business management software and services for small and medium-sized businesses.

## SALES INSTITUTE OF IRELAND

68 Merrion Square Dublin 2  T: (01) 662 6904  F: (01) 662 6978
E: info@salesinstitute.ie  W: www.salesinstitute.ie
**Categories:** Information; Marketing; Networking; Training

The Sales Institute promotes professionalism and standards of excellence in the sales profession in Ireland. It has over 1,300 members. It provides events, education and training for its members.

## SEED CAPITAL SCHEME

Office of the Revenue Commissioners, Dublin Castle, Dublin 2
T: (01) 702 4107  F: (01) 679 9287  E: cillbyrn@revenue.ie
W: www.revenue.ie  C: Cillian Byrnes
**Categories:** Equity

The Seed Capital Scheme repays income tax to people leaving employment to start their own businesses (only companies qualify). Qualifying individuals may claim back the tax paid in respect of up to €100,000 of income in each of the previous six tax years. An explanatory guide is available on the Revenue Commissioners' website.

## SEROBA KERNEL LIFE SCIENCES LTD

15 Molesworth Street, Dublin 2  T: (01) 633 4028
E: contact-ireland@seroba-kernel.com  W: www.seroba-kernel.com
**Categories:** Equity

Seroba Kernel is a European life science venture capital firm with total funds under management of €100m, which invests on average between €5 million and €7 million over the life of each investment, across biotechnology, specialty pharmaceuticals, medical technology, diagnostics, instrumentation and other selected opportunities within the sector that have the potential to fundamentally change medical care.

# SHANNON DEVELOPMENT

Town Centre, Shannon, Co Clare  T: (061) 361555  F: (061) 361903
E: info@shannon-dev.ie  W: www.shannon-dev.ie
**Categories:** Equity; Grants; Incubator; Information; Mentoring;
Training; Workspace

Shannon Development is the Regional Development Agency responsible for development in the Shannon Region. It offers grants and other assistance to businesses in the Shannon region, broadly in line with the assistance available nationally from Enterprise Ireland.

# SLIGO COUNTY ENTERPRISE BOARD

Sligo Development Centre, Cleveragh Road, Sligo  T: (071) 914 4779
F: (071) 914 6793  E: info@sligoenterprise.ie
W: www.sligoenterprise.ie  C: John Reilly, CEO
**Categories:** Debt; Equity; Grants; Information; Mentoring; Training

Sligo County Enterprise Board aims to generate sustainable employment in the county, through development of an enterprise culture, forging of multi-sectoral partnerships, fostering of economic development and provision of direct financial supports. It operates in the micro-enterprise sector, supporting start-up businesses and the expansion of existing enterprises whose employment potential does not exceed 10 employees.

# SLIGO LEADER PARTNERSHIP COMPANY LTD

Sligo Development Centre, Cleveragh Road, Sligo  T: (071) 914 1138
F: (071) 914 1162  E: info@sligoleader.com  W: www.sligoleader.com
C: Michael Quigley, CEO
**Categories:** Community & Rural Development

Sligo LEADER Partnership is supported under LEADER and the Local Development Social Inclusion Programme in achieving local development through the promotion of sustainable enterprise.

# SMALL FIRMS ASSOCIATION

Confederation House, 84–86 Lower Baggot Street, Dublin 2
T: (01) 660 1011  F: (01) 638 1668  E: info@sfa.ie  W: www.sfa.ie
C: Patricia Callan, Director
**Categories:** Information; Networking; Publications; Training

The Small Firms Association is the national organisation exclusively representing the needs of small enterprises in Ireland, and provides economic, commercial, employee relations and social affairs advice and assistance to over 8,000 member companies, as well as seminar programmes and member networking evenings. In addition, its website provides information and services on-line to members.

# SMALLBUSINESSCAN.COM

W: www.smallbusinesscan.com
**Categories:** Information; Networking; Website

The web portal www.smallbusinesscan.com was developed for Ulster Bank by the Drive4Growth Company to respond to the challenges SME owner / managers face in starting, establishing and growing their ventures. It is a one-stop-resource for connections to peers, collaborators, enablers and new markets.

# SOCIAL ECONOMY AGENCY

171 York Road, Belfast BT15 3HB  T: (028) 9077 0502
E: info@socialeconomyagency.org  W: www.socialeconomyagency.org
**Categories:** Community & Rural Development; Co-operatives;
Information; Social Economy; Training

The Social Economy Agency provides support to the co-operative and social economy movement in Northern Ireland.

# SOUTH & EAST CORK AREA DEVELOPMENT LTD

Midleton Community Enterprise Centre, Owennacurra Business Park,
Knockgriffin, Midleton, Co Cork  T: (021) 461 3432  F: (021) 461 3808
E: info@secad.ie  W: www.secad.ie  C: Ryan Howard, CEO
**Categories:** Community & Rural Development

SECAD is supported under LEADER and the Local Development Social Inclusion Programme in achieving local development through the promotion of sustainable enterprise.

## SOUTH CORK ENTERPRISE BOARD

Unit 6A, South Ring Business Park, Kinsale Road, Cork  T: (021) 497
5281  F: (021) 497 5287  E: enterprise@sceb.ie  W: www.sceb.ie
C: Sean O'Sullivan, CEO

**Categories:** Debt; Equity; Grants; Information; Mentoring; Training

South Cork CEB supports the creation of economically-sustainable niche
micro-enterprise opportunities in the manufacturing, internationally-
traded services and highly innovative locally-traded services sectors
through the provision of information, advice, mentoring, management
development and business counselling. It also offers grants and
financial supports.

## SOUTH DUBLIN COUNTY ENTERPRISE BOARD

3a Village Square, Old Bawn Road, Tallaght, Dublin 24
T: (01) 405 7073/4  F: (01) 403 1234  E: info@sdenterprise.com
W: www.sdenterprise.com  C: Loman O'Byrne, CEO

**Categories:** Debt; Equity; Grants; Information; Mentoring; Training

The South Dublin CEB develops and supports local entrepreneurship
and enterprise in the county of South Dublin.

## SOUTH EAST BUSINESS INNOVATION CENTRE

Unit 1B, Industrial Park, Cork Road, Waterford  T: (051) 356300
F: (051) 354415  E: info@sebic.ie  W: www.sebic.ie
C: Denise Stoneman, Administrator

**Categories:** Business Plans; Incubator; Training

South East Business Innovation Centre supports the generation and
development of new innovative enterprises by providing tailored
business consultancy services in Carlow, Kilkenny, Waterford, Wexford
and South Tipperary. It is a member of the European BIC network.

## SOUTH EAST ENTERPRISE PLATFORM PROGRAMME

Research & Innovation Centre, Waterford Institute of Technology,
Waterford Business Park, Cork Road, Waterford  T: (051) 302953
F: (051) 302901  E: ecrehan@wit.ie  W: www.seepp.ie  C: Eugene Crehan

**Categories:** Incubator; Mentoring; Training

SEEPP is a 12-month incubation programme for technology start-ups,
offering training, mentoring and other support.

## SOUTHERN & EASTERN REGIONAL ASSEMBLY

Assembly House, O'Connell Street, Waterford  T: (051) 860700
F: (051) 879887  E: info@seregassembly.ie  W: www.seregassembly.ie
**Categories:** Policy

The Southern & Eastern Regional Assembly was established in 1999, following the designation of Ireland into two regions for the purposes of EU funding. The Assembly is made up of 41 councillors who are nominated by their respective Local & Regional Authorities and their functions are: managing and monitoring the Regional Operational Programme 2007-2013; promoting the co-ordination of public services in the region; monitoring & making proposals in relation to the general impact in the region of EU funding; and making public bodies aware of the regional implications of their policies & plans. The focus of the Regional Operational Programme 2007-2013 is on innovation and the knowledge economy, environment and accessibility, and sustainable urban development.

## SOUTH KERRY DEVELOPMENT PARTNERSHIP

An Tobar, West Main Street, Cahersiveen, Co Kerry  T: (066) 947 2724
F: (066) 947 2725  E: aoriordan@skdp.net  W: www.southkerry.ie
C: Ann O'Riordan
**Categories:** Community & Rural Development

South Kerry Development Partnership is supported under LEADER and the Local Development Social Inclusion Programme in achieving local development through the promotion of sustainable enterprise.

## SOUTH TIPPERARY DEVELOPMENT COMPANY

c/o The Bridewell, St. Michael's Street, Tipperary Town, Co. Tipperary
T: (062) 333450  E: tlg@iol.ie  C: John Devane, Manager
**Categories:** Community & Rural Development

South Tipperary Development Company is supported under LEADER and the Local Development Social Inclusion Programme in achieving local development through the promotion of sustainable enterprise.

## SOUTH WEST ACTION FOR RURAL DEVELOPMENT

94 Church Street, Cookstown BT80 8HX  T: (028) 8676 4714
E: sward@coookstown.gov.uk  W: www.sward.org.uk
C: Charlie Monaghan, Programme Manager
**Categories:** Community & Rural Development

SWARD (South West Action for Rural Development) is the delivery mechanism for the NI Rural Development Programme 2007-2013 for the four District Councils areas of Cookstown, Dungannon and South Tyrone, Fermanagh and Magherafelt.

## SOUTH WEST MAYO DEVELOPMENT

Carey Walsh Building, Georges Street, Newport, Co Mayo
T: (098) 41950  F: (098) 41952  E: info@southmayo.com
W: www.southmayo.com  C: Gerry O'Neill, CEO
**Categories:** Community & Rural Development

South West Mayo Development is supported under LEADER and the Local Development Social Inclusion Programme in achieving local development through the promotion of sustainable enterprise.

## SOUTHERN ORGANISATION FOR ACTION IN RURAL AREAS

The Civic Centre, Lakeview Road, Craigavon BT64 1AL  T: (028) 3831 2587  F: (028) 3831 2488  E: craigavon@soarni.org  W: www.soarni.org
C: Elaine Cullen / Lynn Morrow
**Categories:** Community & Rural Development

SOAR is the Joint Committee and Local Action Group for the Craigavon, Armagh and Newry & Mourne Council areas, responsible for the administration of the Northern Ireland Rural Development Programme 2007-2013 (NIRDP) within the rural areas of Craigavon, Armagh and Newry.

## SOUTHSIDE PARTNERSHIP

The Old Post Office, 7 Rock Hill, Main Street, Blackrock, Co Dublin
T: (01) 209 0610  F: (01) 275 5729  E: info@sspship.ie
W: www.southsidepartnership.ie  C: Marie Carroll, Manager
**Categories:** Community & Rural Development; Information;
Social Economy; Training

Southside Partnership is supported under the Local Development Social Inclusion Programme in achieving local development through the promotion of sustainable enterprise.

## SPADE ENTERPRISE CENTRE

North King Street, Dublin 7  T: (01) 617 4800  F: (01) 677 1558
E: mailbox@spade.ie  W: www.spade.ie
C: Susan Richardson, Centre Manager
**Categories:** Incubator; Workspace

SPADE opened in 1990 in the former St Paul's Church, offering incubator workspace for small businesses.

## STRABANE ENTERPRISE AGENCY

Orchard Road Industrial Estate, Orchard Road, Strabane, Co Tyrone
BT82 9FR  T: (028) 7138 2518  F: (028) 7188 4531  E: info@seagency.co.uk
W: www.strabaneenterprise.co.uk
**Categories:** Information; Training; Workspace

Strabane Enterprise Agency is a member of Enterprise Northern Ireland. It plays a key role in encouraging the development of the local economy. Its mission is to encourage, promote and cultivate an enterprise ethos throughout the Strabane area and further afield.

## SUNDAY BUSINESS POST

T: (01) 602 6000  F: (01) 679 6498  E: sbpost@iol.ie  F: www.sbpost.ie
**Categories:** Publications

Ireland's only dedicated business newspaper.

## SUSTAINABLE ENERGY IRELAND

Wilton Park House, Wilton Place, Dublin 2  T: (01) 808 2100
F: (01) 808 2002  E: info@sei.ie  W: www.sei.ie
**Categories:** Information; Training

Formerly the Irish Energy Centre, Sustainable Energy Ireland is Ireland's national agency for energy efficiency and renewable energy information, advice and support. EU-funded, it provides guidance on the potential for more efficient use of energy in home, office, industry and municipal activities and on the development of renewable energy resources, from commercial projects to domestic applications. In addition, the Centre offers advice on potential sources of funding for sustainable energy initiatives.

## SYNERGY CENTRE

ITT Dublin, Tallaght, Dublin 24  T: (01) 404 2000 / 404 2376  F: (01) 404 2700  E: innovate@synergycentre.ie  W: www.synergycentre.ie
**Categories:** Incubator; Training

The Synergy Centre at ITT Dublin is the innovation centre of South Dublin County, providing office space and business supports to early-stage enterprises. Its focus is on the high-technology and knowledge-intensive sectors and it aims to enable industry and academia to interact to create viable enterprises for South Dublin County that will secure the area's future in terms of job creation, innovation and export potential. It also offers the Synergy Enterprise Programme

## SYNERGY ENTERPRISE PROGRAMME

Synergy Centre, ITT Dublin, Tallaght, Dublin 24
T: (01) 404 2000 / 404 2376  F: (01) 404 2700
E: jos.evertsen@ittdublin.ie  W: www.m50-enterprise.ie
C: Jos Evertsen, Programme Manager
**Categories:** Incubator; Training

The Synergy Enterprise Programme is a one year full-time programme that supports entrepreneurs with a viable business concept, from business planning to first sales with support from experienced entrepreneurs and small business experts.

# TALLAGHT PARTNERSHIP

Killinarden Enterprise Park, Killinarden, Tallaght, Dublin 24
T: (01) 466 4280  F: (01) 466 4288  E: anna.lee@tallpart.com
W: www.tallpart.com  C: Anna Lee, Manager
**Categories:** Community & Rural Development; Information; Training

One of the Area Partnerships funded by Pobal, as part of the Local Social Inclusion Development Programme. Partas delivers its enterprise development and business support service in Tallaght, targeted at the long-term unemployed.

# TCD ENTERPRISE CENTRE

Pearse Street, Dublin 2  T: (01) 677 5655  F: (01) 677 5487
E: bnoone@tcd.ie  W: www.tcd.ie
C: Bridget Noone, Enterprise Executive
**Categories:** Incubator; Training

Originally established by IDA Ireland, the centre is now owned by University of Dublin, Trinity College. It is home to 30 businesses, including the Dublin Business Innovation Centre.

# TEAGASC

Oak Park, Carlow, Co Carlow  T: (059) 917 0200  F: (059) 918 2097
E: info@hq.teagasc.ie  W: www.teagasc.ie  C: Eric Donald, Head of PR
**Categories:** Consulting; Training

Through its rural innovation support service, Teagasc offers mentoring and training for local entrepreneurs starting their own business linked to the rural economy. It also offers training courses at its Ashtown Food Centre and Dairy Products Research Centre, to strengthen in-company capabilities in quality systems, food safety and hygiene, food technology and product development and marketing. Teagasc research centres provide technical services to small and medium food-producing companies on a cost-recovery basis.

## TERENURE ENTERPRISE LTD

17 Rathfarnham Road, Terenure, Dublin 6W  T: (01) 490 3237  F: (01) 490
3238  E: info@terenure-enterprise.ie  W: www.terenure-enterprise.ie
C: Michelle Hannon, Manager
**Categories:** Business Plans; Community & Rural Development;
Incubator; Information; Training

Terenure Enterprise Centre provides business incubator units, business
advice and assistance with business plans, funding applications, etc.
and an enterprise information library for small start-up projects unable
to secure such support from other sources.

## TIPPERARY INSTITUTE

Nenagh Road, Thurles, Co Tipperary / Cashel Court, Clonmel,
Co Tipperary  T: (0504) 28000  F: (0504) 28001  E: info@tippinst.ie
W: www.tippinst.ie
**Categories:** Community & Rural Development; Mentoring; Training

TI provides locally responsive and interactive educational, training,
communication, mentoring and support services to rural communities.
It is piloting a distance learning competency training programme for
owner / managers of SMEs.

## TIPPERARY NORTH COUNTY ENTERPRISE BOARD

Connolly Street, Nenagh, Co Tipperary  T: (067) 33086  F: (067) 33605
E: info@tnceb.ie  W: www.tnceb.ie  C: Rita Guinan, Chief Executive
**Categories:** Debt; Equity; Grants; Information; Mentoring; Training

Tipperary North CEB stimulates a spirit of enterprise and facilitates the
creation of employment and the development of sustainable micro-
enterprises in North Tipperary through support, assistance and
promotional activities whether financial, training or otherwise.

## TIPPERARY SOUTH RIDING
## COUNTY ENTERPRISE BOARD

1 Gladstone Street, Clonmel, Co Tipperary  T: (052) 612 9466
F: (052) 612 6512  E: ceb@southtippcoco.ie  W: www.southtippceb.ie
C: Thomas Hayes, CEO

**Categories:** Debt; Equity; Grants; Information; Mentoring; Training

Tipperary South CEB helps to create jobs by facilitating the establishment, development and expansion of small enterprises in the county. It provides financial assistance, mentoring and training programmes.

## TOLKA AREA PARTNERSHIP

Rosehill House, Finglas Road, Dublin 11  T: (01) 836 1666  F: (01) 864
0211  E: info@fcp.ie  W: www.fcp.ie  C: David Orford

**Categories:** Community & Rural Development

Tolka Area Partnership is supported under the Local Development Social Inclusion Programme in achieving local development through the promotion of sustainable enterprise.

## TOMKINS

5 Dartmouth Road, Dublin 6  T: (01) 202 6700  F: (01) 660 6920
E: post@tomkins.com  W: www.tomkins.ie

**Categories:** Intellectual Property

Tomkins are European intellectual property experts. Established in 1930 by Arthur Bellamy Tomkins, the firm is one of Europe's longest established intellectual property law specialists.

## TOWNSEND BUSINESS PARK

28 Townsend Street, Belfast BT3 2ES  T: (028) 9043 5778  F: (028) 9031
2328  E: admin@townsend.co.uk  W: www.townsend.co.uk
C: Clare Savage, Manager

**Categories:** Information; Training; Workspace

Townsend Enterprise Park is a member of Enterprise Northern Ireland. For over 20 years, it has delivered business support to new and established companies in the Greater Shankill and Lower Falls areas of Belfast. Its mission is: 'to promote social and economic regeneration and employment within our community'.

## TYNDALL NATIONAL INSTITUTE

Lee Maltings, Prospect Row, Cork  T: (021) 490 4177  F: (021) 490 4058
E: info@tyndall.ie  W: www.tyndall.ie  C: Kieran Flynn
**Categories:** Consulting; R & D; Training

The Tyndall Institute's strengths lie in photonics, electronics, materials
and nanotechnologies and their applications for life sciences,
communications, power electronics and other industries. Research
programmes range from theoretical modelling and design to novel
material, nanotechnology, device processing and fabrication, packaging
and integration; and novel systems incorporating these new devices.

## TYRONE DONEGAL PARTNERSHIP

Omagh Business Complex, Gortrush Industrial Estate, Great Northern
Road, Omagh, Co Tyrone BT78 5LU  T: (028) 8225 0962  F: (028) 8224
9454  E: h.sweeney@tyronedonegalpartnership.org
W: www.tyronedonegalpartnership.org
C: Hugo Sweeney, Cross-Border Projects Manager
**Categories:** Community & Rural Development; Cross-Border; Training

Tyrone Donegal Partnership, established in 1996, is a successful cross-
border, not-for-profit organisation which aims to contribute to the
improvement of the social and economic conditions, primarily in the
counties of Tyrone and Donegal and the adjacent counties including
Fermanagh, Sligo and Leitrim.

## ÚDARÁS NA GAELTACHTA

Na Forbacha, Gaillimh  T: (091) 503100  F: (091) 503101
E: eolas@udaras.ie  W: www.udaras.ie
C: Pádraig Ó hAoláin, Chief Executive
**Categories:** Grants; Incubator; Information; Training

Údarás na Gaeltachta is the regional authority responsible for the
economic, social and cultural development of the Gaeltacht region. It
offers grant schemes and incentives to help small and medium-sized
enterprises in the Gaeltacht areas, broadly in line with those available
nationally from Enterprise Ireland.

## ULSTER BANK

Small Business Office, 33 College Green, Dublin 2  T: (01) 702 5225
F: (01) 702 5350 / Group Head Office, 11-16 Donegall Square East, Belfast
BT1 5UB  T: (028) 9027 6017  F: (028) 9027 6033  W: www.ulsterbank.com
**Categories:** Debt; Franchises

Ulster Bank, a member of the RBS-NatWest Group, has a Small Business
Adviser in every branch to guide and advise entrepreneurs through the
start-up process and explain, help and direct them through every aspect
of business banking. Start-up businesses with a turnover below £100,000
(€127,000) qualify for 12 months free banking. Ulster Bank offers
overdrafts, loans, leasing and invoice discounting, as well as Internet
banking and e-commerce facilities.

## ULSTER COMMUNITY INVESTMENT TRUST LTD

13 - 19 Linenhall Street, Belfast BT2 8AA  T: (028) 9031 5003
F: (028) 9031 5008  / Ardee Business Park, Hale Street, Ardee, Co Louth
T: (041) 685 8637  E: info@ucitltd.com  W: www.ucitltd.com
**Categories:** Community & Rural Development; Cross-Border; Debt;
Social Economy; Training

Ulster Community Investment Trust Ltd is the key provider
of social finance, free advice, business support and mentoring to the
social economy sector in Northern Ireland and the Republic of Ireland.

## ULSTER FACTORS

7 North Street, Belfast BT1 1NH  T: (028) 9032 4522  F: (028) 9023 0336 /
Carmichael House, 60 Lower Baggot Street, Dublin 2  T: (01) 676 2240
F: (01) 602 4777  E: enquiries@ulsterfactors.com
W: www.ulsterfactors.com
**Categories:** Debt

Ulster Factors offers an invoice factoring service to facilitate cash flow
for small and medium-sized businesses.

## UNIVERSITIES

See individual entries for: Dublin City University; National University
of Ireland Galway; Queen's University Belfast; University College Cork;
University College Dublin; University of Dublin, Trinity College;
University of Limerick; University of Ulster.

## UNIVERSITY COLLEGE CORK

College Road, Cork  T: (021) 490 3000  F: (021) 490 3612
E: t.weaver@ucc.ie  W: www.ucc.ie/en/ResearchandIndustry
C: Tony Weaver, Industrial Liaison Officer
**Categories:** Consulting; R & D; Training

The Office of Technology Transfer (OTT) at University College Cork is responsible for the commercialisation of the university's intellectual property and managing the university's interactions with industry. It acts to link industry with UCC's research community. UCC has an outstanding international reputation in research across all faculties and a long tradition and expertise in technology transfer, intellectual property, innovation, and in working with industry. The OTT aims to maximise any opportunity that this research presents to provide a return for the economy and the university.

## UNIVERSITY COLLEGE DUBLIN

UCD Research, Belfield, Dublin 4  T: (01) 716 4000  F: (01) 716 3709
E: ucdresearch@ucd.ie  W: www.ucd.ie/research
**Categories:** Consulting; R & D; Training

UCD Research comprises the Office of the Vice-President for Research and the Office of Funded Research Support Services. Research facilities in UCD include seven dedicated Research Institutes, five Graduate Schools, NovaUCD Innovation & Technology Transfer centre and a dedicated Research Headquarters at the heart of the campus.

## UNIVERSITY OF DUBLIN, TRINITY COLLEGE

Trinity Research & Innovation, College Green, Dublin 2  T: (01) 677 5655
F: (01) 677 5883  E: kellym8@tcd.ie  W: www.tcd.ie/research_innovation
C: Michelle Kelly, General enquiries
**Categories:** Consulting; Incubator; R & D; Training

Trinity Research & Innovation actively supports TCD's wider research portfolio, by promoting and managing the interface between TCD researchers, funding agencies and industry. It is also responsible for managing TCD's Intellectual Property, Technology Transfer and Innovation, Commercialisation and Entrepreneurship – the last of which is housed in the TCD Enterprise Centre.

## UNIVERSITY OF LIMERICK

Research Office, Foundation Building, Plassey, Limerick  T: (061) 202686
F: (061) 202912  E: paul.dillon@ul.ie  W: www.research.ul.ie
C: Paul Dillon, Director of Technology Transfer
**Categories:** Consulting; R & D; Training

The Mission of the Research Office is to facilitate the growth of relevant, sustainable research and its dissemination within the communities it serves. It is divided into three sections: Graduate School; Research Support Services; and Technology Transfer. In addition, UL operates the Centre for Entrepreneurial Studies and the Marketing Centre for Small Business.

## UNIVERSITY OF ULSTER

Office of Innovation, Jordanstown Campus, Shore Road,
Newtownabbey BT37 0QB  T: (028) 9036 8019  E: enquiry@ulster.ac.uk
W: www.oi.ulster.ac.uk
**Categories:** Consulting; R & D

The Innovation Services team is responsible for the capture, protection and commercialisation of Ulster's intellectual capital by providing support and advice on intellectual property management; technology licensing; consultancy; spin-out company creation; and industrial collaborations. The University takes a stake in spin-out companies through UUTech Ltd. UU established UUSRP Ltd, a wholly-owned company, to develop and manage its campus-based science research parks. UU operates a number of applied research centres.

## WATERFORD CITY ENTERPRISE BOARD

Enterprise House, New Street Court, Waterford  T: (051) 852883  F: (051) 877494  E: info@waterfordceb.com  W: www.waterfordceb.com
C: Bill Rafter, CEO
**Categories:** Debt; Equity; Grants; Information; Mentoring; Training

Waterford City Enterprise Board provides a full range of supports for micro-enterprises in its region. It provides information and advice on all aspects of establishing and developing a small business, including advice on a range of financial supports available to business.

## WATERFORD COUNTY ENTERPRISE BOARD

Court House, Dungarvan, Co Waterford  T: (058) 44811 F: (058) 44817
E: waterfordceb@cablesurf.com  W: www.enterpriseboard.ie
C: Gerard Enright, CEO
**Categories:** Debt; Equity; Grants; Information; Mentoring; Training

Waterford County Enterprise Board provides a full range of supports for micro-enterprises in its region.

## WATERFORD INSTITUTE OF TECHNOLOGY

Industry Services, Room 2.10, Walton IT Building, WIT Cork Road
Campus, Waterford  T: (051) 302034  F: (051) 378292  E: kkiely@wit.ie
W: www.wit.ie  C: Kathryn Kiely, Industry Services Manager
**Categories:** Consulting; Incubator; R & D; Training

WIT's Industry Services & Technology Transfer Office works within the Office of Research & Innovation to support and develop innovation activity within the Institute. WIT operates research groups in applied optics, Advanced Manufacturing Technology (AMT) and electronics. WIT also operates the South East Enterprise Programme.

## WATERFORD LEADER PARTNERSHIP LTD

John Barry House, Lismore Business Park, Mayfield, Lismore, Co
Waterford  T: (058) 54646  F: (058) 54126  E: info@wlp.ie  W: www.wlp.ie
C: Julie O'Donnell, LES Co-ordinator; Jimmy Taaffe, General Manager
**Categories:** Community & Rural Development

Waterford LEADER Partnership is supported under LEADER and the Local Development Social Inclusion Programme in achieving local development through the promotion of sustainable enterprise.

## WEBPAYMENTS.IE

E: feedback@webpayments.ie  W: www.webpayments.ie
**Categories:** eBusiness; Website

Webpayments.ie is a free and independent resource to help guide you through the process of setting up online payments in Ireland. The site has been setup in response to the difficulty often experienced when choosing and integrating a web payments platform.

## WEST CORK ENTERPRISE BOARD

8 Kent Street, Clonakilty, Co Cork  T: (023) 883 4700  F: (023) 883 4702
E: enterprise@wceb.ie W: www.wceb.ie  C: Michael Hanley, CEO
**Categories:** Debt; Equity; Grants; Information; Mentoring; Training

The West Cork Enterprise Board is a state agency responsible for enterprise development in the West Cork area. It provides advice, training and mentoring services for business development, as well as financial assistance in the form of refundable aid and capital grants, employment grants and assistance towards feasibility studies.

## WEST CORK DEVELOPMENT PARTNERSHIP LTD

West Cork Technology Park, Clonakilty, Co Cork  T: (023) 883 4035
F: (023) 883 4066  E: ian@wcdp.ie  W: www.wcdp.ie  C: Ian Dempsey
**Categories:** Community & Rural Development

West Cork Development Partnership is supported under LEADER and the Local Development Social Inclusion Programme in achieving local development through the promotion of sustainable enterprise.

## WEST LIMERICK RESOURCES LTD

St Mary's Road, Newcastlewest, Co Limerick  T: (069) 79114
F: (069) 61870  E: srowley@wlr.ie  W: www.wlr.ie  C: Suzanne Rowley,
Information & Communication Officer
**Categories:** Community & Rural Development

West Limerick Resources is supported under LEADER and  the Local Development Social Inclusion Programme in achieving local development through the promotion of sustainable enterprise.

## WEST OFFALY PARTNERSHIP

Crank House, Banagher, Co Offaly  T: (057) 915 1622
E: info@westoffalypartnership.ie  W: www.westoffalypartnership.ie
**Categories:** Community & Rural Development

West Offaly Partnership is a voluntary community organisation established in 1994 and has been to the forefront of community education, planning and action for the past 12 years. It focuses on social exclusion and combating disadvantage in the community it serves, especially among the long-term unemployed and those at risk of becoming long-term unemployed.

## WESTBIC

Galway Technology Centre, Mervue Business Park, Galway
T: (091) 730 850  F: (091) 730 853  E: info@westbic.ie  W: www.westbic.ie
C: Mary Ryan
**Categories:** Business Plans; Incubator; Marketing; Training

WestBIC aims to support entrepreneurs with innovative business ideas that they wish to develop in the Border, Midland and Western regions of Ireland. It provides tailored support through the initial stages, from concept to commercialisation, through seven regional offices.

## WESTERN DEVELOPMENT COMMISSION

Dillon House, Ballaghaderreen, Co Roscommon  T: (094) 986 1441
F: (094) 986 1443  E: info@wdc.ie  W: www.wdc.ie
**Categories:** Community & Rural Development; Debt; Equity; Policy

The Western Development Commission is a statutory body promoting economic and social development in counties Donegal, Leitrim, Sligo, Mayo, Roscommon, Galway and Clare. Its activities include: review and development of strategic regional policies for a range of sectors; securing the implementation of major regional development initiatives; and management of the Western Investment Fund.

## WESTERN MANAGEMENT CENTRE

Galway Business Park, Dangan, Galway  T: (091) 528777  F: (091) 528649
W: www.wmcgalway.com
**Categories:** Training

The Western Management Centre offers training and development programmes geared towards the needs of business owners and entrepreneurs.

## WESTMEATH COMMUNITY DEVELOPMENT

2nd Floor, Presentation House, Harbour Street, Mullingar, Co
Westmeath  T: (044) 934 8571  F: (044) 934 8441  E: info@westcd.ie
W: www.westcd.ie  C: Joe Potter, CEO
**Categories:** Community & Rural Development

Westmeath Community Development is supported under LEADER and the Local Development Social Inclusion Programme in achieving local development through the promotion of sustainable enterprise.

## WESTMEATH COUNTY ENTERPRISE BOARD LTD

Business Information Centre, Church Avenue, Mullingar, Co
Westmeath T: (044) 934 9222  F: (044) 934 9009
E: info@westmeath-enterprise.ie
W: www.westmeath-enterprise.ie  C: Christine Charlton, CEO
**Categories:** Debt; Equity; Grants; Information; Mentoring; Training

Westmeath CEB offers a full range of supports for micro-enterprises in
its region. It is a one-stop-shop for business advice and information in
Westmeath County.

## WESTMEATH EMPLOYMENT PACT

3 Fairview Terrace, Patrick Street, Mullingar, Co. Westmeath  T: (044)
933 3829  E: tep@eircom.net  C: Larry Fullam, Co-ordinator
**Categories:** Community & Rural Development

Westmeath Employment Pact is supported under the Local
Development Social Inclusion Programme in achieving local
development through the promotion of sustainable enterprise.

## WEXFORD LOCAL DEVELOPMENT

Cornmarket, Mallin Street, Wexford  T: (053) 912 3994
E: paulaw@wap.iol.ie  C: Bernard O'Brien, CEO
**Categories:** Community & Rural Development

Wexford Local Development is supported under LEADER and the
Local Development Social Inclusion Programme in achieving local
development through the promotion of sustainable enterprise.

## WEXFORD COUNTY ENTERPRISE BOARD

Unit 1, Ardcavan Business Park, Ardcavan, Wexford  T: (053) 912 2965
F: (053) 912 4944  E: info@wexfordceb.ie  W: www.wexfordceb.ie
C: Tom Banville, Acting CEO
**Categories:** Debt; Equity; Grants; Information; Mentoring; Training

Wexford County Enterprise Board offers financial and technical
assistance to both start-up and existing businesses.

## WICKLOW COUNTY ENTERPRISE BOARD

Wicklow County Campus, Clermont House, Rathnew, Wicklow
T: (0404) 30800　F: (0404) 30899　E: enterprise@wicklowceb.ie
W: www.wicklowceb.ie　C: Sheelagh Daly, CEO
**Categories:** Debt; Equity; Grants; Information; Mentoring; Training

Wicklow CEB's services include information and advice, training and mentoring, and financial assistance.

## WORK WEST ENTERPRISE AGENCY

301 Glen Road, Belfast BT11 8BU　T: (028) 9061 0826　F: (028) 9062 2001
E: info@workwest.co.uk　W: www.workwest.co.uk
C: Claire Ferris, Manager
**Categories:** Information; Social Economy; Training; Workspace

Work West is a member of Enterprise Northern Ireland and aims 'to be a commercially viable organisation which seeks to improve the economic and social profile of West Belfast by motivating and enabling enterprising people to establish and expand job creating businesses'.

## WORKSPACE (DRAPERSTOWN) LTD

The Business Centre, 7 Tobermore Road, Draperstown, Co
Londonderry BT45 7AG　T: (028) 7962 8113　F: (028) 7962 8975
E: info@workspace.org.uk　W: www.workspace.org.uk
C: Brian Murray, Chief Executive
**Categories:** Community & Rural Development; Information; Social
Economy; Training; Workspace

Workspace is a member of Enterprise Northern Ireland. As one of Ireland's leading forces for community economic and social regeneration, in addition to providing business support services and business property, the Workspace Group is also involved in: recruitment; training and employment initiatives; energy efficiency and insulation; event management; childcare; and recreational activities. These commercial activities are pursued to generate profits that are then used to benefit the local community.

## XANTHAL LTD

Suite 101, 93 Upper George's Street, Dún Laoire, Co Dublin T: (01) 271 1888 E: info@xanthal.com W: www.xanthal.com C: Anthony Quigley
**Categories:** Consulting; Marketing

Xanthal provides outsourced marketing, sales development and business growth services to start-up and expanding companies. It helps companies formulate and execute their 'go-to-market' plans.

## YOUNG ENTERPRISE NORTHERN IRELAND

Grove House, 145-149 Donegall Pass, Belfast BT7 1DT T: (028) 9032 7003 F: (028) 9032 6995 E: info@yeni.co.uk W: www.yeni.co.uk
**Categories:** Young Enterprise

Young Enterprise is Northern Ireland's foremost business and enterprise education charity, and a member of the Junior Achievement Worldwide network, the world's largest and fastest growing business and economic education organisation, reaching over 8 million young people worldwide.

## YOUNG ENTREPRENEUR

Unit 3 Tom Crean Business Centre, Kerry Technology Park, Tralee, Co. Kerry T: (066) 711 9669 F: (066) 711 9670 E: info@youngentrepreneur.ie
W: www.youngentrepreneur.ie C: Anne Looney
**Categories:** Competitions; Young Enterprise

The Young Entrepreneur Programme is a unique opportunity to explore and develop the talents of all participants. It complements traditional learning by layering workshops, case studies and interaction with key business leaders on top of participants' own ideas. The Young Entrepreneur Programme is a not-for-profit organisation dedicated to illustrating the validity of entrepreneurship as a career choice. Its mission is to help identify, inform, recognise and celebrate Kerry's next generation of business leaders – and their educators.

# OTHER TITLES FROM OAK TREE PRESS